THE
SUMMER
WIND

THE SUMMER WIND

THOMAS CAPANO AND THE MURDER OF ANNE MARIE FAHEY

GEORGE ANASTASIA

ReganBooks
An Imprint of HarperCollins*Publishers*

HarperCollins books may be purchased for educational, business, or sales promotional use. For information please write: Special Markets Department, HarperCollins Publishers, Inc., 10 East 53rd Street, New York, NY 10022.

FIRST EDITION

Designed by Charles Kreloff

ISBN 0-06-039314-9

99 00 01 02 03 ❖/RRD 10 9 8 7 6 5 4 3 2 1

For Michelle and Nina,
With Love

ACKNOWLEDGMENTS AND AUTHOR'S NOTE

This book grew out of my coverage of the Thomas Capano-Anne Marie Fahey murder case for the *Philadelphia Inquirer*. The idea to expand the story into a book evolved out of that coverage. In that regard, I am especially grateful to Judith Regan, who saw this as more than just a true crime story and gave me the chance to write it that way.

I would like to extend my special thanks to members of the Fahey family who were willing to share their thoughts, feelings, and insights. The grace, dignity, and civility that they displayed throughout was admirable. They are the definition of class.

I would like to thank several editors at the *Inquirer* who saw and helped shape versions of this story in its original journalistic form. These would include Nancy Albritton, Chris Conway, Dan Biddle, and Herb Kestenbaum.

A special thanks also to the prosecutors, investigators, defense attorneys, and fellow reporters who were involved in this story from beginning to end, and who graciously took the time to talk with me about it.

The wit, wisdom, and good humor of the press corps that covered the fourteen-week Capano trial turned what could have been an unbearable situation into a memorable event. While it would be impossible to mention everyone, I am especially grateful to Marisol Bello, Sharon Mittelman, Todd Spangler, Terry Spencer, Brian Kasem, Susan Schary, and Bill Ternay who were there from start to finish and whose daily analysis over lunch and occasionally over dinner influenced what follows. And Tim Shaffer deserves special recognition for his exceptional photography.

Thanks to Carrie Budoff, Tanyanika Samuels, and David Lee Preston for reading over my shoulder. Special thanks to Cal Morgan for editing this book with grace and style while under great pressure. And finally and as always to my wife, Angela, for her love, encouragement, and support.

Comments quoted in the text are drawn from interviews or on sworn testimony in court or before a grand jury. Conversations that are re-created come from those same sources or from the diary notes of Anne Marie Fahey, the testimony and notes of Tom Capano, or from transcripts of tape recordings that were entered as part of the trial case file.

The thoughts of the individuals in any particular setting are also based on an analysis of the aforementioned sources and on interviews with either the individuals themselves or with those familiar with the individual and the event.

George Anastasia
July 1999

THE
SUMMER
WIND

1

The cooler wouldn't sink.

It was floating out there in the middle of the Atlantic Ocean, bobbing on the water. Mocking him.

Tom Capano looked at it for a long time; then he turned to his brother Gerry. Gerry looked away. He had made it clear that he wanted no part of this. But Tom needed him. Maybe for the only time in his life, he needed his younger brother's help.

They were out there together, and they had to finish what they had started.

Tom cursed.

The cooler was an Igloo marine model, a fisherman's ice chest. It was about four feet long, two feet high, and two and a half feet wide, made of heavy-duty white plastic. Tom had wrapped a large metal chain around it and secured it with a padlock, but that and its contents still weren't enough to make it sink. The cooler stood out against the blue-green sea, floating calmly about thirty feet away from them.

They were standing on the deck of the *Summer Wind*—which was the name of Gerry's sports fishing boat, and also the title of a melancholy Frank Sinatra song of fleeting romance and the heartache of lost love. But that was an irony that would have been lost on Tom Capano as he stood staring at the damn ice chest, willing it to go down.

"I can't fucking believe you did this," Gerry Capano

shouted. "Why did you get me involved in this? I can't fucking believe it."

They were about sixty miles out, southeast of the southernmost tip of New Jersey. It was late on a hazy Friday morning at the end of June in 1996, the kind of day sailors and fishermen described as "snotty." There was a slight wind blowing out of the southeast. The waves were two to four feet. The sun was trying to break through the heavy mist.

During the ride down to the shore that morning, Tom had assured his brother that everything would be all right. "I'll never let anything happen to you," he had said. But now, as he stood at the back of the small boat, he had nothing more to say to his brother.

Gerry cut back on the dual engines that powered the twenty-five-foot Hydra Sport. He reached for the shotgun he kept in the boat's small wheelhouse: a twelve-gauge Mossberg, silver with a black stock. Gerry kept the gun on board to kill sharks. He used deer slugs. They were more effective than buckshot.

Gerry aimed at the cooler and fired once. There was a dull thud as the slug pierced the plastic. The brothers looked at one another.

Now blood was seeping out of the bullet hole. But the cooler was still bobbing on the ocean's surface. It wouldn't sink.

Gerry cursed in frustration and anger. He powered the engines and swung the boat around toward the cooler, gently pulling alongside. Tom reached over and grabbed for the chain, pulling the ice chest hard against the *Summer Wind*.

Gerry cut back on the engines and allowed the boat to idle. He reached down, grabbed the boat's two anchors, and brought them to his brother.

"You're on your own," he said.

Tom was fighting to get the chain and padlock off the cooler. Gerry walked away, toward the bow of the boat. For three or four minutes he stood there, looking out at the sea. In the distance, he could see another small fishing boat, but otherwise they were alone.

He heard chains and anchors clanging and Tom struggling.

Occasionally his brother would pause and vomit over the side. Gerry didn't know if this was because he was seasick—Tom had a weak stomach; he hated boat rides—or because of the work at hand.

"Are you done yet?" Gerry yelled at one point.

Tom did not answer.

He had gotten the chain off and had the lid of the cooler opened. And he was sickened by what he saw inside. It was the body of a woman. She was tall, with long, thick hair and a large, oval face. Once she had been beautiful, but now her features were distorted. She had been dead for several hours, stuffed inside the cooler before rigor mortis had set in. Along the side of her head, above her left ear, her hair was matted and discolored where the blood from a bullet wound—a wound Tom had inflicted several hours earlier—had coagulated. Her hair, which was auburn, had turned a dark reddish purple around the small head wound.

Using nylon rope he had found on board, Tom Capano secured the anchors and the chain to the body. Then he tilted the cooler and allowed the remains of the woman he had once loved to slip out into the water. Gerry turned when he heard the splash. He saw part of a calf and a foot disappear into the ocean as the now-anchored body began its slow descent. It would take several minutes to reach bottom. They were at a depth of about 200 feet, Gerry knew; he often fished for shark there.

The area was known as Mako Alley.

"I can't fucking believe you got me involved in this," he said again.

Tom Capano didn't hear him. He was throwing up over the side of the boat.

The brothers said very little else that morning. Gerry got a Philips-head screwdriver out of his toolbox, took the lid and one of the handles off the Igloo cooler, and threw them into the ocean. Next he got a hose and washed out the chest, rinsing away the pools of blood that had settled on the bottom of the plastic container.

Minutes later the *Summer Wind* was heading due west, toward shore, at about twenty-five knots. At that point, Tom Capano flung the cooler—now missing a lid and a handle, and with a bullet hole through its side and bottom—into the water.

Gerry pushed the boat to full throttle. The white Hydra Sport 2500 bucked, then lurched forward, skimming the top of the noontime sea. The Capano brothers never looked back.

If they had, they would have seen the large white Igloo cooler bobbing on the water.

It wouldn't sink.

It is a surreal story, a soap opera with an outlandish script. Even some of the jurors to whom the story was later presented seemed perplexed by it all. They heard all the testimony, viewed all the evidence, assessed all the witnesses—and it was still as if the story were some kind of dream, or nightmare: A rich, powerful, and secretly obsessive lawyer carries on clandestine two-year affair with beautiful young gubernatorial aide. He is in his mid-forties, married, with four teenage daughters. She is in her late twenties, model-thin, anorexic, and conflicted. She is a flirt who enjoys—indeed, seeks out—the attention of older men. But she is racked with guilt—guilt rooted in a troubled upbringing and a staunch Irish Catholic background. She tries to end the affair. He kills her. This was a clash of two generations and two cultures; a story of love and betrayal, of wealth, greed, power, and treachery bubbling beneath the thin veneer of respectability that money and political clout can provide. Before it is over, the story is more *Jerry Springer* than jurisprudence.

Brother against brother, lover against lover—the story of the investigation and conviction of Thomas J. Capano for the murder of Anne Marie Fahey is a tale of the values and morals of America at the end of the twentieth century. If the 1990s were, as *Vanity Fair* has proclaimed, "The Tabloid Decade," then the Capano trial was a signal headline for this era when all vestiges of public shame seemed to have faded away.

Self-centered and self-absorbed, Tom Capano testified for eight days at his own trial, confident that he could talk his way out of a murder rap. It was his final miscalculation.

His first was believing that the cooler would sink.

They got back to Stone Harbor, New Jersey, around three that afternoon. All told, the boat trip had taken about five hours, hours that the Capano brothers would be hard-pressed to account for once the investigation started to narrow in on what had happened that morning.

But it would be months before they would have to deal with those particulars. And it would be Gerry more than Tom who agonized the most over the events; Gerry, the youngest brother, the wild one, the one who was always breaking the rules and getting into trouble.

It was Gerry, as it turned out, who had a conscience, who couldn't live with what he had done. Tom, who had killed the woman and stuffed her body into the ice chest, had already begun blocking it out as they drove home from the Jersey shore to Wilmington.

Tom, the oldest brother, the one they called the golden boy, thought he could get away with murder.

A billboard at the city limits proclaims Wilmington, Delaware, "A Place to Be Somebody." It is a small-town vanity that captures both the charm and the hubris of the city, population 71,000, that sits along the Delaware River opposite southern New Jersey and just below Philadelphia. Wilmington is a small, even incongruous spot in the megalopolis that stretches from Boston to Washington, D.C.

Over the last twenty years, by virtue of some canny legislation, Wilmington has become the improbable corporate capital of America, if not the world. Half of the country's Fortune 500 companies are based there. It is a financial Disneyland, though its steel and glass and plastic cityscape is strangely lacking in human qualities. So dependent is the city upon its new crop of finance company denizens that its very identity is defined by their presence.

Where once it was the DuPont Company that set the city's tone, now it is MBNA Corporation, First USA Bank, Mellon, Chase Manhattan, and a handful of other financial giants. Today's downtown Wilmington has been rebuilt around those institutions and the liberalized banking laws that brought them to the city. Banker-friendly legislation passed in the 1980s, including a big cut on taxes levied against financial houses and the gutting of prickly consumer protection laws, turned

Wilmington—the only city of any size in Delaware—into an attractive haven for big banking companies eager to expand their credit card operations.

What could be more American, after all, than buying on credit? Plastic is so much better than cash. America's credit card debt rose from $100 million in the late 1980s to nearly $500 million by the early 1990s, and Wilmington basked in the glory of it all.

The modest skyscrapers that sprung up here were a tribute to corporate America and to the 17.5 percent interest rate that guarantees most credit card consumers a lifetime of debt. Rodney Square, the European-style piazza that opens onto Market Street in the heart of the downtown business district, is surrounded by the old and the new edifices that define Wilmington. The elegant, five-star Hotel duPont sits across the square from the stately, classical Daniel L. Herrmann Courthouse. The other two sides of the square are lined by the old Wilmington Trust Building and the public library, classic examples of beaux arts architecture that date from the 1920s.

But on the corners of the square, jutting up behind the older buildings, are the shiny glass-and-concrete monuments to the new players. The headquarters of MBNA, the largest credit card issuer in the country, stretches over two blocks and will soon include the courthouse building itself, which MBNA will occupy once the city finishes construction on a new justice center a block away. First Union, Corestates, and Mellon Bank occupy the other corners. A block away is the Chase Manhattan Centre, and towering over the southern end of the downtown, a few blocks below Rodney Square, is the pristine First USA building.

Always looking to be good corporate citizens, MBNA executives spearheaded the drive to refurbish the city's Grand Opera House, the centerpiece of a still questionable attempt to pump life back into Market Street after dark. The Opera House is now the locus of all that is distinguished, all that is high society, in the city. It is the venue for the Grand Gala, the annual fundraising soirée that brings out the city's best and brightest, or at least its most powerful and wealthiest. The black-tie affair is like a senior prom for those who make up the city's elite and those who dream of joining them.

Not to be outdone, First USA has given the city its Riverfront Arts Center, where crowds lined up for months not too long ago to view the blockbuster Nicholas and Alexandra exhibition, a celebration of historic wealth, power, and ostentatious elegance that played well in local social and political circles. The Czar would have fit right into Wilmington society.

The development along the waterfront has also included Frawley Stadium, home of the Wilmington Blue Rocks, the city's minor league baseball team. Tickets are at a premium; the quaint, Norman Rockwell-like ballpark is one of the best seats in town during the summer.

Built in the image of its new masters, Wilmington is modern, neat, and conservative, and it's locked up tight by 6:00 P.M.

By that time the stores that line Market Street have been shuttered, and the office workers have headed to their homes in neighborhoods north and west of the downtown area, staying clear of the poorer sections of the city, where many African-American families have somehow managed to miss out on the boom. At the same time, the executives who run the big companies have gotten into their BMWs and Jeep Cherokees and Volvos and headed out to Greenville or one of the other trendy, upscale suburbs, where capuccino bars, gourmet specialty shops, and mailboxes stuffed with Eddie Bauer and J. Crew catalogues announce that life is good and interest rates are solid.

Wilmington is urban lite. There are still the remnants of the city's once solid, ethnic, middle-class neighborhoods, areas that fifty years ago were cultural enclaves for the city's Italian, Irish, Polish, and African-American blue-collar workers. There are also poverty-stricken, crime-ridden neighborhoods that would rival those of Philadelphia or New York. And finally there are the gentrified areas, which look a lot like Alexandria, Virginia, or Haddonfield, New Jersey—neighborhoods of large, sprawling Victorian-style homes on tree-lined streets with manicured lawns and cobblestone sidewalks. Neighborhoods that offer city life with suburban security—though all on such a small scale that "urban" seems too strong a word to describe it.

Wilmington isn't New York or Philadelphia. What's more, it doesn't want to be. More southern in temperament and attitude than Baltimore or Washington, Wilmington has long operated in its own social, political, and cultural time zone. Outsiders consider the place quaint, provincial, marked by a civility that disappeared in most of America's cities back in the 1950s. People on the streets actually smile at strangers, say hello, and pause to engage in conversation. Everyone, it seems, knows everyone else.

This was the Wilmington of Thomas J. Capano as he returned from Stone Harbor on the afternoon of June 28, 1996. He was a player, one of the people who made things happen.

"He was part of the power structure in the city and the state," recalls Celia Cohen, a longtime political writer who is now working on a book about the history of Delaware politics. "At that time, if somebody said we want to get the ten most influential people in the state to a meeting to discuss getting something done, Tom Capano would have been one of those ten. He was intelligent, extremely self-confident, and he knew how to make things happen. People trusted him. And he had a track record to back him up."

Capano could pick up a phone and call an executive at any one of the city's financial houses. He could walk into the mayor's office unannounced. He could meet with the governor or the state's only congressman or with either one of its U.S. senators.

He was forty-six years old, the oldest son of one of the wealthiest families in the city. His father, the late Louis J. Capano, had built many of the suburban housing tracts that sprung up around Wilmington during the construction boom of the 1960s and 1970s. The family fortune stemmed from the construction company Louis Capano had founded, and from the real estate holdings in which he had wisely invested and on which Louis Capano Jr., one of Tom's younger brothers, had expanded.

But while Louis Jr. was clearly the family moneymaker, Thomas Capano had been the pride and joy of his immigrant parents, Louis and Marguerite Rizzo Capano. He was the son who was going to take the family to the next level—not financially, but socially and politically. There was a daughter,

Marian, who was five years older than Tom, and there were three younger brothers, Louis Jr., Joe, and Gerard.

Louie and Joe were rough-and-tumble characters, happy to work in the construction trades, anxious to follow in their father's footsteps. Gerry, who came along late in life—he was thirteen years younger than Tom, eleven younger than Joe—was the spoiled baby of the family, a big kid who never really grew up.

Tom was the smart one, the one who was always reading books. Tom was the standout student-athlete at Archmere Academy, the private, boys-only Catholic prep school he attended in the mid–1960s. He was the president of the student council, one of the senior class leaders, a delegate to Boys State. He starred on the football and track teams. He went on to Boston College, and then to the college's law school.

"Every mother loves her children equally," Marian Capano Ramunno would recall sadly after everything fell apart for her brother. "But there is always one child who is easier to like. Tom was easy to like. He never gave my parents a bit of trouble. He was the golden boy."

There was a standing joke within the family. Marguerite Capano, like any mother, would brag about the accomplishments of her sons, whatever they might be. Louie did this. Joey did that. Gerry did the other. But when she referred to her oldest son, it was always as "My Tommy." After they had all reached adulthood, the others in the family would mock Tom and chide their mother.

"His name is Tommy, Ma," they would say with a laugh. "Not 'My Tommy.'"

Louis Capano Sr. cried when his oldest son graduated from law school in 1974. It was a dream fulfilled. Wealthy by dint of his own hard work, Louis Capano always felt like an outsider in the social and political circles that defined Wilmington. He had come to this country as a boy from Italy with his father, Thomas, after whom he would name his first son. The elder Thomas Capano was a stone mason from a small village in Calabria who had brought his family to America to find a better life. His relatives had settled in the Wilmington area earlier, but while they found opportunity, they also encountered institutional bigotry.

Louis Capano Sr., who dropped out of school as a teenager

to learn a trade, was a carpenter. One of his first jobs as a carpenter's apprentice was to build the outhouses that were still in use behind many of the row houses in Wilmington's Little Italy. The immigrant Thomas Capano and his son Louis were men who worked with their hands. They were good at what they did, but sometimes that didn't seem to be enough.

Through the early 1960s there were still deed restrictions in some areas of the city that prohibited the sale of property to Italians or Jews. Blacks, of course, weren't even considered. There was no way they would be able to buy a home in those neighborhoods. In fact, it wasn't until the urban riots of 1968—when the Delaware National Guard occupied the city for nearly a year—that the rights of African Americans were tacitly recognized and their status as second-class citizens began to erode.

Even after the Capanos and dozens of other Italian families accrued substantial wealth and moved from the cramped quarters of the city's Little Italy to larger homes in the immediate suburbs, they still faced limitations. For years, Italians—along with other ethnic groups—were denied membership in the Wilmington Country Club. Louis Capano was one of several prominent Italian Americans who helped fund and build the Cavalier Country Club so that he and his friends would have a place of their own. It was a small victory that provided some satisfaction, but it reinforced the feeling that Italians were outsiders, not part of the mainstream, not worthy.

But Thomas Capano, the grandson and the son of Italian immigrants, was a lawyer. He could move in circles that had been forever closed to his father and grandfather. He would have the status and the prestige, the social standing, they had been denied.

He would have it all.

The brothers got back to Wilmington at a little after 5:00 P.M. on June 28, 1996. They were riding in a Chevy Suburban that Tom had unexpectedly borrowed that morning from his estranged wife, Kay. First they stopped at the Acme parking lot near Trolley Square, the trendy shopping center a few blocks from the center of town. Gerry had left his pickup truck there that morning.

Gerry got in his truck and followed Tom back to the house on Grant Avenue. This was the house Tom had moved into in September after separating from Kay. It was a stately two-story in a neighborhood of well-kept, expensive homes. Mike Castle, the congressman and former governor, lived across the street.

During the ride back from Stone Harbor, Gerry and Tom had agreed on an alibi of sorts, an explanation for why they had gone down to the shore that morning. Gerry wrote it all down on a yellow Post-it note and put the note inside his checkbook.

At Grant Avenue, Tom asked for another favor. He needed to get rid of a couch. Stained with blood, it was still in what Tom called the "great room," the den/dining area where the murder had occurred. He needed Gerry's help carrying it out of the house.

The brothers entered the house through the garage. As they did, Gerry saw a rug that had been rolled up and partially cut in pieces. Like the couch, the rug was stained with dried blood.

Gerry didn't ask any questions. He didn't want to know.

He helped carry the couch to the garage. It was a large, rose-colored four-seater with a woven pineapple-like design in the fabric. Gerry noticed the stain right away. It was about shoulder high against one of the back cushions. He told Tom he should cut the stain out before they dumped the couch.

Tom got a knife and cut deep into the cushion, hollowing out the area and pulling away the fabric and the discolored interior. He threw the remnants into a trash bag near the rolled-up rug. Then he and Gerry lifted the couch onto the back of the Chevy Suburban and headed out to a construction site off Foulk Road near Route 202, where Louis J. Capano & Associates had a contract to renovate an office complex for First USA.

They got to the construction site at a little before 6:00 P.M. No one was around. Gerry tried to rip one of the legs off the couch to make it look damaged, so that no one would be surprised to see it discarded. Then he and Tom heaved it into a large Dumpster. Gerry climbed up and threw some debris around, covering the couch.

Tom watched in a daze. He had been awake for nearly thirty-six hours, and there was still more to do.

After Gerry left, Tom went back to Grant Avenue, threw

the rug and the trash bags from the garage into the back of the Chevy, and headed over the Delaware Memorial Bridge to Penns Grove, New Jersey, where the family owned a Holiday Inn. He pulled up to a trash bin behind the hotel, where he discarded the rug and the trash bags.

Fifteen minutes later he was back in Wilmington. He bought gas for the Suburban, filling the tank, then drove directly to his wife's house on Seventeenth Street, where Kay and their four daughters—Christy, sixteen, Katie, fourteen, Jenny, thirteen, and Alex, eleven—lived. The two oldest girls had recently returned from a trip to Italy with their uncle Louis and his wife, Lauri Merten, a professional golfer. Tom was anxious to see his daughters. Even after the separation, they had remained close. He stopped by the house on a regular basis, and the girls spent most Saturday nights with him at Grant Avenue. In fact, one of the reasons he had rented the large house was so that each of his daughters would have her own room and could entertain friends during the time they spent with him. He had put a phone and a boom box in each bedroom. There was a big-screen television in the great room on the first floor, and another in the recreation room in the basement. He had put a pool table in the dining room right under the chandelier.

He was always amazed at his girls, at how easily they got along, at how they always seemed to attract crowds. Wherever they went, they seemed to be the center of attention. Others might have described the Capano girls as spoiled and pretentious; Tom Capano saw them as privileged and special. Like their father, they gave off an aura of entitlement.

A generation after their parents and grandparents had been shunned and discriminated against, the Capanos took pride in being a part of the society that had once looked down on them. Their membership in the Wilmington Country Club proved it: They had arrived.

When he got to Seventeenth Street, the girls told Tom Capano that they'd rented a movie and ordered some pizzas. Kay was out. Tom ate a slice and then fell asleep, surrounded by his beautiful young daughters, who laughed and giggled as they watched a romantic comedy.

Capano awoke with a start at around 10:30 P.M. He said good night to the girls, told them he would pick them up the next day, and headed out the door. He drove two blocks to a home on Delaware Avenue, pulled into the driveway, opened the back door with a key, and punched in the alarm code. Then he headed up the steps to the second-floor bedroom suite, where he knew Debby MacIntyre would be waiting.

She was already in bed. She had been expecting him for an hour. They were both tired. They kissed and fell asleep, slipping easily into a routine established during the fifteen years that they had been secretly seeing one another. The next morning they made love and then went downstairs and had breakfast.

Tom told her he had to run some errands and that he'd be calling her later. He said he'd decided to replace the rug in the den of his home on Grant Avenue. He said he was looking for something smaller, maybe an Oriental.

It was a little after 11:00 A.M. on Saturday, June 29, 1996.

Investigators who would later re-create Tom Capano's actions in the hours following Fahey's murder were amazed at the callousness of it all. Eight hours after dumping the body of a woman he professed to love into the Atlantic Ocean, Tom Capano happily shared a pizza and fell asleep watching a movie with his unsuspecting teenage daughters. Twelve hours after that, he made love to another mistress, a woman he would ultimately try to frame for the murder that would soon consume his life. In the span of thirty-six hours Capano had shot Fahey, disposed of her body, had sex with MacIntyre, and then carefully and meticulously set out to remove all evidence of his crime.

And never once, those who saw him during that period said, did he show any sign of remorse or sadness.

2

In the end, it always came back to this: Anne Marie Fahey was dead because she had said no to Tom Capano.

After all the theories and the speculation and the bizarre, outlandish, and incredible testimony had been offered and the jury had reached its verdict, that was the bottom line: Capano killed her because she refused to resume their affair.

It had taken her over two years to get to that point, however, and that was what gave the story its intrigue, what turned the murder into the spectacle it became. Tom Capano was a poster boy for the self-indulgent, self-absorbed machismo of the decade that had given us O. J. Simpson, Joey Buttafuoco, Marv Albert, Latrell Sprewell, Dick Morris, and Bill Clinton. Anne Marie Fahey was a cover girl for the materialistic and out-of-focus value system that lies at the heart of Generation X.

Fahey was the victim, there is and could never be any doubt about that. Her lifeless body was laying at the bottom of the Atlantic Ocean wrapped in chains and an anchor. She had been preyed upon by Tom Capano, manipulated and controlled and taken advantage of. But for the longest time she hadn't seen it that way. Fahey had been thrilled and excited by the attention of this suave, powerful, and sophisticated lawyer who was unlike anyone else she had ever met—certainly unlike any of the young men she had ever dated. For years she was seduced by the aura of Tom Capano, and the nature of the seduction itself seemed part and parcel of the morality of the times: an era when celebrity—even on a local level—was more important than character, when status meant more than integrity, and when money was the common measure of an individual's worth.

The investigation of Fahey's disappearance and suspected murder dominated political and social life in Wilmington from the day she was reported missing. For the next two and a half years, it would be *the* story in the city. Before it was over, Capano the well-regarded lawyer and local celebrity would be unmasked as a philanderer who had cheated on his wife almost from the day they were married, as a libertine who enjoyed watching his mistress have sex with other men, as a control freak who had to have everything his own way, and as a self-centered individual who wouldn't take no for an answer.

Tom Capano, the son who always did the right thing, at some point had gotten things skewed. Somewhere along the way, like many other politicians, sports figures, and celebrities, he came to believe that the right thing was whatever he chose to do. Capano had missed or forgotten one of life's most important lessons: You cannot do whatever you want to whomever you want whenever you want.

For Fahey, it was the other side of the same worn and soiled coin: You cannot have whatever you want whenever you want it. Life is a series of choices. There are no guarantees. This is America, not Utopia.

From Anne Marie Fahey's diary, March 3, 1994:

I have fallen in love w/a very special person whose name I choose to leave anonymous. We know who each other are. It happened the night of my 28th birthday. We have built an everlasting friendship. I feel free around him, and like he says, "He makes my heart smile." He deserves some happiness in his life and it makes me feel good to know that I can provide him w/such happiness. Who knows if anything serious will ever happen between the 2 of us (I only know what I dream.).

Ciao, AMF

The entry was the first reference to Tom Capano by Anne Marie Fahey in a series of personal notes she entered sporadically in a floral-covered diary that her brother Robert and sister-in-law, Susan, had given her as a Christmas present three months earlier.

It was one of several items detectives pored over in the early morning hours of June 30, 1996, as they opened investigation No. 96–16037: the disappearance of Anne Marie Fahey, single, white female, age 30, height 5-foot-10, weight 128 pounds.

The missing person report came in a little after midnight. The call was made by Kathleen Fahey-Hosey, Anne Marie's older and only sister. There were also four older brothers. Anne Marie was the baby of the family, the one they all tried to look out for. She was, her sister and brothers knew, a troubled young woman; her outgoing and seemingly carefree personality was a front, a facade. Behind that exterior was a woman full of insecurity and self-doubt, a woman who questioned her looks, her intelligence, and her ability. On her best days she could be striking, with a radiant smile, a terrific figure, and a presence that would turn every eye in the room her way. But she herself may never have known it.

Psychologists—of whom Fahey had seen her share—say it all starts with the face looking back at you in the mirror each morning. You have to like who you see there, and too often Anne Marie Fahey did not.

The product of a largely dysfunctional family, Anne Marie had been burdened with a poor and unhappy childhood. Her mother had died when she was nine. Her father had disappeared a short time later into the abyss of alcoholism. He lived for eleven more years, bringing misery and discomfort to his children as he struggled and most often failed to perform the functions expected of a parent. The Faheys lived in a middle-class neighborhood in Wilmington, but the family often went without heat and sometimes even electricity as bills went unpaid and what little money Robert Fahey Sr. made as an insurance salesman went to buy the liquor that had become the focal point of his life.

Later, Tom Capano would refer to the Faheys as "white trash." The description stung the family, because they knew that there was a basis, however far back in their past, for the label. Most of the siblings had no time for their father. They had largely raised themselves, and whatever they had made of their lives had been in spite of him, not because of him.

Only Anne Marie had made peace with her father when he died. She was studying at Wesley College in Dover at the time. He was an alcoholic and a diabetic and had never been much of a factor in her life. He had left Wilmington during her sophomore year in high school, moving to Newark; she had decided to stay to finish at Brandywine High School, where she had friends and was a standout on the basketball and field hockey teams. She had already been spending weeks, if not months, away from the house, living with friends whose parents felt sorry for her and who willingly took her in.

As a teenager, Anne Marie Fahey was already adept at creating her own reality, ignoring the harsh, uncaring atmosphere at home. If she found any solace, it was in the memory of her mother and in the warmth of her maternal grandmother, Katherine McGettigan—"Nan"—who taught her about family and gave her a sense of who she was, however fragile and incomplete that sense would turn out to be.

From Anne Marie Fahey's diary, March 24, 1994:

> My boyfriend (Tomas) asked me today if I wanted to be a girlfriend and live alone and he would pay rent for my room. I need to think. I love him, but . . . he has four children (girls) and a wife. I will be a silent girlfriend. Oh, my god.
>
> Today is the day my father died! How sad. My dad was a bad father, but he was the only father I ever had so therefore I loved him. I do not think that he consciously meant to be a bad father,—he just had no clue! He really made my life very sad & lonely. I will never forget the pain he caused me. He forced me to lie to protect my identity.

Finding out who Anne Marie Fahey was proved to be a major part of the investigation detectives opened that summer evening in 1996. Her diary provided some clues, but she had hidden her identity from so many people for so many years that after she was gone it was hard to reconstruct it. Everyone saw a piece of Anne Marie, usually a piece she wanted them to see. But few people really knew who she was.

Perhaps no one did.

Or, perhaps, sadly, it was Tom Capano who knew her better than anyone.

They had met in the spring of 1993 at a political function, a fundraiser for a Democratic Party women's club. Capano, who moved in both city and state political circles, attended using a ticket purchased by his wife, Kay. Fahey was the scheduling secretary for Governor Tom Carper, and she and a coworker had gotten tickets to the function at their office. As part of the governor's staff they often appeared at such fundraisers, for both political and practical reasons. Young, single, career-minded, and living on barely-making-it salaries—Fahey was earning $31,500 a year—women who staff political and government offices often view a luncheon or dinnertime fundraiser as both a chance to socialize and an opportunity for a free meal.

Fahey walked up and introduced herself to Capano. She was the youngest Fahey, she said with a smile. She was sure he knew her sister, Kathleen, who had worked on several Democratic political campaigns in the city, and her brothers, nearly all of whom had worked at one time or another at O'Friel's.

O'Friel's Irish Pub, in the heart of Wilmington, was owned and operated by the Freel brothers, Edward, Charles, and Kevin, perhaps the most politically active and astute group of power brokers and kingmakers within the local Democratic Party. Ed Freel, in fact, was the secretary of state and the man who had helped Anne Marie get her first job as a secretary in the congressional office of Tom Carper two years before.

When Carper gave up his congressional seat and was elected governor, Anne Marie came north—came home, in fact—to serve as his scheduling secretary.

Charles "Bud" Freel and Capano had masterminded the political career of the late Daniel Frawley, a city councilman and mayor. Freel, Capano, and Frawley had become friends in the early 1980s, when they played together at the Wilmington Rugby Club. The beer bashes that inevitably followed rugby matches involved the usual mix of wine, women, and song, but also included serious and semiserious political discussions. Frawley's political career grew out of the scrum where he, Capano, and Freel butted heads with rival rugby clubs and from the beer-soaked parties that followed.

When Frawley was elected mayor in 1984, Capano became the city solicitor. And when Frawley was in danger of blowing the job because of his own penchant for booze and broads, it was Bud Freel and Tom Capano who brought him back in line.

"Dan Frawley was the quintessential frat boy," said one longtime Wilmington political operative. "He was the guy in the toga with the bottle of beer in one hand and the half-naked blonde in the other. Capano was the one who told him to hang up his toga and put on his business suit, that he was the mayor and had to start acting like it."

It was a lesson Frawley never completely absorbed. Instead, during his second term in office, he appointed Capano chief of staff. At that point Capano, who had been hiding his own sexual encounters for some time, became the man who ran the day-to-day operations of the city—the de facto mayor.

The third Freel brother was Kevin, who managed the family bar as well as the occasional political campaign and who, on the side, was a Shakespearean actor. He would later emerge as the unofficial spokesman for the Fahey family during the investigation into Anne Marie's disappearance. Whenever a member of the out-of-town media showed up to do a story on the Fahey case, the reporter would invariably end up at O'Friel's Irish Pub, drinking a bottle of black-and-tan at the long, highly polished bar as Kevin provided the background on the plays and the players in the convoluted case. He was born to the role, which allowed him to dip deeply into his experience and background in politics, the bar business, and the theater.

His description of Anne Marie was a classic, and it would show up in half a dozen different stories about the case. She had a smile that would light up a room, Kevin Freel would say, as if he were finding the words for the first time. And a laugh that would make your heart skip a beat.

"This place could be packed during happy hour on a Friday afternoon," Freel would continue. "And over the din of all that noise you would hear her laugh and you would know that Annie was in the room."

The Freels, the Capanos, and the Faheys would all become a part of the story, as would the governor, the former governor, and dozens of other politicos and lawyers and wives and girlfriends and lovers. The overlapping relationships that surfaced as first investigators and then reporters began to scrutinize the lives of Anne Marie Fahey and Thomas J. Capano were surprising to outsiders who stumbled onto the case. But to those who lived and worked in the city, the reaction was always the same.

"That's Wilmington," they would say.

From Anne Marie Fahey's Diary, April 24, 1994:

> I had a great day on Friday. My friend and I went to his house to eat. What a house! He enchants me. During the weekend my thoughts were devoted to Tomas. I am afraid because I am in love with a man who has a family. I need to realize that our relationship will never be anything other than a secret. I fantasize my life with him all the time. He is very gentle, intelligent, handsome and very interesting. Why does he have to be married??? More information later.

There were dozens of entries in the diary that detectives began to review the night Anne Marie Fahey was reported missing. Not all focused on Capano, whom she referred to as "Tomas." There was also a detailed account of her battle with anorexia, and some disturbing comments about her attitude toward food. There were references to the psychological counseling and therapy she was receiving and the Prozac she was taking. An entire section of the diary was devoted to a trip to Ireland she and her brother Brian—whom she lovingly referred to as Seymour—had taken in the summer of 1994 with money left by their grandmother, who had passed away late in 1992. Anne Marie still grieved for the woman, whom she had loved perhaps more than anyone in the world; the trip to Ireland was a bittersweet memorial to Nan.

There were also references to "PJ": Paul Columbus, an old boyfriend with whom she had been involved in a rocky relationship for several years. And there were several pages devoted to a brief romance in the summer of 1994 with another young man, a romance for which Anne Marie had held high hopes, but that never really went anywhere.

The diary entries were like her life, filled with gaps and unexplained blank spaces. There would be weeks without any entries, then a rapid-fire succession of comments, some coming one day after the other.

Detectives opening a missing person investigation would look to the diary for leads, hints of what might have happened, of who might know where she was or what had become of her. Anne Marie's relationship with Tom Capano was a logical starting point. While only the last entry in the diary mentioned Capano's full name, there were three other notes found in Fahey's apartment that night, one written on the letterhead of Capano's law firm, that hinted at their relationship. And there were friends, questioned first by members of Fahey's family and then by police, who knew bits and pieces of the secret love affair they had been conducting for more than two years.

But it was the last entry in the diary, from Easter Sunday 1996, that set the tone and provided the signature phrase for the investigation. It was the first and only time Anne Marie Fahey mentioned Capano by name. And it was not a flattering reference.

From Anne Marie Fahey's diary, April 7, 1996:

Happy Easter! Well, . . . another yr. has passed since my last entry and man o' man has a lot happened. I've been through a lot of emotional battles. I finally have brought closure to Tom Capano. What a controlling, manipulative, insecure jealous maniac. Now that I look back on that aspect of my life—I realize just how vulnerable I had become. It hurts me when I think about that year. For one whole year, I allowed someone to take control of every decision in my life.

3

Detective Robert Donovan of the Wilmington Police Department was on call the weekend of June 29, 1996, and consequently drew the Fahey assignment. By the time he arrived at the tiny third-floor apartment in the 1700 block of Washington Street, where Anne Marie had lived for the past two years, there was already a crowd. The missing woman's sister, her boyfriend, several of her friends, and, most interesting of all from Donovan's perspective, two members of the Delaware State Police were jammed into the four-room apartment.

Donovan, a burly, street-smart cop who had been on the job for ten years, had been forewarned. He had received a call from the duty desk at a little after midnight with the assignment to check out a missing persons report.

"But there's more," the sergeant said.

"Oh?" asked Donovan.

"The missing woman works for the governor," said the sergeant on the duty desk. "And there's another surprise."

"Yeah?" said Donovan.

"Some people from the governor's security detail are already on scene."

Donovan, who had recently made detective after working the streets in uniform for years, wasn't often surprised by what he encountered on the job. Work enough Saturday night details in Wilmington and you develop a keen sense of cynicism. It's

easy to get emotionally buried in bar brawls and domestic violence complaints that leave people bruised and bleeding,
sometimes dead. One case runs into another; you become
numb with the routine.

But Donovan quickly realized that there would be nothing
routine about this case. In theory, this was a missing persons
investigation. But from the beginning, everyone involved
sensed that it was more.

Politics change things. And this certainly was political;
Donovan knew that from the get-go. The presence of members
of the governor's security detail—Lieutenant Mark Daniels
and Detective Steven Montague had responded to a call from
Ed Freel, the secretary of state—merely served to underline
the fact. Throw the name Capano into the mix, and the case
moved to another level. Donovan knew that Capano was
wealthy and wired. He had money and power and connections—a Wilmington trifecta.

Capano had been the mayor's chief of staff when Donovan
joined the Wilmington Police Department. Donovan also knew
that Capano had been a former state prosecutor before he had
worked in the mayor's office, and that after he left the mayor's
office he had served as chief counsel to Governor Michael
Castle.

In one of those neat little Delaware twists, Castle had left
the governor's office after serving the maximum two terms permitted by law. He then ran for the state's only seat in the U.S.
House of Representatives; this was the seat vacated by Tom
Carper, Fahey's boss, who had left Congress to run for governor. Castle and Carper had, in effect, traded positions. Castle
was a Republican, Carper a Democrat, but both had the support of the powers that ran the state. At the highest levels in
Delaware politics, labels were not important. It was all about
access and getting things done and being part of that elite
group who knew what was best for the city and the state. These
were the people who were always in a position to make the
decisions that mattered. Some were to the manor born; if your
name was DuPont, for example, and you wanted to play in politics and government, there would always be a seat at the table
for you. Others had to earn their way by playing the game

according to the rules: Don't make waves; don't call too much attention to yourself; don't publicly criticize a political opponent; and whenever in doubt, always err on the side of the banks, the investment brokers, the people with the money. It was a paternalistic and patrician form of democracy, and it was what Delaware was all about.

Capano had a seat at the table. He had worked for Mayor Frawley, the Democrat, and for Governor Castle, the Republican. After he left the governor's office in 1992 he joined the high-powered law firm of Saul, Ewing, Remick & Saul, which was headquartered in Philadelphia but had opened an office in Wilmington. Capano was a good fit at the firm. Its forte was government bond work, and it handled most of the big financial borrowing deals for the city and the state. Who better to open doors and provide the kind of access required in that line of work than a man who had sat beside and counseled a mayor and a governor?

By the time Anne Marie Fahey disappeared, Tom Capano was a partner with the firm and the manager of its Wilmington office. He was pulling in about $250,000 a year. He also had a draw from his family's real estate holding company and a very liberal law firm expense account that allowed him, unbeknownst to the firm, to bill lunches, dinners, and business trips—many of which, it would turn out, he shared with his mistresses.

There were several different ways to measure and describe Capano's wealth at this time, but perhaps the best was uncovered by investigators when they began to track his credit card purchasers and look at his bank statements.

Early in 1996, Thomas J. Capano was carrying a balance of $173,190.13 in his checking account at the Wilmington Trust Bank. The account would fluctuate from time to time, but it never dropped below $125,000. That was his *checking* account. His overall net worth, according to a financial workup done by his own accounting firm a few years earlier, was in excess of $5 million. His brothers, who ran the family's construction and real estate businesses, were worth millions more.

Bob Donovan, who had a somewhat lower balance in his personal checking account, knew about the world in which

Tom Capano lived, worked, and played, though he was hardly a part of it. He had seen Capano around City Hall when he was chief of staff: One of Capano's duties was to oversee the public safety department. As a street cop Donovan had had one encounter with the wealthy lawyer. "There had been a series of break-ins in his neighborhood," Donovan remembers. "We did a stakeout and set up a surveillance from his backyard on Seventeenth Street. I met him then, but I doubt if he remembered me."

Donovan was about six foot three, slightly overweight, with a Marine-style crew cut and a nonchalant, disarming manner. He had grown up in a Wilmington suburb and had always wanted to join the state police, but when he applied there hadn't been any openings. He joined the Wilmington Police Department instead; in the mid–1990s he was living with his wife and two young children, a boy and girl, in one of the city's middle-class neighborhoods, counting the days until they could move to the suburbs. Wilmington has a limited residency requirement for its cops: after twelve years on the job, a police officer can live outside the city. Donovan, whose parents had a small farm with horses downstate, wanted his kids to experience life outside the city.

"Bobby's a good cop," said a veteran investigator who watched the case unfold. "But if anybody had realized what was involved in the beginning, he'd have never gotten the assignment. He'd only been a detective for a short time and one of the veterans would have grabbed it away from him."

Fortunately for Donovan, by the time the case took off he was the point man. By then it was too late; there was no way he could have been excluded from the investigation. Call it fate or happenstance, but it was as if an outside force were setting things up and putting people in place during the early days of this investigation—an outside force that was going to ensure that the investigation moved forward, that it would not, as Capano hoped, be swept under the rug.

Donovan brought the right temperament and attitude to the case. He was patient, focused, willing to do whatever needed to be done. He had enough experience to be cynical, but he hadn't been at it long enough to become jaded. He had a habit of chewing on a paper clip as he poked through an investigative file or jotted down notes on a phone trace. He tended to listen more than he spoke

He liked being a cop, enjoyed figuring things out. And in his own way, Bob Donovan was good at it. One of his greatest attributes was his lack of pretense. This would prove crucial to the case that he was about to open.

One of the things Tom Capano counted on was that the investigation into Anne Marie Fahey's disappearance would remain in the hands of local investigators. He didn't see how it could go any other way. Capano knew his connections would allow him to monitor all that was going on. It wasn't necessarily that he thought the locals were incompetent, but Tom Capano was extremely confident in his ability to anticipate their moves and stay two or three steps ahead of them. He saw it as a game and he thought he knew the rules.

Later that summer he would brag to a friend about how the investigation was going nowhere. "The Faheys are white trash," he said. "By Labor Day this will all be forgotten."

Bob Donovan was one of the reasons it wasn't. The others were a baby-faced federal prosecutor named Colm Connolly, whose Boy Scout looks hid the heart of a bulldog, and a buttoned-down veteran FBI agent named Eric Alpert, whose dry wit and unassuming manner belied a quiet, determined confidence.

Donovan set the tone that first night. Sensing that a dispute over turf would be petty and counterproductive, he welcomed the state police into a case that was clearly within his own purview. Later he would ask for help from the federal government; eventually he was glad to cede direction to the U.S. Attorney's Office, which effectively took over the case.

Ultimately it was Donovan working the streets, Alpert working the electronic trail, and Connolly patiently reconstructing the story from the emerging patchwork of evidence who formed the heart of the team that brought Tom Capano down.

Within weeks of Fahey's disappearance, they were certain that she was dead. And they were convinced that Capano had killed her. But it would take nearly two years—and the addition of a secret and until this writing little-known undercover operation run off the books out of the Wilmington office of the Bureau of Alcohol, Tobacco and Firearms (ATF)—before they were able to put together enough evidence to make an arrest and bring Capano to trial.

The process began around 3:30 A.M. on June 30, 1996, when Donovan, Montague, Daniels, and Wilmington Police Sergeant Elmer Harris left the Fahey apartment at 1718 Washington Street and drove over to Capano's home at 2302 Grant Avenue, about five minutes away.

The diary notes were one of the reasons the investigators wanted to question Capano. But there already were other references to the relationship. Friends of Fahey's who were reluctant at first to even mention her affair had finally opened up to Anne Marie's sister, Kathleen Fahey-Hosey, and then to the investigators on the scene.

Kathleen had gone to her sister's apartment that night with Anne Marie's boyfriend, Michael Scanlan, and two of her close friends, Ginny Columbus—Paul Columbus's sister—and Jill Morrison. Scanlan, a young banking executive who had been dating Anne Marie since September, knew nothing about Anne Marie's involvement with Capano. Morrison and Columbus, who worked with Fahey in Governor Carper's office, knew a little. When Kathleen first found the diary, she pulled them aside, out of Scanlan's earshot, and asked what exactly they knew about the relationship between her younger sister and this lawyer.

Robert Fahey's wife, Susan, also spoke on the phone that night with Kim Horstmann, another friend of Anne Marie's and a woman who probably knew more about the Fahey-Capano affair than anyone else. Horstmann, trying to protect Fahey's privacy, said nothing in that first phone conversation. But after she hung up, she dialed Capano.

This was nearly two hours before Donovan and the others showed up at his door. She told him that Anne Marie's family had reported her missing, that no one had seen her for three days. She asked if he knew where Anne Marie was.

Capano was surprised by the call. It wasn't the way he thought things would play out. He knew Fahey had taken

Friday off, and figured she would not be missed until she failed to show up for work Monday morning. Now Horstmann was on the phone talking about a missing person investigation and telling him that the governor's office and the state police were already involved.

Capano told Horstmann that he had taken Anne Marie to dinner Thursday night and had dropped her off at her apartment later that evening, around 10:00 P.M. That was the last time he had seen her. He said he thought she was going to the shore that weekend with her. In fact, he was adamant about it.

"Why isn't she with you?" he asked.

Horstmann and Fahey had rented a house at the South Jersey shore, but the lease expired that weekend. They had never planned to be there, she told Capano.

"Maybe she just wanted to be alone, you know how she can be," Capano said. "I'm sure she'll turn up at work on Monday morning. I'm totally confident of it. We both know that she has the potential to do this. "

Horstmann said that Capano had sounded calm. She found it curious that he seemed more surprised that the state police were involved than he did that Annie was missing.

In fact, Fahey's family had become concerned when she had failed to show up for a dinner date with her brother Robert and his wife, Susan, earlier that Saturday evening. She and Scanlan, a thirty-one-year-old executive in the community affairs department of MBNA, were supposed to drive over to Robert's home in Newtown Square, Pennsylvania, and then go out to dinner at a local restaurant.

It was a chance for Robert and his wife to get to know Scanlan better. Anne Marie had already told Kathleen that Scanlan might be "the one." Kathleen was excited. She thought Anne Marie and Michael were a good fit. He was her age and had a good job and a secure future. He could bring stability to her life. In addition, she thought that Scanlan—tall, with a solid swimmer's build and the aw-shucks manner of a young John Wayne—was a nice guy. And God knew Annie deserved a nice guy for a change. While sitting on the beach at the Jersey shore earlier that month, the two sisters had joked about wedding plans, and Anne Marie had told Kathleen who she would have in her wedding party if Scanlan asked her to marry him.

Robert Fahey called Scanlan at a little after 9:00 P.M. that Saturday night to ask why he and Annie hadn't shown up for dinner. Scanlan said he hadn't heard from Anne Marie for two days; in fact, she hadn't returned three of his phone calls, and he assumed the plans had been canceled. Scanlan then called Kathleen to ask if she had seen Anne Marie. She hadn't seen or heard from her since Wednesday night. Scanlan told Kathleen he'd pick her up, and the two of them would drive over to Anne Marie's apartment together to look for her. Columbus and Morrison, who received phone calls from Kathleen, headed that way as well.

The moment Kathleen walked into the third-floor apartment, she knew something was wrong. She had asked Anne Marie's landlady, who lived on the first floor, for the key. She was concerned about her sister, she said; perhaps she had slipped and passed out. Maybe she was lying up there in the apartment unable to call for help.

Kathleen and Scanlan walked up the two flights of stairs and let themselves in. The first thing Kathleen noticed was the smell from the kitchen. Garbage in a plastic bag in the trash receptacle was rotting. The stench was overwhelming. That was the first sign of trouble: Anne Marie Fahey was extremely neat, even obsessively so. Friends called her "Anal Annie," and with good reason. Everyone knew what a crazy neatnik she was. Everyone joked about it. The first thing Anne Marie did when she woke up in the morning was make her bed. She wasn't even out from under the sheets when she began to straighten them out. She kept all her shoes in their original boxes, neatly stacked at the bottom of her clothes closet. If they came stuffed with paper or with cardboard inserts to hold their shape, that paper and those inserts were put back in the shoes each time she took them off and placed them back in her closet.

She folded her dirty laundry and piled it neatly in a basket until she was ready to do the wash. She never left a dirty dish in the sink. Never threw a pair of jeans, a sweater, or a dress over the arm of a chair or left a shirt hanging on a doorknob. At work, she had the paper clips in her desk drawer lined up in order. She had a row of pennies all facing heads up in the same direction. Pens and pencils were neatly arranged by color and size. So were her notepads and her Post-its.

"Anne Marie was just orderly," her sister said. "She wouldn't even leave a spoon in the sink."

Kathleen knew her sister would never have consciously left the apartment in the condition she found it.

"There was a terrible smell when we first got in the apartment from . . . vegetables and spinach and stuff that were in the trash," Kathleen recalled. "There were dry packages of, like, rice and pretzels on the counter. The trash was pulled tight as if somebody was going to lift it out. And on top of it was a water bottle."

In the bedroom, the comforter had been pulled down off the pillows and bunched up. Several of her shoeboxes were scattered about the room. There was a plastic dry cleaning bag on the floor in the clothes closet. A floral dress was flung over a chair.

There was one other item that caused Kathleen to pause as she looked about the bedroom. There was a gift box from Talbots, an upscale women's clothing store that Kathleen and Anne Marie both favored.

A week earlier, on a Saturday afternoon, Annie and Kathleen had been shopping and Annie had stopped in at Talbots and tried on an expensive taupe-colored pantsuit. Kathleen had chided her sister about the outfit.

"How could you afford something like that?" she asked, eyeing the price tag. The outfit cost nearly three hundred dollars. "And where would you wear it?"

Anne Marie got upset. She said she would wear it to work.

Kathleen also remembered how thin her sister had looked trying on the outfit. Annie was five foot ten. The suit was a size four.

"I hadn't realized how much weight she had lost," Kathleen said as she recounted that afternoon. "Whenever she came out to my house she'd be wearing jeans and a baggy sweater or sweatshirt. When she tried on the suit, I saw how thin her shoulders were, how skinny she was."

Anne Marie acted annoyed and told Kathleen not to worry about it. She put the pantsuit back and they left the store.

Now a Talbots box was sitting in the middle of the floor in Anne Marie's bedroom. When Kathleen opened it, the seal was still on the tissue paper. She peeled it away and saw that the box contained the taupe pantsuit, the one she knew her sister couldn't afford.

Kathleen Fahey-Hosey called the Wilmington Police and reported her sister missing. Then she called Ed Freel, the secretary of state, and asked for his help. That's how Daniels and Montague from the governor's security detail ended up in the apartment before Donovan that night.

As they searched the apartment, they found Anne Marie's pocketbook and her wallet, which contained her driver's license and credit cards and a few dollars in cash. They also found her passport. Anne Marie's car, a green Volkswagen Jetta, was parked out front. But the keys to the apartment and the car were missing.

Kathleen also found the diary. And three notes, which she quickly realized had been written by Tom Capano.

One of the notes was undated and unsigned, but from the references in the text Kathleen knew it had been written back in November. It appeared that Tom Capano had been lending her sister some money to help pay for a dinner party at the Saloon, a swank Philadelphia restaurant where the Fahey clan had celebrated the birthday of Kathleen's husband, Patrick Hosey.

The note, printed in a clear, clean style, ended with a personal and troubling reference: "Annie, I will miss you next week more than you can imagine. It would help a lot if we could be together on Sunday night. . . . I promise to get you out of the house as early as you like on Monday morning. Please consider it. And please accept this gift in the spirit in which it is given. All I want is to make you happy and to be with you. I love you."

The two other notes were written in the same clear hand. Both were signed "Tom," and one was written on the letterhead of Saul, Ewing, Remick & Saul. The one dated May 2, 1996, referred to another gift of money from Capano, this time apparently to help pay for the repair of a crack in the windshield of Anne Marie's car.

"Please accept this," the note read in part. "The windshield stresses you and it's dangerous. I would do more if you'd let me (like replace the Jetta with a Lexus 300ES Coach Edition). Maybe some day . . .

"Tom."

The note on Saul, Ewing letterhead was dated June 25, just five days earlier. It also made reference to a loan Capano had apparently given her sister to help get over a rough spot when she was low on cash.

"Just add this to the balance," it read. "Consider it a consolidation loan (That's a joke.). Kidding aside, you should not be penniless for several days in case of an emergency (like an overpowering yearning for a latte). I'd have sent more but I know you'll have a hard time even accepting this. Please accept it in the spirit in which it's given. And don't spend it on Jill!

"Tom."

After the police left to interview Capano, Kathleen continued to search through Annie's apartment, looking for any other hints of where she might be or who might know what had happened to her. She called her brother Robert four or five times through those early-morning hours, and shared some—but not all—of her thoughts with Michael Scanlan, who stayed on along with Ginny Columbus and Jill Morrison.

Kathleen let no one else read the diary, however. She was upset at herself for looking at it, and felt guilty for violating her sister's privacy. But she couldn't ignore the words on the page—particularly the last entry, written two months earlier, on Easter Sunday. The comments about Capano were troubling. But there was even more. It shocked and upset Kathleen to think that her sister had kept a part of her life hidden from her family. She knew Anne Marie had been seeing a therapist, that she had some emotional problems. But she never knew about the eating disorder. The first hint of that came in the last diary entry.

Eventually she would learn—along with the entire city, it sometimes seemed to Kathleen—about all of her sister's problems. About the anorexia and the bulimia and about how she tried to starve herself and fought to keep her weight down by taking laxatives, sometimes as many as fifteen during the course of a day.

Kathleen, who shared Anne Marie's classic good looks and bright smile, got her first inkling of what was to come as she sat in her baby sister's apartment in the early-morning hours of June 30, 1996, and read the last diary entry her sister would ever write.

From Anne Marie Fahey's diary, April 7, 1996 (continued):

Five weeks ago I was diagnosed w/Bulimia. My weight is currently 125 pounds. Pretty skinny, but I want more. My brother Robert is the only sibling that knows anything. Most likely that will remain the case. At this point, I'm afraid to share this news with Michael. I don't want him to run. I truly love him,—I'm afraid of what he might think of me. Michael is the most wonderful person. This is the first "normal" relationship I've ever had, and I can't screw it up!

4

He was wearing a bathrobe and appeared tired when he opened the door to the police shortly after 3:30 A.M. But he wasn't surprised to see them. He let them in and led them to the great room. He sat in a wicker chair. They sat across from him on a couch shaped like the letter C.

Tom Capano told the detectives who came to his home on Grant Avenue that morning that he already knew Anne Marie Fahey was missing. He said he had had a call a few hours earlier from Kim Horstmann. Until that moment, he said, he'd thought Fahey was at the Jersey shore with Horstmann. He was almost certain, he said, that that was what Annie had told him she intended to do for the weekend.

He said he and Fahey had gone to dinner earlier that week. At first he thought it was Wednesday night, but later corrected himself and said it was Thursday. They went to the Ristorante Panorama on Front Street in Philadelphia. It was one of her favorites. He knew the owner.

Capano said he had picked Fahey up at her apartment around 6:30 P.M. They went in his Jeep Cherokee. She was wearing a light-colored floral dress. Donovan noted the description. It sounded like the dress found draped over the chair in Fahey's bedroom back at the apartment. The couple had had a seven o'clock reservation. He described what they had for dinner: She had had fish, he one of the chicken dishes. He paid for the dinner with a credit card, and, as was his habit, let Anne Marie tabulate the tip and sign the bill. He always had trouble figuring out the percentage. And besides, he hadn't been very happy with the service.

They had ordered the grilled calamari as one of their appetizers. It was one of Annie's favorites. But the waitress had brought fried calamari instead. He was going to complain, but Annie told him not to bother. She didn't want to embarrass the waitress.

He said they left the restaurant a little after 9:00 P.M. and drove back to his house to pick up some things—a bag of groceries that included rice, bananas, spinach, strawberries, and soup and the gift he had gotten her from Talbots. No, he said, maybe the gift was already in the Jeep. He wasn't sure about that. He had ordered the pantsuit especially for her after she had complained about her sister, Kathleen—"Cass," she called her— and the remarks she had made when they were out shopping on Saturday.

The gift was a little surprise, something to cheer her up. The food was his way of trying to get her to eat. He knew about her anorexia and bulimia. He said it was important that there was food in the apartment, that there shouldn't be any excuse for Anne Marie not to eat.

He said he dropped her off a little before 10:00 P.M. He put the perishables in the refrigerator, put the other food on the counter, checked her bedroom air conditioner—it was always stuffy in her apartment—used the bathroom, and then left.

He might have stopped at the Getty station, the one on Lovering Avenue across from Gallucio's Tavern, to pick up some cigarettes on the way back to his place. Donovan made another note.

Mark Daniels was asking most of the questions, which surprised Capano. He thought he detected some annoyance on the part of Donovan and Harris, as if the state police were horning in on what should have been a Wilmington Police Department investigation.

In fact, Donovan preferred having someone else ask the questions; it freed him up to watch Capano react. Sometimes a person's look could say more than his words. This morning, however, Capano wasn't giving up very much. He said he was tired. He had, as was his habit, taken some extra-strength Tylenol before going to bed to help him relax. But otherwise he was calm, in control. He politely refused to let the investigators walk around the house. His four daughters were asleep upstairs, he said, and it was the middle of the night.

But he was willing to answer their questions and to do anything else he could to help with their investigation. He was sure Anne Marie would turn up.

She was a bit of an "airhead," he said, and could be "very unpredictable." She had been having a hard time lately, dealing with her eating disorder and trying to find herself. She wasn't happy with her job, and she had had that fight with Cass. Anne Marie complained, Capano said, that her sister always "put her down."

Daniels asked Capano if his relationship with Fahey was sexual. Capano was not happy with the question, but he answered it. He said it had been, but not recently. He said the last time they had had sex was about six months earlier. Now they were friends. They went to dinner once a week or so. They would talk on the phone almost every day. She confided in him. In the past, he said, she had talked about suicide, about just popping all her pills and then going to sleep forever. She was frustrated by her constant battles with depression, anxiety, and anorexia. He said she was on medication, but it bothered her, nauseated her and kept her up at night. She was having trouble sleeping.

He would buy her gifts, like the air conditioner in her bedroom or the pantsuit; he bought her groceries from time to time, and sometimes lent her money. She always said she would pay it back, and sometimes she did. But he never cared. He was happy to do it. She was always broke, struggling to make ends meet. Sometimes she would go to work without any money in her pocket; just the week before he'd sent thirty dollars over to her at her office because she was out of cash. It was three days until payday and she didn't have a cent.

He was sure, he said again, that Anne Marie had told him she was going to the shore with Kimmy that weekend. Now he knew that wasn't the case, because Kimmy had told him otherwise, but he was certain that was what Annie had said.

Daniels asked Capano if he thought the circumstances—Fahey disappearing after their dinner date, no one hearing from her for forty-eight hours, her failure to show up at her brother's—seemed "suspicious."

"She probably just went off somewhere to be alone, without telling anyone," Capano said. "I'm sure she'll show up for work on Monday."

Daniels asked Capano if Anne Marie Fahey was in his home at that moment.

"No, she isn't," Capano said with an air of certainty that Donovan interpreted in two ways: Fahey wasn't in the house, and the interview was over.

One of the problems with the early stages of the Fahey investigation was the crime scene: The police didn't know where it was. If Fahey had been abducted, where had it happened? There was no sign of a forced entry to her apartment. Even if there had been, by the time police got to the scene it would have been compromised by Fahey's sister and her friends, who had been poking around looking for hints as to where she might have gone.

If it was Capano's home on Grant Avenue, they had no access to it.

And no matter where the crime scene may have been, they were late. If Capano was to be believed, Fahey had last been seen alive around 10:00 P.M. on Thursday, June 27. This was Sunday, June 30, around 4:00 A.M., more than forty-eight hours after the fact.

Later in the morning, Donovan, Daniels, Montague, and Harris fanned out around Fahey's neighborhood doing a door-to-door, asking if anyone had seen anything unusual in the last two or three days. They also searched a small park across from Fahey's apartment. Montague arranged for a state police helicopter to fly over the park and along the Brandywine Creek and down to Valley Green Park, an area where friends said Anne Marie would frequently go if she wanted to be alone to read or "sort things out."

The searches turned up nothing.

Later that morning, back at the apartment, Robert Fahey

and Kathleen Fahey-Hosey began calling all of Anne Marie's friends. Then they went through her phone book and called any number they found. Eventually they would be joined by two other brothers, Kevin and Mark. One of the first calls went to Brian, their youngest brother, the one who was closest to Annie, the one whose easygoing, soft-around-the-edges personality reminded them of Anne Marie at her best.

Brian was in Ecuador, visiting with his fiancée's family. He had been gone a week. Anne Marie was supposed to pick him up at the airport on his return.

Brian, who taught fifth grade at the Friends School in Wilmington, had jokingly told his brothers and sisters not to call him in Ecuador "unless somebody died." As soon as he got the call, he booked a flight back. By Tuesday morning he had joined the vigil at his sister's apartment. Over the next six weeks, there was never a time when one of the Faheys wasn't at 1718 Washington Street. Even as hope faded, as it became more and more obvious that Annie wasn't coming home, someone was there just in case. They hoped someone would call about their missing sister. Or that Annie herself, out there somewhere, would get to a phone and call for help.

That call, of course, never came.

But in the beginning, the only person who knew for certain that it wouldn't was Thomas J. Capano. And among the many things the Faheys will never forgive him for is the fact that he allowed them that false hope, allowed them to wait and wonder in agony, allowed them to imagine what might have happened to their sister.

"It was a deep, dark black hole and there was no way out," Robert Fahey said of the weeks he and his brothers and his sister spent watching and waited on the porch and in the apartment for some word about Annie, the little sister they had all promised their mother they would watch out for.

Donovan, Daniels, and the other investigators spoke with Capano one more time that Sunday. After trying unsuccessfully to reach him by phone that afternoon, they drove to Grant Avenue. He wasn't there. So they headed over to his wife's house on Seventeenth Street. Donovan remembered the house from the stakeout several years earlier. It was around 2:30 P.M. when they spotted Capano pulling out of the driveway; after a brief conversation they arranged to follow him back to Grant Avenue, where he agreed to escort them through the house as they searched the various rooms. He also allowed them to search his Jeep Cherokee.

"The officers noted that the house was spotless with nothing out of place," Donovan later wrote in an affidavit. "They did not receive permission to search in any drawers or closets. Mr. Capano's demeanor had changed since the night before [actually earlier that same day], as he seemed very agitated. He stated that he wished he had not said some of the things he told the officers earlier that were private in nature."

Donovan and the others left the house around 3:00 P.M. They had now been working on the case nonstop for fifteen hours.

Police investigations are built on shreds of information. One of the first people Donovan sought out after the interviews with Capano was the attendant at the Getty station, where Capano said he had stopped to buy cigarettes after dropping Fahey off around 10:00 P.M. that Thursday night. The attendant said he closed the station at 9:30. He did not remember anyone coming by after hours and asking to buy a pack of cigarettes.

Daniels had arranged to place an item in the Wilmington *News Journal* that ran on Tuesday, July 2. It was a small piece with a picture of Anne Marie and a story about her disappearance. The fact that Fahey was the scheduling secretary to the governor got the story on page one. There were two phone numbers listed in the article, one for Daniels and the other for Donovan.

The next day Daniels got a call from Lisa D'Amico, a beautician who worked at Michael Christopher Hair Designs out on Pennsylvania Avenue. Anne Marie had missed an appointment there on Friday. D'Amico was her stylist.

As the investigation proceeded, those working the case were struck by how inconsistent Fahey was. She went to great lengths to keep her affair with Capano a secret from her family, but she blurted out details about the relationship to those who weren't nearly as close to her—D'Amico among them. The young beautician told Daniels that during her last appointment back in May, Fahey had seemed "excited and happy" about how her relationship with Michael Scanlan was progressing. At the same time, however, Fahey told her that Capano was "crazy and he scared her." She and Capano had gotten into several heated arguments because she wanted to end their relationship. She complained to D'Amico that Capano was always trying to give her unwanted gifts, that he would show up at her apartment unannounced, and that sometimes she refused to let him in, which made him even angrier. Fahey had told her hairdresser that Capano could be violent, that he would grab and shake her while he screamed and berated her. He would holler about how Fahey had "ruined his life." He would say that he had left his wife for her and now she was rejecting him.

Fahey said she couldn't take it anymore. She was frightened and nervous. She told D'Amico she was worried that Capano might hurt her.

At around this same time, Donovan interviewed Al Franke, a restaurant manager and friend for whom Fahey had once worked. Franke said Fahey told him she had had an affair with Capano, but that it was over. He said Fahey told him she wanted Capano out of her life, that he was "possessive" and "controlling."

Over the next four days the disappearance of Anne Marie Fahey became a bigger and bigger story in Wilmington. Each day's headline in the *News Journal*, the local paper, ran in larger type; each piece of new information was more sensational than the last. The second-day story reported that she had last been seen having dinner in Philadelphia with a Wilmington attorney and political insider. By day three, Capano had been identified by name. "NO TRACE OF CARPER AIDE," said the headline on the first lengthy piece about Fahey's disappearance. Then came "SEARCH SET FOR CARPER ASSISTANT," a story that announced plans for a massive search on July 4 in and around Brandywine Park.

More than 300 people turned out on the Fourth of July to

join in the search for Fahey. They included family members, friends, coworkers, and one ex-boyfriend. Paul Columbus led one of the groups that searched the park that day. He told reporters that he and Anne Marie had dated for nearly four years and were still friends.

"In a way, I hope we don't find anything . . . anything bad," he said before leading his group through a section of the park. "I don't know of any enemies, or even people who disliked her."

The search turned up nothing. By July 6, the *News Journal* had already started running a chronology that began as follows: "June 27: Anne Marie Fahey and Thomas J. Capano go to Philadelphia for dinner at Ristorante Panorama, an upscale Front Street restaurant. It is the last independently confirmed sighting of Fahey in public." The headline that day also indicated that the story had reached yet another level: "CLINTON OFFERS FEDERAL AID FOR FAHEY SEARCH."

Tom Capano left town on July 2, as soon as he realized his name had been publicly tied to the Fahey case. He had already been planning to spend the July Fourth weekend at his family's home in Stone Harbor, and now it seemed wise to leave a day early. By that point, he had already contacted a lawyer, Charles Oberly III, a longtime friend. Oberly, the former Delaware State Attorney General, had advised him not to make any further statements—not to the police, and certainly not to the media—until he, Oberly, had a better sense of where the investigation was going.

Capano's mother had a home on the beach in Stone Harbor at 113th Street. It was a few blocks from the bayside home Gerry had in that same tony South Jersey shore town. Capano's daughters and some of their friends were expected down for the weekend. Katie and a girlfriend, in fact, had driven down with him on July 2. The house was valued at more than $1.1 million, with two large decks overlooking the beach, a two-car garage, and a large fireplace, and it was big enough to accommodate everyone. His mother, Marguerite, always liked having a big crowd, and the traditional Fourth of July gathering marked the official start of summer season.

On Wednesday, July 3, Capano was sitting in the living

room of the beach house, smoking a cigarette and talking on
the phone. When he looked up, Charles "Bud" Freel was
standing there in front of him.

"What the hell are you doing here?" Capano asked.

"I'm here for the Faheys," Freel replied.

For the next two hours, the former political allies talked in
circles.

Freel first asked if Capano had kidnapped Fahey and was
holding her somewhere. If he were, then Freel was there to ask
that he give her up. Capano looked at Freel as if he had lost his
mind.

"Don't be ridiculous," he said. Then he repeated the story
he had already told Horstmann and the police—that the last
time he had seen Fahey was when he dropped her off
Thursday night after their dinner date.

Capano said he was upset with himself over some of the
things he had told investigators when they came to his house,
things that were private and personal, things between him and
Anne Marie that were no one else's business. He was not, he
said, going to submit to another round of interrogation when all
the police were interested in "were the dirty details of how
often we had sex and where we had sex."

"I'm not going to violate the trust that Annie has in me,"
Capano said, making a point of referring to Anne Marie in the
present tense. He then went into great detail with Freel about
all the things he had done for Fahey, about the gifts and money
he had given her and the help he had tried to offer her with her
eating disorder. He was worried, he said, that he would be
made the scapegoat in this thing. He already was concerned
about the political ramifications of what was going on. He then
offered several different scenarios of what might have happened, ranging from suicide to a random abduction, perhaps
when Anne Marie had gone out jogging. Or maybe somebody
had come to her door and snatched her away. Or maybe she had
just taken off to be alone. She was like that, he said, moody and
unpredictable.

Freel, always the political realist, told Capano that the most
important thing was that he cooperate with authorities. His
silence was being perceived by the public as an indication that

he had something to hide. If he didn't want to talk about their sex life, fine, don't answer those questions, Freel said.

"But you've got to cooperate," Freel told Capano. "This is going to steamroll. Before you know it, we'll have *Hard Copy* in Wilmington."

Capano said he would think about what Freel had said. He also said he would like to speak directly, "man to man," with Robert Fahey and asked Freel if he could arrange either a meeting or a phone call.

Freel, who had come directly from visiting with the Faheys at Anne Marie's apartment on Washington Street, said he would try. He left Stone Harbor that afternoon, driving back to Wilmington against the flood of traffic that was pouring into town for the start of the Fourth of July weekend.

Capano would remain in Stone Harbor for the rest of the weekend. A phone conversation with Freel the next day began with angry recriminations and lots of shouting after Capano asked Freel if he had been wearing a wire when he came to see him the day before. But it ended on a cordial, if not friendly, note, as Capano promised to return home on Monday and talk with police. He also said he would call Robert Fahey at a number Freel had gotten for him.

Capano would do neither.

On the Fourth of July, as some 300 people fanned out across Brandywine Park looking for Anne Marie Fahey, Thomas J. Capano was in Stone Harbor, where his brother Gerry was hosting a family barbecue. His daughters, several of their friends, and his mother, Marguerite, were all present for the kickoff of another summer season at the shore.

That same afternoon, about fifty miles further down the coast, Ken Chubb was out fishing for the day with his family about ten miles off the Indian River inlet in central Delaware. The Chubbs were getting ready to head back to their summer cottage when Chubb's adult son spotted something floating in the water. It looked like an ice chest or a cooler, the kind used to store fish. Chubb swung his boat around. His son reached down, grabbed the chest, and pulled it on board.

It was a large Igloo marine model, white plastic. It looked

to be brand new, but it was missing its lid and a handle, and had what appeared to be two fresh bullet holes, one through the side and one through the bottom. In fact, as he looked at it, Chubb realized the holes might have come from one shot— entry and exit wounds, so to speak. It was curious, Chubb thought. Why would anyone shoot a hole in a brand-new fishing cooler?

When he pulled his boat back into dock an hour later, he called out to one of his friends. "Look what we found," he said, holding up the cooler.

That weekend, as the search for Anne Marie Fahey intensified, Ken Chubb took the lid off his old fish cooler and rigged it to the body of the new Igloo model he had found floating in the Atlantic Ocean. He got some epoxy and patched the two bullet holes. Then he added a new handle.

The cooler was as good as new. It still had the bar code on the bottom; it had been purchased at a Sports Authority.

For the next seventeen months, Ken Chubb used the cooler to store his catch whenever he and his family went out fishing.

5

"In order to understand why my sister was easily manipulated by a guy like Tom Capano, you need to understand the frailties of her nature," Robert Fahey said. "She was vulnerable. She was a beautiful woman. Young, single, with a wonderful personality. But she had insecurities that were . . ."

Fahey, the third oldest of the brothers, pauses, looking for the right phrase to explain a complicated and complex situation. ". . . higher than average, let's say. He dazzled the shit out of her. Gave her access to things she never had on her own . . . This guy made a career of preying on vulnerable women."

It took the Faheys weeks to come to grips with the fact that Anne Marie was dead. Each day that passed during the summer of 1996 moved them a little closer. All five siblings got there on their own, but all five arrived at about the same time. And concomitant with their acceptance was their belief that Thomas J. Capano was responsible for their sister's death. Seeing that he was brought to justice would become the focal point of their lives for the next two years.

The six weeks the Faheys spent watching and waiting on their sister's porch and in her tiny apartment became a wake of sorts for the Irish Catholic clan, a chance to talk about Annie and share memories with others who loved her. But there was also a sense of guilt, shared in varying degrees by the siblings. They wondered why they hadn't known more about Anne

Marie's relationship with Capano, why she hadn't come to them, particularly when she was trying to end it and he was harassing her. They had been putting all the pieces together, gathering information from her diary, from her friends, and— from time to time and in the smallest increments imaginable— from the investigators working the case.

The authorities didn't share information with the Faheys; that was never the way it worked. But on occasion they would ask a question in such a way that they provided the Faheys with a glimpse of their sister's other life.

Did the Faheys know, for example, that Anne Marie had gone on a trip with Capano to a luxury vacation resort in Virginia in August 1995? Were they aware that Capano had bought her a round-trip plane ticket to Spain for Christmas that year? And that she had refused the gift? Did they know about the angry confrontation in Anne Marie's apartment a short time after that, when Capano threatened to take back all the gifts he had ever given her? Were they aware that after two months of hardly any contact early in 1996, Capano and Anne Marie started going out again in the spring? That he would take her to a fine restaurant almost every Thursday night? That while she told some people she was deathly afraid of him, she implied to others that they were friends now, that their relationship had evolved, that there was a part of her that would always love him even though both agreed it was time to move on?

The Faheys knew nothing about the relationship between Anne Marie and Capano. If they had, they thought, she might still be here. That was one of the things they always came back to as they sat on the porch sharing memories and clinging to the fading hope that their baby sister was still alive.

Annie had the power to end the affair, to protect herself, but she didn't realize it—that's what struck Robert. He frowned as he admitted this, and the top of his prematurely bald head turned red with anger. At the age of forty Robert Fahey was an executive with Cushman & Wakefield, a major Philadelphia real estate development firm, although at first glance he seemed more like a stern high school principal. Only the soft look in his eyes as he spoke about Anne Marie broke the facade. Robert maintained that if only she had told someone in the governor's office—Carper himself or Daniels or Montague—then word would have gotten back to Capano to back off, to leave her alone.

"She didn't realize the power was there," Robert said. "These were people who could talk to Capano on his level, people who had as much, if not more, power than he did . . . but I think she was ashamed. She didn't want us to know she had gotten involved with a married man. And I think she was worried about a scandal and the impact it might have had on the governor. He was about to start his campaign for reelection."

Kevin, a thick, barrel-chested insurance salesman and the oldest of the Fahey brothers, proposed an even more direct approach.

"She got in over her head," he said. "She got in with the big boys and, unfortunately, she paid with her life."

It was typical of Anne Marie, he said, not to be confrontational even as she was attempting to break up their romance. "It was like her to try to remain friends with this guy," Kevin Fahey said. "She would want him to like her. She wouldn't want to hurt his feelings. That's just the way she was."

On the other hand, he and his brother Mark, the second oldest, had no problems with confrontation. "If she had told us, we would have marched down there and kicked his ass," Kevin said.

Of course, this was all after the fact, and to a large degree it was meaningless. "What if" and "if only" became part of the Fahey family mantra that summer, as the four brothers and sister tried to make sense of their sister's disappearance. But even as they tried to understand the whys of what had happened, they and the investigators working the case were still searching for the whats and hows of Anne Marie's disappearance and death.

They would never find them.

It was—and remains to this very day—a murder case without a body, without a cause of death, and without a murder weapon; a case where the prime suspect was a former prosecutor who knew how the system worked and, even more important, how to work the system.

*   *   *

"You learn from the time you're five years old that people die," Robert Fahey said. "Grandparents. Parents. Generally, you don't look backward. The last person I ever thought would die, let alone be murdered, was my baby sister."

Annie was the one who had needed watching over; now, coupled with the grief and the uncertainty, the Faheys fought the nagging sense that they had all let her down. They had always been protective and tolerant, maybe too tolerant, of Annie, the one-time tomboy who had grown into a sophisticated but insecure beauty. People meeting Annie for the first time were always struck by her vivacious approach to life. But her brothers and sister knew that that was just a shell, beneath which she was an emotionally frail and easily manipulated young woman. Her anorexia was the proof. Experts would later testify that she was a classic sufferer. She had low self-esteem and little self-confidence. She hated her body, particularly her legs, which she thought were large and manly, and her breasts, which she felt were too big. She thought there were few things in her life that she was able to control. The one thing she could was the amount of food she put in her mouth.

From Anne Marie Fahey's diary, March 2, 1994:

> My family and some of my friends (Jill, G.R.) are worried about my weight loss. I, on the other hand, am quite pleased! 5 more pounds to 130. I am starving myself as well as avoiding situations where food is involved. I now think of food as poisonous. I cannot ever imagine eating a sandwich! (too much food). I'll be okay. I will stop before it gets out of control.

Annie was at home on the morning her mother died, back in March 1975. The Faheys were living in a house out near Concord Pike in Wilmington at the time. Robert Fahey Sr. was selling insurance on a somewhat regular basis. Kathleen Fahey, who had been a secretary at the DuPont Company in downtown Wilmington when they met, had given up her job to devote her time to her family. Staunch Catholics, the Faheys had six children in the first twelve years of their marriage. The large family and Robert Fahey's fluctuating income—as an insurance salesman he depended on commissions—sometimes made life at home tough. But Kathleen McGettigan Fahey brought a warmth and a quiet determination to the house that provided her children with a sense of security. Now she could no longer offer that to them. She had been diagnosed with lung cancer the previous summer, and her health had been steadily deteriorating.

Annie and Kevin were the only children in the house that morning. The others had gone off to church. It was a Sunday. Annie didn't know what had happened, but she knew her father was upset; he was extremely nervous, and his eyes were filled with tears. He didn't explain anything. He just said he wanted her to stay in the basement for a little while with the family dog. He held her hand and walked her down the stairs, then shut the basement door behind him as he returned to the kitchen. He forgot to turn on the basement light.

He called a funeral director and then summoned his brother-in-law, who was a Catholic priest, making arrangements to have his wife's body removed from the house without his youngest daughter seeing it. It was an act of kindness that turned traumatic.

Because Robert Fahey Sr. forgot about Annie. She sat in the dark basement with the dog that morning for more than an hour—a period of time that seemed far longer to an already traumatized nine-year-old. Finally, her uncle, the priest, asked where she was, and her father remembered. The priest opened the door and found little Annie shivering, holding the dog and quietly sobbing.

Few people who were close to Anne Marie ever knew about that day. It was one of her secrets, part of the sadness she carried around inside of her. She confided to only a few close and trusted friends that from that morning she had always been afraid of being locked away and alone in the dark. Tom Capano was one of the people she told. At the time he was her confidante and her lover. Later, he would use that fear to manipulate her.

The death of their mother left the Fahey children largely on their own. Their father lost more and more bouts to alcoholism, and became physically and verbally abusive at home. It seemed as though he was always screaming or hollering at someone. Annie spent a lot of time hiding under the kitchen table.

Her grandmother would come over most weekends to help out, lending a bit of stability to the troubled home, but over the years the children drifted further and further away from their father and closer to one another. "It was a one-day-at-a-time existence," Brian Fahey said of his childhood. "Sometimes there was enough to eat, sometimes there wasn't. . . . There was never any plan. We tried to look out for each other as best we could."

Sometimes when the bills hadn't been paid and the utilities got turned off, Annie would get up early and arrive at school before the other kids. She would head for the gym, where she would take a shower, enjoying the luxury of the hot running water her classmates took for granted. Annie tried to maintain a sense of normalcy at school; she was a fair student, a good athlete, and, although she never thought so, an attractive young woman. She spent her junior and senior years living in a home with Kevin and Robert, both of whom were out of college and working at the time. Her father had lost their home in Wilmington in a sheriff's sale and moved to Newark. Kathleen and Brian were away at school. Mark was out of the house and drifting; he eventually would do battle with many of the same demons that consumed his father.

Annie would earn money babysitting and working after school as a waitress. She passed the time at the homes of friends, sometimes sleeping over for days at a time. The summer after she graduated from Brandywine High School in 1985, she and a girlfriend got jobs at Bethany Beach and spent the season living and working at the shore. It was, she later told friends, one of the best summers of her life.

College for Anne Marie was a series of ups and downs. She chose Wesley, in Dover, which at the time offered a two-year program in political science, her major. She played field hockey and basketball, and did well enough in her studies to be accepted as a transfer student to the University of Delaware in Newark. But she never fit in at the larger state university. She went into a deep depression while at Newark, and also had one of her first serious bouts with anorexia, although no one in the family was aware of it. She dropped out and returned home to Wilmington, working at odd jobs and trying to find herself.

Two years later, when Wesley College started a four-year program in political science, Anne Marie headed back to campus. Eager for a career in politics or international relations, she spent a semester at the University of Granada in Spain and came back raving about the country and the people. An amazing mimic and a quick study, she was speaking nearly fluent Spanish by the time she returned. She enjoyed the earthy sensuality that was part of the Spanish culture, the sense of family, the love of good food and wine, and the passion—none of which had been part of her own upbringing. She had recreated herself, it seemed; Anne Marie had become "Ana Maria."

After graduating from Wesley she went to Washington, where she wrangled an internship with the Organization of American States. But she had to return to Wilmington on weekends to work in a restaurant in order to support herself; Anne Marie Fahey would always struggle financially. She hated asking her brothers and sister for help, but occasionally had to do so. At the same time, her brother Mark was struggling with his life, tending bar—perhaps not the best idea, given his own problems.

Kevin and Robert, on the other hand, were fairly successful. Both had homes in the Pennsylvania suburbs; Kevin was selling insurance, Robert was in real estate. Kathleen had married Patrick Hosey. She was a therapist at a rehabilitation center in Bryn Mawr, Pennsylvania, and was about to start a family. Brian was teaching. Like Anne Marie, he was fascinated with Spanish language and culture.

Despite what they had been through—or perhaps because of it—the Faheys were making it. Mark had problems that would continue to haunt him and cause the other siblings concern, but everyone else seemed to have a clear path before them—all but Annie. Then, in 1991, she walked into Carper's congressional office while in downtown Washington and struck up a conversation with some of the staff. Before long, they were all laughing at this outspoken, outrageously funny, tall, attractive, unpretentious woman from back home. She was looking for work, and there was a staff opening. She was interested; so were they. But they would have to clear it with the congressman's chief of staff, Ed Freel. Someone made a quick phone call to his office. In the middle of the conversation, Anne Marie jumped on the line.

"Fast Eddie," she said. "It's me, Annie. How ya doin'? They wanna hire me."

She got the job.

A year later she headed back to Wilmington, first working on Carper's gubernatorial campaign and then in the governor's office as his scheduling secretary—a job that carried more clout than her $31,500 a year would suggest. "She made up his schedule," said a political insider. "She knew who he was seeing every day, every hour. If you needed to get to Carper, Annie was one of the people who could get you access, or deny it. People would dismiss the job as, 'Oh, she's just a secretary.' But it was politics. And in politics, access is everything. She had more power than she knew."

She moved into a house on North Clayton Street with two other women, including one of her oldest and dearest friends, Jackie Vinnersley. Vinnersley owned the property, a neat, two-story brick two-family with bay windows and a tidy front porch. The house was just off the corner of West Ninth Street in Little Italy. Vinnersley was fixing up the property; she was engaged, and she and her husband would eventually make it their home. But when Annie first came back to Wilmington, Jackie had more than enough room for her.

They had been best friends since the seventh grade, and Jackie knew everything about Anne Marie. She knew about her old boyfriends and her failed romances. She knew about her family problems and her difficult childhood. Annie had even lived for a time at Jackie's house when she was in junior high school and things had gotten tough at home. Now she was back in Wilmington, ready to start a new career and reestablish ties with people she loved. It was a good time for Anne Marie, a time when she began to believe in herself.

The only long-term, serious relationship she had had was with Paul Columbus. She and PJ had dated for about four years, beginning during her second enrollment at Wesley. For a long time Anne Marie believed that she and Paul would end up together, but he had had trouble finding himself and they both decided they were better off apart.

Maybe, in that regard, they were too much alike.

"I always thought my life would be with PJ," she wrote in one diary note after she had returned to Wilmington, "but not anymore. I wish him well and there's a part of me that will always love him." In another she wrote that "I realize I deserve more than what PJ is able to offer."

It was in the spring of 1993, as she was establishing herself as Carper's scheduling secretary, and reestablishing her ties to the city of Wilmington and the people she had grown up with, that Anne Marie Fahey spotted Thomas J. Capano across the room at a political fundraiser.

She thought he looked sophisticated. He had a beard and glasses and moved about with an air of self-confidence that she found attractive. She was sure he knew her family, so she walked up and said hello. After that, he would joke with her whenever he called the governor's office on business. She liked the attention and didn't try to hide the fact that she was flirting with him.

"When are we going to lunch?" she would say.

Capano would laugh and promise to set something up. He liked the attention of the younger woman. He found her attractive. She made him smile.

That summer, their paths crossed again at another political fundraiser, this time at the Hotel duPont. Capano's law firm had bought a table, and Anne Marie and members of the governor's staff were sitting at another table nearby. They made eye contact, smiled, and waved. Later, Capano was out in the hallway smoking a cigarette when Annie and Ginny Columbus emerged from the ladies room.

Capano watched them walk toward him and smiled. But he was clearly making more eye contact with Columbus, whose dark good looks were breathtaking, than with Anne Marie. She noticed right away and made a joke about it. "Heh, Capano," she said in her typically forthright manner. "What are you looking at her for? I'm the one you're supposed to be taking to lunch."

They had lunch the next week in one of the fancier dining rooms at the Hotel duPont. They began talking on the phone on a regular basis. More lunch dates followed. Then he started stopping around the house, sometimes during the day. They played Trivial Pursuit; Capano was good at it—he had a knack for retaining information. They would see each other at Mass on Sundays. They both went to Saint Anthony of Padua, which was around the corner from the house on Clayton Street in Little Italy, the neighborhood where Capano's grandfather had lived and where his father had grown up.

Capano would attend Mass with his wife, Kay, and their daughters. His oldest, Christine, was thirteen at the time; she was, ironically, about as close in age to Fahey as he was. Once, on a Sunday morning, Capano was driving his daughter Jenny to church—she was about to make her First Communion and was wearing her lavish white Communion dress—when he spotted Annie on the corner and stopped. She walked over and he introduced her to his daughter. She told Capano how beautiful Jenny was. She told the smiling little girl that she was a friend of her father's from work. And at that point, while both she and Capano were aware of what was going on, that was all they were.

Anne Marie found their lunch dates romantic. He was kind and caring and sensitive and listened to her. What's more, he seemed to be interested in what she had to say, what she thought. He was older and more worldly than anyone she had ever dated. He treated her like a princess. Money was never an issue. He had more than she could ever imagine. They flirted with one another constantly. Annie loved to tell dirty jokes, and Capano loved to hear her tell them. They would hint at sex, talk around the issue, look into each other's eyes and know what the other was thinking. But they never acted on it.

It was a long, slow, sensual dance to music only they could hear.

But some people started to notice.

Jackie Vinnersley, for example, came home one night from the gym to find Capano and Anne Marie sitting in the living room sharing a bottle of Merlot, Annie's favorite, which Capano had brought over. This was sometime in the fall of 1993, Vinnersley later told investigators.

"As soon as I walked in, I detected something," she said. "I just felt uneasy. Body language tells a lot, and you could just tell the way they were sitting that there was some contact there. I mean . . . I don't know. It was kind of a more than friends type of thing."

Vinnersley knew Capano was married with kids. She wondered about that. It was strange, she thought, for a married man to be over at night sharing a bottle of wine with her single roommate. She also noticed the way Annie was dressed.

"She's not promiscuous at all," Vinnersley said, still speaking in the present tense about Anne Marie even though she had been missing for months at the time she gave her statement. "She's very reserved, conservative. Never had guys over to the house. But that night . . . her cleavage was showing. I mean . . . her blouse was down and that's unusual for her because she usually has conservative shirts on and things like that."

Later that night, after Capano left, Vinnersley asked Anne Marie about the visit.

"What's going on?"

"Nothing, we're just good friends," said Fahey.

"He's a married man. Why is he over here drinking a bottle of wine?"

Fahey laughed it off. They were friends, she insisted. From work.

Capano would show up from time to time at the house that fall. He would always make a fuss over Vinnersley, telling her what a great job she had done fixing it up, offering her legal advice about the coffee shop she was planning to open. "He would bend over backwards to be nice, and I just thought it was false," she said. "Like he would say about the house, 'Oh, the house looks great. You did this and you did that. Annie tells me you stained the floors.' And he just went over a little too much and I just thought it was just false."

Capano took Annie and Jackie to lunch a few times when he was preparing some legal papers for her business. He did the work for free, as a favor to Annie. And Vinnersley remembered how he always acted the gentleman, always placed the lunch order with the waitress, always picked up the tab. On the way back, as they walked along the street, he would make sure that he walked on the outside, closest to the curb. And he would tell them, two young women sixteen years younger than he and clearly from another generation, that that was the way he was raised, that that was what a man did when he was out with a woman.

Vinnersley found Tom Capano a little pretentious. She also was put off by the fact that Capano would always greet her with a hug and a kiss on the lips. He considered it a normal greeting; she didn't. "I thought this was kind of a little bit odd," she said. "I'm not a kissy-kissy person. You kiss your relatives, kiss your husband or whatever. I was a little uncomfortable about that."

Capano would attribute her discomfort to her background. She was English, he would say, implying that the British were stiff and cold. He was Italian, and everybody knew Italians were warm and passionate. Like the Spanish. Anne Marie hung on his every word.

In January, they went out on their first date to celebrate her twenty-eighth birthday. He made reservations at the Ristorante Panorama, one of his favorite places. He and she both knew the relationship was about to move to the next level.

It snowed that night, a terrible storm that forced several restaurants to close. Instead of the Panorama, they ended up at the Chart House, located right on the Delaware River waterfront in Philadelphia. When they returned to her house on Clayton Street that night, neither of her roommates was home. That night they made love for the first time.

"I was crazy about her," Capano said in describing the first few months of their affair. "And she seemed to feel the same way about me."

There would be more dinners and lunches, and secret meetings at her house when she knew her roommates wouldn't be in. Sometimes they'd meet there for lunch and make love instead. Then they'd both head back to their offices and call each other on the phone like high school sweethearts.

"She made me laugh," Capano said. "She was a very down-to-earth person. . . . It was very easy to have fun with her."

*   *   *

From Anne Marie Fahey's diary, March 7, 1994:

We (Tomas and I) had lunch on Friday at the Shipley Grill. It was very good. I hope that tonight he will visit me before working in Philadelphia. I am alone in my house tonight drinking a beer and listening to music (*When Harry Met Sally*). We have problems because he has a wife and children also. I don't want to be in love, but I can't help it. By god, please don't judge me! . . .

No news on the weight loss. I am stuck at 135 pds, and it's pissing me off! I can't starve myself any more than I already am. I suppose I should be thankful that I have not gained any weight either. I still avoid situations where there is food involved . . . When I lose my last 5 pds, I will treat myself.

Where is my friend?

Ciao, AMF.

6

Bud Freel was right: *Hard Copy* would be coming to Wilmington. But *Inside Edition* got there first. The tabloid television show ran a piece on Anne Marie Fahey's disappearance on July 11, 1996, one day after the *New York Times* devoted nearly one-third of its National Report page to the story. *Inside Edition* offered the typical splashy tabloid report, heavy on the politics and the social standing of the principal players in the drama. The *Times*, by contrast, offered a lengthy, detailed, and dry report under the headline "TENSE VIGIL FOR FAMILY AS A SISTER DISAPPEARS." The story included a large photo of Kathleen Fahey-Hosey and her brothers Brian and Robert standing on Anne Marie's porch, and a large blowup of the missing persons flier that the Faheys and their friends had posted all over the Wilmington area and all along the Jersey shore, offering a $10,000 reward for help in locating Anne Marie.

Donovan continued to work the case through the holiday weekend and into the next week. He met with the FBI for the first time on Monday, July 8, the day Capano came back to Wilmington from Stone Harbor. With the help of the feds, Donovan got court authorization for a Dial Number Recorder, or DNR, to be placed on Capano's phone line at 2302 Grant Avenue. The device, placed without Capano's knowledge, would allow investigators to keep tabs on all calls coming into or going out of the house and would list those numbers and the addresses attached to them. There was no way to record the conversations—investigators didn't have any justification to seek a wiretap at that time—but the recorder would show whom Capano was calling and who was calling him. One number turned up frequently, almost on a daily basis. It was to a residence on Delaware Avenue not far from where Capano's wife lived. The phone number was registered to Deborah MacIntyre, a fortysomething private school administrator and former wife of David Williams, a lawyer who had worked in the same law firm as Capano back in the late 1970s and early 1980s. Before the investigation was over, Donovan would come to know MacIntyre very well. And through MacIntyre, he and the prosecutors working the case would have a much more complex and troubling picture of Thomas J. Capano.

Capano got back to Wilmington that Monday, but despite his promise to Freel, he did not sit down with the police investigating Fahey's disappearance. He said his lawyers, Oberly and two others who were also representing him, had advised against it at that time. There was nothing to be gained. He had told the police everything he knew, and he was not going to get into a discussion about his personal life or Anne Marie's that had nothing to do with her disappearance.

In fact, Capano was already working spin control, as he had been from the first day. One of the first people he called on Friday morning, June 28, even before he left for Stone Harbor to dump the body, was his longtime friend Keith Brady. Brady, in his late thirties, was the Delaware Deputy Attorney General, the number-two law enforcement official in the state. He answered directly to Jane Brady (no relation), the state's Attorney General. Capano had left a message for Keith Brady that Friday morning about getting together for drinks later that night. Brady had not returned the call, but the following Tuesday morning, July 2, before leaving for the shore, Capano reached Brady and the two had a brief discussion. By that point, Brady already knew Fahey was missing and that Capano was the last person to have seen her alive. Brady and Capano went back several years. When Capano was chief counsel to Governor Castle, Brady was deputy counsel. They worked in the governor's office for more than two years and often socialized as well. Both were married. But both, it would turn out, had a rather loose interpretation of their marriage vows.

Brady's secretary would remember that her boss wasn't especially anxious to speak with Capano when she left him a note about the June 28 call. She said he complained that Capano "talked too much about his personal life." Brady, for reasons that would become clear much later, kept notes of their July 2 conversation so that if he were called upon to describe what was discussed—as he correctly surmised that he would be—he would be able to give a fairly accurate account.

The notes, scribbled in longhand on a sheet of paper that he eventually turned over to authorities, recorded a series of one-line comments that were either verbatim transcriptions or paraphrases of what Capano told him that day. They included Capano's description of his last night with Fahey, his reaction to the investigation, and some of his thoughts on Fahey and what might have happened to her. Among other things, Capano mentioned twice that Fahey had taken Friday off because she didn't want to go to Dover. Fahey, like much of the governor's staff, worked out of two offices, one in Wilmington and the other in Dover, the state capital. With the end of June came the final session of the state legislature for the fiscal year. Business shifted to Dover. Fahey had scheduled Friday off in part so that she wouldn't have to drive the hour to the capital for work that day. Brady's notes of his conversation with Capano included these comments:

- Blown away by it.
- Spooked by it; by the way the cops are treating him.
- Had become good friends.
- She told him she was taking Friday off.
- Didn't want to get dragged to Dover.
- 3:00 A.M. cops came.
- Had to take sleeping medicine.
- They thought I was hiding her out.
- She wanted time to herself; didn't want to go to Dover.
- 2:00 P.M. Sunday backing out of house; 2 cops were following me.
- Kim told him he's a suspect.

- I thought she would stroll in Monday and when she didn't show up "I died."
- Serious head case, under psychiatric care.
- Was OK, but kind of down.
- Didn't leave there thinking she was going to kill herself.
- I'm afraid of the cops.

Brady was just one of the people with whom Capano had begun to spin his story. Another, of course, was Oberly, who eventually went on national television to defend his client against the "unfounded allegations" that surrounded the Fahey investigation. Capano, Oberly argued, had become an easy target for an investigation that was going nowhere.

While Capano declined to meet with authorities, he did sit down with another close friend, public relations consultant J. Brian Murphy, on July 9. At Murphy's urging, the two drafted a statement that Murphy wanted Capano to release to the press.

Murphy had been part of the old Dan Frawley–Wilmington Rugby Club set. He dabbled on the fringes of city and state politics, and always seemed to be involved in some type of consulting work that depended on a government contract. His connections to Capano helped in that regard. He also was indebted personally to Capano, who had lent him money at least once in the past—about $15,000 to help pay private school tuition for one of Murphy's kids. Murphy would turn out to be one of the last Capano loyalists. Sitting in a coffee shop in the Hotel duPont early in November 1997, just days before Capano would be arrested and charged with Fahey's murder, he adamantly defended his friend.

"There's no way the Tom Capano I know could do something like that," he had said then. "It's just totally out of character. This has ruined his life. He's devastated by it."

Even at that late date, people like Murphy and Oberly were holding onto the belief that Fahey might still turn up, that stranger things had happened, that perhaps she had amnesia and was living out on the West Coast or somewhere down South. Someone had told Tom that Anne Marie had been spotted at the Newark, New Jersey, airport, Oberly said. He then recounted the story of a woman who had gone missing for ten years—*ten years,* he emphasized—before she was found living an entirely new life with a new family and set of friends, out in Seattle or somewhere else in the Pacific Northwest.

Capano helped plant those seeds, and his friends who wanted to believe him unwittingly played a part in fostering the fiction. Capano used them as he would use so many others over the next two years.

The statement he and Murphy drafted on July 9 was never released. Others in Capano's camp, including his lawyers and several other politicos who were meeting to discuss how he should handle the growing public relations crisis, counseled against it. Murphy was in a minority of one when he urged Capano to go public with what they had written. Murphy believed his friend, and believed what was contained in the seven-paragraph press release, entitled "Statement by Thomas J. Capano in the Disappearance of Anne Marie Fahey."

> The disappearance of Anne Marie Fahey remains as much a mystery to me as it does to her family and friends. I can only say I share the gut-wrenching emotions of Anne Marie's family and pray for her safe return.
>
> While I can do nothing to end the speculation of the public and press, I can state for the record the pertinent facts of my last meeting with Anne Marie.

The statement then repeated Capano's version of the events of June 27, how he had dropped Anne Marie off after dinner and then driven home.

> While Anne Marie had some problems, there was nothing out of the ordinary in either her conversations or behavior that would lead me to believe anything was amiss. I am at a complete loss to explain what caused her disappearance.
>
> It is difficult to respond as to how others may characterize our relationship. Frankly, the nature of our relationship is and will remain a matter between Anne Marie and myself. What is relevant and important is that Anne Marie and I are good friends and parted company good friends that evening.

*   *   *

The statement then detailed how Capano had learned that Anne Marie was missing and how he had expected her to show up for work on Monday, July 1, as he had told authorities.

"I have and will continue to fully cooperate with investigators," the statement continued—somewhat disingenuously, given the position Capano and his lawyers had taken. "As much as anyone else, I want to know Anne Marie's whereabouts.

"I will not be granting interviews or making further statements. I want to thank my friends who have offered their many kind words of support and encouragement and ask all concerned to pray for Anne Marie's safe return."

Months later, when Donovan and the others got their hands on the statement, they were struck nearly dumb by its arrogance. That the statement had not been released to the public was immaterial. That was a strategy decision; it had nothing to do with the content of what Capano intended to say. What riled Donovan and the others working the case most was the fact that when Capano sat down with Murphy to craft his elaborate plea, he knew all too well that no amount of praying was going to bring about Fahey's safe return.

The same day that he met with Murphy, Capano put in a call to Robert Fahey. It wasn't at the time or to the number that Freel had suggested, so Capano was fairly certain he wouldn't get Fahey directly. It was better this way; he could leave a message instead. The recording he left ran for several minutes on Fahey's voice mail at Cushman & Wakefield; like the statement prepared with Murphy, it was another performance in Capano spin control.

Robert, this is Tom Capano.

It's Tuesday, it's after twelve, twelve-thirty-nine P.M. on July 9.

I think you know from Bud that I really want to speak to you and anybody else in your family who cares to. Um, Bud tells me you're maybe not really interested in speaking to me and I guess I can understand, uh, Robert, um, I don't know what to say, um, ah, I really, ah, I really do want to talk to you. I, I, I, if you would consider that, please call me.

My number is . . . I'm in and out a lot, so um, you'll get my voice mail, and um, I'd like to see you face-to-face if you're willing to do that. Um, I have some things I want to show you. I have some things I want to tell you.

Um, I care for Anne Marie a great deal, Robert. Um, I don't know I guess apparently from what Buddy's telling me that that hasn't come through and I don't understand what. Um. And I know I'm babbling because I'm out of my freaking mind with uh, everything, but if you'll consider it I'd really like to do it, ah, ah, anytime, any place, anywhere. And, um, there's one thing, if you decide you don't want to talk to me, there's one thing I want you to know. Um, I have talked to the police twice.

I have told the police I will talk to them as many times as they want. But I am not gonna talk about ancient history.

Anne Marie has a right to privacy and I have a right to privacy and I am not going to tell them details of things we did a year ago or eight months ago or all this incredible personal stuff they want to know from me, OK? Stuff they've already tried to ask me that I am not going to answer. It's got NOTHING TO DO WITH ANYTHING. I'll tell you if, if you want to know, but I am, I am not going to have all those details on the front page of the newspaper and I will talk to them about anything else in the world. I will talk to them about last Thursday night. I will talk to them about anything, but I am not going to talk about ancient history and I just am not budging from that. Maybe you can't understand that, but, um, I'm sorry but it's irrelevant. It can do nothing.

I mean, do you and Kathleen want to read stuff in the newspaper? 'Cause you know it's going to leak. It's personal. So, well, I said I'd stop. I know I'm rambling but I desperately would like to talk to you; have you hear from me everything and let you ask me anything you want to ask me. OK, my number is . . . I wanted to come see you all at that apartment, but I know that Kathleen would just frankly gouge my eyes out. Ah, I'll stop.

Please call me, Robert.

Robert Fahey played the message over and over. He couldn't believe it. He made a copy and quickly turned the original over to the authorities working his sister's case. He had no intention of talking directly with Capano. He was sickened by the man, by his self-pity, and by his unbelievable hubris.

"The phone call speaks to a level of arrogance that is foreign to people with even a minimal level of morality or concern for others," Robert said months later as he recounted that phone message and his reaction to it. "Twelve days after he brutally murdered Anne Marie, he called to talk about how the publicity was affecting him. Not once did he express any concern about her whereabouts nor what happened to her. . . .

"He was trying to create a reason not to cooperate so he wouldn't look bad. It had nothing to do with the fact that our sister was missing. It was all about what this was doing to Tom Capano. This whole thing was about self-preservation."

7

On July 24, 1996, the Fahey family made one last attempt to get Tom Capano to tell authorities what he knew. In a letter addressed to him at his law office, they wrote: "As the last person to be seen with Anne Marie, one would hope that you would do the right thing—come forward and share all you know about Anne Marie's disappearance.

> Your team of lawyers has been effective at communicating for you but very ineffective at helping us find our sister. Do what your father Louis would expect of one of his sons— come forward and share all you know about Anne Marie's disappearance.
> Imagine, if you will, that this case involved one of your four daughters ... We are talking about someone's life, please help us today.
> Sincerely, The Fahey Family.

Tom Capano ignored their plea.

The Faheys were novices in the world of criminal justice. They knew that an investigation, especially a murder case without a body or a cause of death, wouldn't unfold as quickly as a television drama. But they had no idea how tedious and mind-numbingly microscopic a murder investigation, particularly one built almost entirely on circumstantial evidence, could be.

"They never told us what they were going to do," Kevin Fahey said of the meetings his family would have with Connolly, Donovan, and Alpert. "But they told us they had a game plan. They said it might take some time. They said we had to be patient and trust them. They said they would only have one shot to do this and they had to do it right."

"I don't think any of them ever had an investigation like this," Robert Fahey added. "And they went at it twelve to fourteen hours a day, sometimes seven days a week. They just never let up."

Robert Fahey quickly came to realize that Connolly was the one who would dominate the case. And at first he was taken aback by the brash prosecutor.

"When we met him for the first time—he's got this little baby face, a peach fuzz kind of face—I questioned his age and experience. He was thirty-two [actually, he was thirty-one at the time], but he looked about twenty-eight. I said to myself, 'Oh shit, we got the young kid on the block.'"

But as Fahey watched Connolly tenaciously go about the business of building a case, his opinion changed.

Most of all, he was struck by the fact that the young prosecutor was offended by the idea that Capano's wealth, status, and connections—what Connolly sometimes referred to as Capano's "aura"—might somehow help him get away with murder. That was not the way the system was supposed to work. It sounded almost trite—like a line from one of the old movies that Connolly loved and frequently quoted—but he believed in the American justice system, in the need for society to play by the rules, and in the absolute necessity for those who broke the rules to face the consequences.

Connolly's and Capano's careers had followed some of the same tracks. Like Capano, he had attended Archmere Academy, but Connolly left after his sophomore year when his father, who worked for DuPont, was transferred to a plant in the Philippine Islands. His father had grown up in the Bronx; his mother spoke with a soft Irish brogue that belied her immigrant roots. Colm was the oldest of four children, a golden boy in his own right. Like Capano's, Connolly's life was a dyed-in-the-wool American success story. After graduating from high school in the Philippines, he attended the University of Notre Dame, perhaps the only Catholic university in America that could cast its shadow over Boston College. He spent a year studying at the London School of Economics before enrolling at Duke University Law School, where he earned his law degree. He had worked for private firms in New York and Philadelphia during his summers while at Duke, but he knew he wanted to be a prosecutor, and he got a job in the U.S. Attorney's Office in Wilmington after he graduated. He was married. His wife, Anne, was also a lawyer. She had graduated from Dartmouth College. The two had met at Duke. At the time the investigation began they had two sons, a two-year-old and an infant. Before it was over they would have another, and Anne Connolly would be expecting again.

Intelligent, clever, and somewhat precocious, Connolly kept his personality under wraps whenever reporters were around. The only thing he offered to the media during the entire investigation was that phrase all federal prosecutors learn their first day on the job: "No comment."

But he had a lot to say in the private meetings where he and Donovan and Alpert mapped out a strategy. The idea was to cast a broad net over Capano and those closest to him, and then slowly draw the net tighter and tighter until someone asked to be set free. At that point, Connolly said, they'd approach their potential informant and "make him an offer he can't refuse."

When Connolly, Donovan, and Alpert began assembling their profile of the Capano family, Thomas was the brother who, on paper at least, appeared the least likely to be the focus of an investigation.

Louis Jr., on the other hand, had already had one go-round with the FBI. Back in 1989 he found himself in the middle of a political bribery and kickback investigation involving a New Castle County councilman who was suspected of soliciting payoffs from developers in exchange for favorable zoning decisions. Louis, who had passed some money on to the councilman, agreed to wear a wire and helped the FBI carry out a sting that resulted in the councilman being indicted and, eventually, convicted and sentenced to jail. Along the way, Louis admitted to some questionable campaign contributions to the councilman and other politicos, but because of his cooperation in the bribery-kickback case, he faced no charges.

According to several insiders familiar with the investigation, Tom Capano had helped steer his brother clear of the criminal mud pile, and helped arrange the cooperation that allowed Louis and the Louis Capano & Sons Construction Co. to come out unscathed.

Two years later, in a case Connolly and the others found haunting, Joe Capano was arrested on charges of kidnapping and rape. The victim was a woman with whom Joe Capano, who was married, had been having a longtime affair; at one point she had been a babysitter for his children. Friends would later claim that the charges were all a misunderstanding, that the victim, who was thirteen years younger than the then-forty-year-old Capano, had wanted to have them dropped.

The original police complaint alleged that on Halloween night in 1991, Joe Capano went to the woman's home and assaulted her, ripping two telephone lines out of the walls and flipping over a television in the process. From there, the complaint alleged, Capano forced the woman to go with him back to his home, where he held her against her will for nearly twelve hours and forced her to have sex with him at least three times and in at least three different ways.

Ultimately, Joe Capano pleaded guilty to lesser charges contained in a criminal information filed by the State Attorney General's Office. The Attorney General at that time was Charles Oberly, who was now representing Tom in the Fahey case. Joe Capano's lawyer was Joseph Hurley, a top criminal lawyer in Wilmington. Hurley would also serve briefly on Tom Capano's defense team.

Joseph Capano pleaded guilty to downgraded charges of assault, criminal mischief, unlawful sexual contact, and unlawful imprisonment. Sentenced to three years' probation and sixty hours of community service, he was also required to pay a fine and court costs that totaled about $9,000 and to continue with psychological therapy sessions that had begun with court approval shortly after his arrest and release on bail.

Before Joe Capano formally entered his guilty plea to the reduced charges in the case, Hurley got an assurance from state prosecutors that they would not oppose an attempt to withdraw that plea should the victim bring any civil action against Joseph Capano. In a motion requesting that guarantee, Hurley described his client as "a man of relative substance" and said he was concerned "since we cannot be sure what the complainant's future intentions would be" with regard to any civil action. The formal guilty plea to the charges, he argued, left his client "in dire circumstance of vulnerability."

The Capano family fortune, at least on some level, appeared to be more important than the Capano family reputation. No civil action, however, was ever filed, and the guilty plea was never withdrawn.

In one other motion that spoke to the nature of the relationship, the woman's lawyer asked that Joe Capano be required to return to her "any and all photographs and negatives taken by the defendant of the victim depicting her in various stages of undress." Hurley initially opposed that motion, arguing that Joseph Capano "is entitled to his memories and he is entitled to his possessions." But on the day of sentencing, Hurley turned five photographs in a sealed envelope over to the woman's lawyer, according to court documents.

The third Capano brother, Gerard, had no arrest record but a questionable reputation. He lived a fast life, primarily off his inheritance. He was part-owner of a landscaping business that did most of its work for Capano-owned apartment and office complexes and shopping centers. But Gerry was something of an absentee manager. While the summer was the busy time of the year for his business, he spent most of June, July, and August at his home in Stone Harbor, where, ironically, he contracted with a local landscaper to care for the grounds around his home.

He owned boats and Jet Skis and fast cars and lots of guns. At one time he was into cigarette boats, those sleek speedboats that had been part of the backdrop of *Miami Vice* in the 1980s.

But Gerry later switched to fishing boats. He had owned the *Summer Wind* for several years, but was always on the lookout for something bigger and better.

An avid hunter, he spent thousands of dollars each year on trips to Alaska, Montana, and other exotic locales to bag big game. He had twenty-one different guns—pistols, shotguns, rifles—registered in his name. He was constantly buying, selling, or trading automobiles, some classics and some hot rods that he would drag-race at area tracks.

Gerry's social life revolved around a fast crowd of young Wilmington-area blue-collar types who moved along the fringes of the drug world. Gerry had a reputation as a big drinker, a guy who liked to party. He had been thrown out of several high schools for drug use, a habit that carried over to his adult life. Cocaine and marijuana were his recreational drugs of choice.

He would later be described by a friend as "a spoiled rich kid who never grew up because he never had to," and by one of Tom Capano's own lawyers as "a typical screwed-up rich kid who never had to earn anything in his life . . . a poster child for the Me Generation." The lawyer, Joseph Oteri, went on to depict Gerry Capano as a "longtime drug user and booze-hound" whose brain was "like a fried egg."

Gerard Capano would eventually concede that the descriptions fit. But in the summer of 1996, as Connolly began building his case, none of the brothers was giving up anything to authorities. There was no need—not yet. They were rich, impertinent, and secure. They were Capanos.

"When this all broke and we started to hear about Tom threatening and harassing Annie, about how he was controlling and manipulative, people couldn't believe it," said Kevin Freel as he sat at a table in his pub one afternoon. "Tommy was always the good brother."

There was a time back in 1994, in fact, when Tom Capano seriously considered running for the office of Attorney General of Delaware. Some politicos believed he had a real shot at becoming the top law enforcement official in the state. Freel and his brothers, however, counseled against it. They believed that Louis's and Joe's criminal problems would have made it an uphill battle, particularly in the more conservative southern part of the state.

Tom Capano also had mixed feelings about jumping into a political campaign. He enjoyed being the power behind the throne, but he wasn't certain he wanted to come out front.

"He had a lot of trouble with the glad-handing part of a campaign," said another insider. "There were only so many chicken dinners he could go to downstate before he would get disgusted with it all. He knew that. Tom always thought he was smarter than everyone, and he wasn't real good at hiding it. That can turn off voters."

At the time he was considering the run for Attorney General, Tom Capano was a partner and the manager of the Wilmington office of Saul, Ewing, Remick & Saul. He was making big money and was still a mover in the world of politics. He decided he didn't need the aggravation—or the pay cut—that would come with running for and then, if elected, serving as Attorney General.

Two years later, he was a suspect in the most politically sensational criminal case in the history of the state.

"People couldn't believe it," Kevin Freel said. "I mean, they knew the problems the brothers had had, but no one ever thought Tom would get himself involved in something like this. He wasn't that kind of person. At least that's what we used to think. We were sitting here talking about that one night and somebody said, 'Yeah, he's acting just like a Capano.'"

Connolly began to sift through the already substantial file that Donovan had built when he joined the case in mid-July, looking for leads and ways to move the investigation forward. There were clearly more questions than answers. And there were even some bits of information that seemed to support Capano's version of events.

The woman who lived in the second-floor apartment at 1718 Washington Street, the apartment right under Anne Marie's, told detectives she heard footsteps around 10:00 P.M. on June 27. She remembered that she was watching a movie, *The American President*, on cable that night. And at about the time

the movie was ending, which was around ten, she heard someone walking in the apartment above her. She thought, however,
that she only heard one set of footsteps, not two. She said she
went to bed a short time later, and heard nothing else.

Capano, of course, said both he and Anne Marie were in the
apartment at around that time. And that he left a few minutes
after arriving.

In addition to Anne Marie's car keys, it seemed that a topaz
ring was also missing. The ring was a favorite of hers, and she'd
often worn it with the floral dress she had on that night. A pair
of jogging shorts, running shoes, and a T-shirt were also unac-
counted for.

Detectives learned that at 11:52 P.M. that night someone
had dialed *69 from Anne Marie's phone to check on the last
call that had come in. The last call was one of two made by
Michael Scanlan that night, asking Anne Marie to join him for
drinks at Kid Sheleen's, a popular Wilmington bar. Investigators
discovered that there were a dozen unopened messages on
Fahey's voice mail spanning a period from late Thursday night,
June 27, through Saturday evening, June 29. Family members
and friends said Annie was fanatical about checking her messages; one of the first things she would have done after arriving
home, they all insisted, was to check her voice mail. And if she
were going to be away from home for several hours, she would
invariably call and check her messages from wherever she happened to be.

The *69 call was puzzling to investigators. It meant that
someone was in Fahey's apartment shortly before midnight on
June 27. If it was Fahey, why hadn't she checked her messages?
Why had she simply dialed *69 ?

Capano said he was home at that point. His home phone
records indicated that shortly after midnight he had called his
voice mail at his office at Saul Ewing. That call seemed odd to
Connolly and Donovan. Why not wait until morning? Did
Capano intend to return a business call after midnight? Or was
his call to the office voice mail, which he knew would create a
time and date record, an attempt to establish an alibi, to
demonstrate that he was in his home as he said he was that
night?

Even that was inconclusive. It was a five-minute ride at best from Fahey's apartment on Washington Street to Capano's home on Grant Avenue. Whoever punched *69 into her phone at 11:52 P.M. could easily have been at Capano's home by midnight.

The phone records proved nothing. They just raised more questions.

Capano's credit card records also seemed to be leading nowhere. There was one from the Sports Authority back in April. There were several from restaurants, including Ristorante Panorama on the night of June 27, but Capano had already told investigators he and Anne Marie had had dinner there that night. The card also confirmed Capano's assertion that they had left around 9:15 P.M.; the bill had been paid at 9:12. There was one other purchase that was curious. On Saturday morning, June 29, Capano's Visa statement showed that he had spent $308.99 at the Wallpaper Warehouse, a store located on Route 13 out near the New Castle County Airport.

Connolly and Donovan looked at each other.

"Why would someone with Capano's money who was leasing a home go out and buy wallpaper?" Donovan asked.

"It doesn't make sense," Connolly said.

Ruth Boylan, who looked like a grandmother out of a Norman Rockwell painting, never figured to be a key witness in the Anne Marie Fahey case. But she provided Donovan with one of the first big leads in the investigation. Boylan was a housekeeper. She cleaned homes in and around the Wilmington area. She had been doing it for years and had an excellent reputation for both efficiency and dependability. When Capano moved into the home on Grant Avenue he hired her to come in once every other week to clean the place. She kept her schedule on a wall calendar. She penciled him in for Mondays. Donovan went to see her late in July.

Boylan said she had cleaned Capano's home on June 24. She said he called her before her next scheduled visit, July 8, and told her to skip it.

"He said he had been away and the house wasn't dirty," she explained to Donovan. Since Capano had been in Stone Harbor for the previous week, that made some sense.

Boylan said she next cleaned Capano's home on July 22. She checked her calendar to be sure. It was the fourth Monday of the month. Donovan asked what kind of condition the house was in. She said Capano's home was never really dirty, that there was nothing unusual in that regard.

Donovan typed up his notes of the interview and added it to the growing file as he and Connolly sat in the prosecutor's office puzzling over the Wallpaper Warehouse receipt.

"Lemme call out there," Connolly said.

He looked up the number in the Wilmington phone book. He dialed and then smiled. The voice on the other end of the line had answered with the words, "Airbase Carpets."

Wallpaper Warehouse also did business as Airbase Carpets. In fact, the store sold more rugs than wallpaper. Within minutes Connolly and Donovan were exchanging high fives. Capano, they learned, had bought a rug that Saturday morning—a cheap imitation Oriental.

Why did he need a rug?

That night, in the rain, Donovan was back out banging on Ruth Boylan's door.

"I just have a few more questions," he said.

Then he quickly got to the point. Had she noticed anything different in the house when she cleaned it on July 22?

A light went off in Boylan's head. "Of course," she said.

The sofa that had been in the so-called great room, the combination den and dining area, was missing. And the rug that covered nearly the entire floor had been taken up and replaced by a smaller rug, an Oriental.

Boylan described the sofa as rose in color, with a pineapple-swirl design on the fabric. As Donovan continued to question her, she said it had seemed to be in "very good" condition. She said the original rug had been a tight weave, nearly wall-to-wall, beige in color, and practically brand new. In fact, investigators learned that Capano had purchased the rug when he moved into the house back in September after separating from his wife. Part of the lease agreement was a stipulation that the tenant would provide rugs to cover and protect the hardwood floors.

"There was not a spot or a worn place on it," Boylan said of the rug Capano had replaced.

Donovan typed her comments into another report.

Then he, Connolly, and Alpert sat down to brainstorm. The conclusion was obvious: Capano must have removed the sofa and rug from his house because they had been tainted somehow. Most probably, they had been stained with blood.

"We figured he wrapped her body up in the rug," Donovan said later.

Finding the rug and the sofa, they felt certain, would lead them to the body.

Alpert came up with the first lead in that regard. He got a call from the project manager who was working for Louis Capano & Associates on the First USA office renovation job out on Foulk Road near Route 202. The project manager, a man named Shaw Taylor, was troubled, and said he wanted to talk to someone investigating the Fahey case. He wasn't sure if the information he had was important or if it even meant anything. But he wanted someone to know.

Shaw met with Alpert and another FBI agent at a truck stop outside of Wilmington. He wasn't taking any chances. He had been around Wilmington long enough to have developed a healthy respect for the Capanos' power and influence.

Shaw told Alpert that on Monday, July 1, he was ordered to have the construction debris Dumpsters at the job site hauled away and emptied. He said none of the receptacles were full, and that it was several more weeks before they were scheduled to be taken to two nearby landfills, one on Cherry Island near the Delaware River and the other out on Route 13 south of Wilmington. He said when he asked his immediate superior why the Dumpsters had to be removed, he got no explanation. He said he ultimately learned that the order to have the Dumpsters taken away ahead of schedule had come from Louis Capano Jr.

He said it didn't make sense economically to haul away half-full Dumpsters. But when he persisted, he was told, "Don't ask questions, just do it."

Several other small pieces of information surfaced toward the end of July, as Donovan and Alpert continued to work sources and follow leads and Connolly began to filter and process their raw data.

A clerk at a drugstore not far from Capano's home remembered a man fitting Capano's description coming in on Sunday, June 30, and asking about household cleansing products. The customer wanted to know which product was the best for removing bloodstains.

During the last week in July, Donovan conducted lengthy interviews with Kim Horstmann and Jill Morrison, two of Anne Marie's closest friends, and with Lisa D'Amico, the hairdresser. Alpert interviewed Michele Sullivan, a psychologist who was treating Anne Marie for her emotional problems and her eating disorder.

Sullivan's last appointment with Fahey had been on the afternoon of June 26. She told Alpert that she was aware Fahey had had an affair with Capano. In fact, she said, one of the things they were working on during the therapy sessions was developing Fahey's confidence to a level where she could successfully end the relationship and walk away.

The therapist told Alpert that Fahey had told her she was "frightened" of Capano. She said Fahey told her that "Capano had stalked [her] and threatened to expose their relationship to others in order to force Fahey to continue the relationship." Sullivan said she had encouraged Fahey to report the harassment to the Attorney General's Office, but that Fahey had not done so.

Sullivan also told the FBI agent that she thought the only reason Fahey would have gone to dinner with Capano on June 27 "would be to break off the relationship." She said she couldn't believe that Fahey "would have willingly gone to Capano's house that night." She also said that Fahey "was not suicidal and was looking forward to the future."

The next day Alpert drew up a twenty-page probable cause affidavit that Connolly submitted to a federal judge in order to obtain a search warrant for Capano's home on Grant Avenue, for his Jeep Cherokee, and for a Chevy Suburban that belonged to Capano's estranged wife, Kay. Investigators had learned Capano had borrowed the Suburban from June 28 until June 30.

The affidavit provided a running outline of the investigation, with references to most of the individuals who had been questioned by authorities. It would be revised and expanded on several times over the next year as investigators learned more about Capano. The affidavit was sealed and did not become public until the following January. But for those with access to it, paragraph twenty-two provided the stark, bare-bones theory of what investigators believed had happened on June 27, 1996: "There is probable cause to believe that Thomas Capano took Anne Marie Fahey without her consent from the Panorama Restaurant in Philadelphia to his home at 2302 Grant Avenue in Wilmington, Delaware, and that he killed her at his residence."

Before the search warrant could be executed, however, Connolly's boss, Greg Sleet, called over to the Delaware Attorney General's Office and asked for a meeting. Ferris Wharton, the state prosecutor, showed up in the U.S. Attorney's Office a few minutes later.

Connolly and Richard Andrews, head of the criminal division and Connolly's immediate supervisor, were waiting for him. The future of the Fahey investigation would be determined that afternoon.

"We've got enough probable cause to get a search warrant for Tom Capano's house," Connolly said.

Wharton, a veteran prosecutor, knew what was coming next. There were, Connolly and Andrews explained, two ways to handle it. Either the federal government could hand everything over to Wharton and let the state take over the case from that point, or the state would have to back away and let the feds move forward on their own.

Wharton said it took him about thirty seconds to make up his mind.

"It was a no-brainer," said the lanky, affable state prosecutor. "I knew the resources they could commit versus the resources we could commit. . . . As much as we would have liked to have known what was going on, it made more sense for them to take the case."

Wharton looked at Connolly and Andrews, who had just finished explaining that if the feds went forward no one in

Wharton's office would be involved. No one, not even Wharton's boss, state Attorney General Jane Brady, would be briefed about the status of the investigation. Because of stringent federal grand jury secrecy laws, the state would be effectively out of the loop for the duration of the investigation.

"Do it," Wharton said.

Federal agents, with assistance from the Wilmington Police Department, swarmed over and through Capano's home for eleven hours the next day, executing the search warrant. Newspaper photographers and television cameramen stood outside the well-appointed home in the upper-class neighborhood recording the event. In brief comments, authorities said the search warrant was being executed in conjunction with a kidnapping investigation. From that point on, Thomas J. Capano was publicly identified as the prime suspect in the disappearance and suspected murder of Anne Marie Fahey.

During the search, investigators found two tiny specks of what appeared to be blood along a baseboard in the great room. It fit the theory that Connolly, Alpert, and Donovan were working: Fahey had been killed in the room where the sofa and rug had been. DNA experts testing the specks against a blood-bank sample of Anne Marie's would later confirm that the blood was, in all probability, hers. Other documents, records, and notes seized that day provided additional leads.

Capano, looking somber, stood by as his house and the backyard were turned inside out.

"He looked as if the wind had been knocked out of him," Connolly said of Capano that day, which was the first time he had ever seen Capano in person.

The specks of blood would prove crucial to the investigation. In the mind of the investigators, they confirmed the working theory of the case. And they provided a comfort zone that Connolly, Alpert, and Donovan could retreat to when things got tough.

"There were nights," Alpert said later, "when I'd be up until two o'clock in the morning pacing the floor trying to figure this out, wondering how he was able to get away with this, wondering if he was that smart or we were just missing something."

All three of them had had nights like that. Sometimes they would call one another. Sometimes they would simply pace alone in the dark.

They were certain that they knew what had happened, that Tom Capano had killed Anne Marie Fahey. They were less certain that they would ever be able to prove it.

It started as a rumor.

But it was quickly confirmed by Donovan and Alpert.

Early in July, Gerry Capano had sold his twenty-five-foot sports fishing boat, the *Summer Wind*. He had bought a larger, more expensive boat, a twenty-nine-foot Black Fin that cost $105,000.

Donovan and Alpert had been picking up reports that Tom and Gerry Capano had been in Stone Harbor on June 28 and that they had gone out fishing that day. The investigators knew that Tom Capano wasn't into fishing. Why would he go out on the boat?

The rumor hinted at the answer. It was something the buyer of the *Summer Wind* had told a friend, and the friend had mentioned to someone else, and so on until it worked its way back to Donovan.

When the *Summer Wind* was sold, there was a piece of equipment missing.

The boat didn't have an anchor.

8

... I talked with Tomas last night ... Our relationship is finished. He told me I need to find a man without children who has a lot of time for me, because I am very special and deserve much more. Well, after he said that I was very sad and I cried all night. I know it is my problem and my fault. Because from the beginning I knew what I was getting myself into ... I have dreams about him and me making love and living together—but it will never happen.

After he left, I was so empty, sad, lonely. I told him things that were hidden inside me. I feel so comfortable w/him,—I can say anything. I watched him get in his car and drive away. I went to bed and cried myself to sleep.

Ciao, T, I love you.
AMF

The relationship between Capano and Fahey was confusing and contradictory, particularly for the investigators trying to put it together after the fact. The picture that emerged from her diary notes and interviews with her friends was of an affair that had run hot and cold over a two-year period. In the end, in the weeks and months leading up to Anne Marie's disappearance, it was Capano who was desperately trying to hold on, and

Fahey who was trying to break away. But there were times when Capano had tried to end it. And during those periods, it was Fahey who appeared to have become obsessed.

Part of the explanation, of course, was that she was a troubled and immature young woman who thought she was in love. Or, perhaps more to the point, who wanted to be in love. She was in serious counseling at that point, the beginning of 1994, and her psychologist, Bob Connor, had become a trusted friend with whom she shared most of her thoughts and even some details about the relationship with Capano. Connor was aware of her eating disorder, and had gotten her on Prozac as a way to deal with her depression, but the drug didn't appear to be working. It gave her headaches and made her sick. But she felt that Connor's counseling sessions were helping her come to grips with her life. Later, she would write that he was one of the few people who really knew her. At that point, she would have said that Capano was another.

What investigators came to realize, however, was that Fahey didn't really know Capano very well in the early months of their love affair. And by the time she figured him out, it was too late. As Donovan, Alpert, and Connolly worked up a profile of Thomas J. Capano, one of the traits that emerged was his uncanny ability to zero in on needy women, anticipate what it was they wanted, and then offer it to them. Capano was an emotional predator who seemed to like the chase as much, if not more, than the conquest. He was adept at juggling affairs and relationships, compartmentalizing his life and his loves. He could be the dedicated husband, the loving son, the caring father, the sensitive boyfriend, and the sensual lover. As the case against him unfolded, investigators would come to learn that he was all those things, but never simultaneously.

And never to the same woman.

From Anne Marie Fahey's diary, April 28, 1994:

> Tomas called today at ten-thirty and told me, "Love you." We decided that we will still see each other. All morning I wondered if he would call (I prayed he would, however I vowed to myself that I would not call him). Our conversa-

tion was good, but I felt a little sad. He is going to Canada from Wednesday until Friday for law school. Poor thing! Ciao Tomas. I love you!

My session w/Bob today was quite tearful. I cried a lot as well as informed him of my eating disorder. I realize how poor of an eater I've become and that it's not healthy, however, it feels great every time I get on the scale if the needle has decreased from b–4. My ideal weight is 125. I can do it! I now weight [sic] 133. 8 more pounds. I could easily do that in a week! I also feel that my world is so out of control and the only thing I can control is my food intake. I know one thing, Prozac is not for me! Bob is aware, so I suppose we'll take it from here.

Cheers—AMF

The trip to Canada that Fahey mentioned in her diary was for a legal seminar in Montreal that Capano attended. It had to do with bond work, which had become his specialty at Saul, Ewing.

Montreal in the spring is lovely. The Canadian city is like a piece of Europe in North America, a place of Old World charm and culture. Old Montreal, with its stone buildings and ornate church steeples, could easily be mistaken for the nineteenth arrondissement in Paris.

April in Paris is, of course, the ideal. But Montreal is not a bad second choice.

While Anne Marie Fahey wrote lovingly of her Tomas in her diary that week, Capano left for Montreal and the "boring" law seminar he told her he would be attending. Kay Capano stayed home with the girls. But Capano was not without companionship. He took his other girlfriend, Debby MacIntyre, the former wife of his one-time law firm colleague and a woman who had once been a good friend of Kay's. Capano and MacIntyre had been carrying on a secret affair since early in 1981. She was independently wealthy—Capano referred to her as a "trust fund" baby—and attractive without being beautiful. A short, well-built woman, she swam to stay in shape, but she lacked Fahey's striking features. She dressed conservatively and looked the part of the buttoned-down school administrator she was. But she had other attributes and interests. MacIntyre, Capano would later say almost boastfully, "had as strong a sex drive as any woman I ever met. She enjoyed sex very, very, very much. . . . As much as I did."

She was the woman, he said, who introduced him to pornography and three-way sex, allegations she would later dispute. She didn't deny that they watched porno films or that she had sex with other partners while Capano was present, but she said she took part at his urging and only because she loved him and didn't want him to leave her.

Debby MacIntyre said she never knew about Anne Marie Fahey. Fahey, likewise, never knew about MacIntyre. They each played a different part in Capano's life. Each had a spot, a compartment. That's the way he liked it.

Anne Marie Fahey's diary went silent about Capano for nearly nine months after those April 1994 references. That summer she had a brief fling with a young man named Michael Hinds. Her brother Robert had introduced them. From her diary entries she appeared more infatuated with him than he was with her, and she noted sadly that she expected him to dump her.

"I am so paranoid that I am not pretty, smart, fun, exciting enough," she wrote as the brief affair was ending.

In July she and her brother Brian left for a two-week vacation in Ireland with the money left to them by their grandmother, Katherine McGettigan. Nan had died in November 1992, leaving each of her grandchildren a small bequest of $2,500. Annie had been reluctant to take the money; she felt guilty, as if she were somehow getting rich off the death of a woman she dearly loved. It was Bob Connor, her therapist, who suggested using the money to finance a trip to Ireland.

They visited Limerick, Dublin, County Cork, Cape Clear, Dingle, Galway, Donegal, and Kilmacrennan, the old homestead of the McGettigan clan and the town where her grandmother once lived. They also drove over to the nearby town of Milford, where her grandmother had once owned a pub, the White Heather Inn. Brian and Anne Marie were delighted to find it still in operation.

Anne Marie came away from the trip with an even greater sense of family and a better idea of who she was and where she had come from. She found warmth and love in the old country, and her absence from home made her aware of the warmth and love that were there for her as well. In one diary note midway through the trip, she mentioned that she and Brian had called their sister Cass at home "to let her know we were alive." Cass told Anne Marie she missed talking to her so much that she called Anne Marie's answering machine in Wilmington just so she could hear her voice.

"I got to say hello to Buster Brown!" Anne Marie noted in her diary. The reference was to her nephew Kevin, Cass's then two-year-old boy. Anne Marie was his godmother.

Brian and Anne Marie spent several days at the end of the trip with relatives, and Anne Marie wrote about how enchanted she was with the people and the country. One of their cousins, Susie, reminded her immediately of Nan.

"Nan lives on through Susie," Annie wrote. "She looks and acts just like her. . . . After a few minutes, I felt totally at home. As if I had known these people my whole life."

There were no references to Capano in the diary notes during that period, but investigators later learned that he had given her $500 as a gift just before she left. He thought she would use the money to buy a plane ticket for a short hop over to Lisbon, though in the end she decided she didn't have enough time. But when she returned, Capano told her to keep the money. She called him on the phone once from Ireland, but he told her not to do it again, that it was too expensive. He said he thought he was being considerate, given her financial situation. She later told friends she was hurt by his blasé attitude.

From Anne Marie Fahey's diary, July 25, 1994, from County Cork:

> I have my grandmother to thank for the relaxation I am experiencing right now. Without her this trip would not have been possible. Of course, I would rather have her w/me, but we all must die.

Kim Horstmann knew more about Anne Marie's relationship with Capano than anyone else, and during the first few months of the investigation she became a primary source for Donovan, Alpert, and Connolly. Eventually, she would tell her story to a grand jury, and would testify for the prosecution in the murder trial.

Horstmann had known Fahey since 1988. They met when they both were spending time in Sea Isle City that summer. They had mutual friends, and started spending more and more time together during the weekends. Unlike Stone Harbor and Avalon, two trendy and upscale South Jersey seashore communities to its immediate south, Sea Isle City is without pretense. A combination family resort and weekend party town, Sea Isle is a laid-back, cutoffs-and-T-shirt answer to Avalon and Stone Harbor's stonewashed, prepped-out enclaves.

On weekends Sea Isle would fill up with middle-class twentysomethings. Once you parked your car on Friday night—assuming you could find a parking space—there would be no reason to get in it again until you left for work early Monday morning. There were a half-dozen bars and clubs within a three-block area in the center of town, and they catered to every taste and mood. Hard rock and heavy metal at the Ocean Drive, locally known as the OD. Acoustic guitars and folk music at the Dead Dog Saloon. Classic summertime rock-and-roll, with the occasional sing-along, at the Springfield Inn. Cozy what's-your-sign romancing at the La Costa and Braca's Cafe. It was the perfect place to spend a carefree summer weekend. Single and attractive, Fahey, the striking brunette, and Horstmann, a sassy blonde, fit right in.

By 1994, they were the best of friends. Horstmann worked in Philadelphia for a financial investment firm, living outside the city, in the Pennsylvania suburbs. Throughout the fall, winter, and spring, she and Annie talked on the phone several times a week and got together on many a Friday or Saturday night. That summer they rented a place in Sea Isle for the second half of the season, beginning on July 15. When Annie got back from Ireland, she spent most weekends at the shore with Kim. It was there that Horstmann first learned about the affair with Capano, which—despite the absence of any reference in the diary at that time and despite the brief fling with Michael Hinds—was apparently still going strong.

Horstmann noticed that Fahey frequently referred to "her friend Tom" or "Tommy." Annie said he was someone she had met at work, and that he often took her out to lunch or dinner. Horstmann figured there was more to the story, but decided to wait for Annie to tell her. Before the summer was out, she did.

"She told me that she was having an affair," Horstmann recalled, "and how difficult it was because he was a married man and he had four children. . . . She said he was a very successful, powerful lawyer, very big in the Delaware community, and came from a very wealthy family."

And, Fahey said with a smile, he treated her "like a princess."

"He would take her to these wonderful dinners," Horstmann later told a grand jury as she recounted her conversation with Anne Marie. "And he would buy her wonderful gifts and she felt she could confide in him and tell him anything about her; that she would be completely honest about her life with Tom. And she felt that, you know, he was treating her like no other man would be able to treat her."

Fahey also told Horstmann about the guilt and shame she felt for beginning a relationship with a married man, a man who left her bed to return to his home and his family.

As a "devout Catholic," Horstmann said, Fahey felt "terrible guilt" and had trouble coping with the fact that she was the other woman in an adulterous affair. She also worried about what her family would think if anyone found out.

When Bob Donovan interviewed Horstmann in July 1996, he asked her about that. "It was difficult," Horstmann said, "because she loved him and he really loved her and, you know, he was talking about leaving his wife and how difficult . . . she did not want the responsibility of having him leave his wife for her and . . . but then she didn't know if she could ever meet a man that would take care of her the way Tom took care of her, or treat her the way he treated her. He treated her, you know, like a complete gentleman and so she was very confused."

Horstmann said Fahey often asked her advice and wondered aloud about where the relationship was going.

"Was she trying to deal with it or was she thinking seriously about making this a long-term relationship?" Donovan asked.

Horstmann said Anne Marie swung back and forth emotionally over that very issue. She talked about making it long-term, but then she would say, "It's never going to work. My family will freak out. My family will completely . . . I couldn't live with it. I couldn't do that. It would upset my family too much."

A minute later, Anne Marie would talk about how kind and caring Capano was and wonder if she would ever meet anyone like him.

"Will anybody ever love me the way he loves me?" she would ask Horstmann. "Will anybody treat me the way he treats me?"

Horstmann said she believed she was the only one Annie had told about the relationship. She was sure that she was the only one to ever see Tom and Annie together and at ease with one another.

In the fall of 1994, Capano arranged to take Annie and Kim to dinner together in Philadelphia. He said he wanted to meet her, that Annie had told him so much about her and that she, Horstmann, was the only person who knew they were seeing one another. They went to DiLullo Central, another posh Philadelphia restaurant.

Over the course of the investigation, Donovan would compile a list of the restaurants Capano frequented in Philadelphia. They were all top-of-the-line, four- and five-star eateries. Most specialized in Italian cuisine, which allowed Capano to play up his ethnicity, emphasizing his passion, his zest for life, his soul. In addition to DiLullo's, a Capano restaurant tour would include stops at Panorama, La Famiglia, the Saloon, and La Veranda, all among the best and most expensive in the city.

It was also no accident that the restaurants were located in Philadelphia, not Wilmington. Capano boasted about his discretion, offering it as a kind of justification for his behavior. It was part of his twisted code of nobility. He said he never took one of his girlfriends to a restaurant in the Wilmington area when they were on a romantic date. He said Wilmington was a small, gossipy town and he would never do anything to embarrass his wife, Kay. In fact, he often chided his male friends for

THE SUMMER WIND   89

being less circumspect, telling them they should think about their wives' feelings.

"She's the mother of your children," Capano would say. "Don't embarrass her."

Although frequently—perhaps chronically is the better word—unfaithful to his wife of twenty-six years, Capano said he was always discreet. And he said it in such a way that it sounded like he believed that should count for something, that in some way that should excuse, or at least diminish, the fundamental impropriety of his behavior.

Asked about how Capano and Fahey acted toward one another that night in DiLullo's, Horstmann said, "They were a couple."

"They would hold hands across the table or I saw them kiss once," she said. "It looked like they were enjoying each other's company."

The raid on Capano's home at 2302 Grant Avenue on the morning of July 31, 1996, ended the first phase of the game of cat-and-mouse that Connolly had begun playing with Capano when he took over the case. While the search warrant affidavit filed by Alpert would not be unsealed for another six months—and only after members of the news media pressed the court to make the document public—the search warrant itself provided enough information for Capano and his lawyers to determine where Connolly was headed.

Among the items being sought, according to the warrant, were "hairs, fibers, blood, semen and any bodily fluids and parts of Anne Marie Fahey and Thomas Capano" as well as "any weapons or objects which could be used to inflict blunt force injury or strangulation." Also any "tools" or "devices . . . and other objects which could be used to dismember or conceal body parts, hairs, and fluids." The gruesome inventory of what investigators were looking for also included "cleansers, soaps, detergents, solvents, and chemicals that could be used to conceal, dissolve, or dismember body fluids or parts."

Finally, investigators were looking for "letters, notes, diaries, journals, calendars, files, memoranda, receipts and records which would provide proof of an affair between Capano and Fahey and establish that Fahey had been attempting to end their relationship and that Capano [had] attempted to prolong their relationship by black mail, threats, gifts, and harassment."

Agents and detectives searched every room and went through every drawer and closet in the home while Capano and his lawyers watched. They also dug up sections of the back yard and brought in trained dogs to sniff and search. They weren't sure what they were looking for. But they were fairly certain that they were examining a crime scene, a scene that had been dramatically altered in the month since the crime had taken place and that had probably been scoured clean with detergents and bloodstain removers.

The rug and the love seat, of course, were gone. And if, as police now believed, the great room was where Anne Marie Fahey had been killed on June 27, 1996, most of the blood that was spilled that night had been cleaned up. Two specks might not be enough to make a case, especially since there still was no body and no confirmed cause of death.

But it was a start.

Connolly had cast his net in a wide circle. Now he would begin pulling it slowly tighter.

9

On August 5, 1996, Tom Capano and his lawyers received a letter from the U.S. Attorney's Office informing them that he was now the subject of an ongoing criminal investigation into the disappearance of Anne Marie Fahey. For Capano, the so-called "target letter" merely confirmed what he knew on July 31, when the search warrant was executed at his home on Grant Avenue. From that point on, Capano told anyone who would listen that he was being made a "scapegoat," that he didn't know what had happened to Anne Marie Fahey, but that he was concerned because the case had become "politicized." He implied that both Governor Carper and, more astonishingly, President Clinton were out to get him, that they both found it in their best interest to make him a target.

"I've been around long enough to know how things work," Capano said cryptically, without clearly explaining the reason for the high-level political conspiracy. No one, with the possible exception of Capano's mother, Marguerite, put much stock in the conspiracy theory. Investigators saw it as an outgrowth of Capano's ego, arrogance, and blossoming paranoia.

One of the nastier rumors that surfaced around this time, and one that Capano was happy to keep alive with a wink and a knowing smirk, was that Fahey had had a relationship with her boss, the governor, and that some of the references in her diary to "Tom" were references to Carper, not Capano. It was grist for the rumor mill that was now running twenty-four hours a day in Wilmington. Who was the "TC" in Anne Marie Fahey's life, Tom Capano or Tom Carper? The question floated around the political and social circles in which Carper, Capano, and Fahey had traveled, but there was nothing of substance to tie the missing woman to the governor romantically.

As for the President's interest, Clinton had offered help to his good friend Tom Carper when he learned that Fahey had turned up missing. That offer, however, had little to do with the U.S. Attorney's Office taking over the case. And at the time, Clinton had more important things to focus on than a missing person investigation in Delaware. He was in the middle of a reelection campaign, among other things. And he would soon have his own extramarital problems and even less of a reason to single out Capano for special attention. That August, the President received a gift from the young woman who would soon become a central part of his life, Monica Lewinsky. She gave the President a tie. He already had given her a cigar.

After the raid, Tom Capano never spent another night in the house on Grant Avenue. He first moved into his brother Louis's mansion out in Greenville. A few months later he moved again, this time back into the home where he had grown up, a sprawling stone colonial off Weldin Road in Brandywine Hundred, just north of Wilmington. For nearly a year, until the day he was arrested, Tom Capano lived with his mother, Marguerite. The golden boy had come home.

They wore white environmental suits and masks and carried rakes and shovels. They used a backhoe and an earth mover. For five days, under the hot August sun, FBI agents and Wilmington police officers sifted through the stale and rancid debris, poking open plastic trash bags and combing through rubbish at the Cherry Island and Delaware Recyclable Products landfills. They were looking for a bloodstained couch and rug, and maybe a gun or some other potential murder weapon. They also believed that their search might turn up all or parts of Anne Marie Fahey's body.

But even though the landfill operators had directed them to the general area where the Dumpsters from the Capano construction site had been emptied more than a month earlier, they found nothing.

"That stuff had been ground up so much it was impossible to tell what it was," said Donovan. "We could have been holding a piece of the couch and not known it."

"It was disappointing," said Connolly of the fruitless, foul-smelling search. "And it reeked. It was hot, then it rained on us. It was disgusting."

While the landfill search was under way, Tom Capano visited a psychiatrist for the first time. Notes of that session and two subsequent meetings were eventually introduced as evidence at his murder trial.

During the first session, on August 16, 1996, Capano said he had had nothing to do with Anne Marie Fahey's disappearance and had never displayed any violence toward her. In a somewhat rambling discourse, he also commented on the specks of blood that had been found in the great room on Grant Avenue. He didn't know whose blood that was, but he said it could have been Fahey's. He said that as a method of birth control they often had sexual intercourse while she was having her period, and claimed that might explain why her blood was in his house.

Capano said that Fahey had a heavy menstrual cycle. Connolly would later call Fahey's doctors to the witness stand to refute that. The doctors testified that Fahey had problems with her period, sometimes skipped a month, and that her bleeding was light rather than heavy.

It was one of the sadder moments in a tragic case. Anne Marie Fahey had spent her brief lifetime jealously guarding her privacy. Now, in a packed and public courtroom, the entire world was learning all her secrets, including the nature and regularity of her period.

Capano went on to tell his psychiatrist that the last time he had seen Fahey was when he dropped her off at her apartment after dinner on the night of June 27. When he first learned she was missing, he said, he believed that she had taken off for the weekend to "collect her thoughts." Now, six weeks later, he thought that she had been the victim of "random violence in the neighborhood," or that she had committed suicide.

A week later, in a second session, Capano said he was feeling tremendous "grief over her disappearance." It was, he said, "the loss of someone I cared deeply about." And he returned again to the question of Fahey's blood in the great room. Now he said that they had fought that night, that Anne Marie had punched and pushed him during an argument over his insistence that she seek clinical treatment for her anorexia. He said that when he tried to stop her from punching him, she got a bloody nose.

Several other people close to Capano were called before a federal grand jury that August as Connolly opened up the investigation and began to focus on those closest to his target. One of the first was Louis J. Capano. There would also be a long, legal battle with Lauri Merten, the professional golfer who was married to Louis. This would lead to more public discussion of the Capano family and its marital woes. The Capano brothers and their affairs became one of the backstories in the case, which was begining to sound more and more like a soap opera. Louis was carrying on an extramarital relationship, and Merten had tapped the phone in their home in an attempt to catch him. The feds believed she had inadvertently picked up some conversations between Louis and Tom. Connolly wanted those tapes, but Merten refused to give them up, a position that was later upheld by the U.S. Third Circuit Court of Appeals. The story eventually made it to the normally sedate pages of *Golf World* magazine, under the tabloidish headline "THE TANGLED TALE OF LAURI MERTEN." The story went on to allege that, in a snit over her husband's escapades, Merten had taken a golf club to his posh BMW. Both husband and wife later claimed that the damage to the car resulted from an accident in which the car scraped a bridge abutment.

Louis Capano Jr. was first subpoenaed to appear before a federal grand jury in Wilmington on August 29, 1996. That morning, just before his appearance, he and his brother Tom had a conversation in the bathroom of Louis's mansion. Tom had been a guest at the house for nearly a month and was aware that Louis was about to go in front of the grand jury. Louis had tried to block the appearance. His lawyers had told Connolly he would exercise his Fifth Amendment right against self-incrimination and decline to answer any questions.

Connolly countered by arranging a grant of immunity. Nothing Louis told the grand jury could be used against him. Still, at Tom's urging, he lied.

That morning, Tom had asked Louis not to tell investigators that he had dumped a sofa in the trash at the construction site. He also asked Louis to say that on Friday morning, June 28, Tom had stopped by his house around 8:00 A.M. to go over some business papers. This would be consistent with the alibi story he had earlier arranged with Gerry.

Louis knew the sofa was in the Dumpster that he had ordered removed from the construction site. And he knew the feds had been out to the landfills looking for it. But he made no mention of it in his testimony that day. He also fabricated a tale about Tom showing up at his house on June 28.

What he did not tell the grand jury was the story his brother first told him on June 30 just hours after he had been awakened and questioned by police.

Tom called Louie that morning and asked him to stop over at the house on Grant Avenue. When he arrived, Tom escorted him out onto the screened-in porch at the back of the house. The girls were upstairs, getting ready for Mass. It was around 11:30 A.M.

"You're not gonna believe what happened last night," Tom Capano said.

During that conversation, Tom Capano told his brother that Anne Marie Fahey was an emotionally troubled woman with whom he had been carrying on an affair for almost two years. He said the affair was over, but that they were still friends. He said that he had taken her to dinner Thursday night and it now appeared that he was the last person to have seen her alive. He said the police were suspicious and he was afraid they suspected him of some wrongdoing.

He insisted he had taken her home that night.

But for Louie he added another twist to the story.

He said that after dinner, they had gone back to his house. Capano said he went upstairs to use the bathroom and when he came down, Anne Marie Fahey had slit her wrists. He said they were superficial wounds, but that she had gotten blood all over the sofa. He said he bandaged her up and took her home. And the next day he got Gerry to help him put the sofa in the Dumpster on Foulk Road.

Tom Capano also told Louis that he had put some of Fahey's "personal belongings," things she had kept at his house, like her hairbrush and nightgown, in the Dumpster as well. He said he didn't want Kay to find out about the affair. He and Kay were seeing a counselor and trying to salvage their marriage.

Nearly everything Tom Capano told his brother Louis that Sunday morning was a lie.

Louis, in turn, lied about the lies to the grand jury.

During his questioning by Colm Connolly, the two quickly fell into verbal sparring. After a series of preliminary questions, Connolly cut to the heart of the matter and asked Louis why he had ordered the Dumpsters emptied on July 1.

"I did it because I had told my brother Tom I would have the Dumpsters dumped," he said.

"Did Tom ask you to have the Dumpsters dumped?" asked Connolly pointedly.

"No, he did not," replied Louis Capano.

"Why did you offer to remove the Dumpsters for Tom?" Connolly shot back.

"That is a much longer answer," said Louis.

"We have a lot of time," replied Connolly.

With that, Louie launched into a lengthy account about his meeting with his brother on June 30, leaving out the part about Fahey's alleged suicide attempt and the bloody sofa.

Louis told the grand jury that his brother was nervous and worried that his wife, Kay, might find out about the affair with Fahey. That was why, Louis said, *he* suggested to Tom that if any of Fahey's belongings were in the house on Grant Avenue he should get rid of them. Louis said he told Tom to throw them in the construction Dumpster out on Foulk Road and that he would make sure it was emptied.

"What items did he say he would put in the Dumpster?" Connolly asked.

"He didn't tell me," said Louis.

Connolly and Louis Capano continued their verbal tap dance for nearly an hour. Along the way, the prosecutor was able to paint a picture of Louis Capano for the jury, a picture he wanted the jurors to have for future reference. Connolly knew this was just the opening salvo in his battle with the Capanos. Louis would end up back before the grand jury on two other occasions. He would also feel the heat generated by Connolly's multipronged attack. The IRS would open an investigation into his financial dealings, and the FBI would focus on the way he tried to influence other witnesses who ended up in front of the same grand jury, including his girlfriend, Kristie Pepper. Louis Capano had spent the night of June 27 at Pepper's home while his wife, Lauri, was out of town for a golf tournament.

Connolly clearly established Louis Capano as a person of wealth. Through his testimony the jurors learned of the various Capano-related businesses in which he was involved; they got a description of his house and pool, they learned that he drove a white BMW 700 with a sun roof, that he and his wife had three phones in their house—Louis couldn't remember the number for the one in the garage—and that they also had two cellular phones and two car phones. Louis also described his somewhat fragile relationship with other members of the Capano family.

"Your mother has a beach house in Stone Harbor, is that right?" Connolly asked.

"Yep, yes she does," said Louis.

"What's the address?"

"One-hundred Thirteenth Street and the ocean. That's all I know."

"Do you speak with your mother frequently?" asked Connolly.

"She would like me to speak with her more frequently," replied Louis.

Asked if he was in Stone Harbor with the rest of the family over the Fourth of July weekend, Louis said no. He had been at his own seaside home in Rehoboth Beach, Delaware, he said.

Louis was not on the best of terms with either his mother or his sister, Marian. In fact, he and Marian's husband, a local attorney named Lee Ramunno, had been feuding for years. Ramunno had once had him arrested for assault.

"Have you spoken with Lee Ramunno in the last two months?" Connolly asked.

"I haven't spoken to Lee Ramunno in the last ten years," Louis Capano shot back without missing a beat.

Throughout the questioning Connolly continued to circle back to the Dumpsters and why Louis had ordered them emptied. He got Louis to repeat how he had encouraged Tom to throw away any of Anne Marie's personal belongings.

"I told him . . . that if he didn't want his wife to know and he didn't want the police to see her pajamas there, whatever else, just to throw it away," Louis said.

"You had a lot of Dumpsters there," said Connolly. "Did you tell him which Dumpster to use?"

"No," said Louis Capano.

Two or three questions on an unrelated matter, and then Connolly was back at it.

"How did you know to have the Dumpsters removed?"

"I'm not sure I understand your question," Louis said. "I told him I was going to have the Dumpsters removed."

"But he didn't tell you for sure whether he would put something in the Dumpsters," Connolly said.

"I assumed he would and it didn't matter," Louis retorted. "I just told him I would have them dumped. If he [had] something to put in [them], fine. If he didn't, fine."

Connolly also asked Louis Capano if his brother Gerry had recently sold a boat. Louis said he had.

He asked about Debby MacIntyre. Louis said he knew her and knew that his brother Tom had recently begun dating her.

"I know he and Debby are friends," Louis Capano told the grand jury. "I know, for example, he was with her last night. I have no idea if he was with her before last night or whatever. I really don't know."

Louis Capano said his brother Tom did not discuss his affairs with him, that until Anne Marie Fahey had disappeared he was unaware that his brother had any relationship outside his marriage.

*   *   *

Connolly was sure Louis Capano had violated his immunity agreement, that he had not been completely truthful with the grand jury. But that was a pressure point to be pushed at a later date. What Connolly couldn't be sure of was how much Louis Capano actually knew about what had happened to Anne Marie Fahey.

Connolly, Donovan, and Alpert knew they would be talking with Louis Capano again before the investigation was over. Getting him on the record and under oath was the first step in squeezing the truth out of him.

Gerard Capano was another matter. He had been with Tom on June 28, less than twelve hours after authorities now believed Fahey had been killed. Both brothers had been in Stone Harbor. They might have gone out on Gerry's boat; that was what Donovan and Alpert were picking up. And now the boat had been sold, without an anchor. The collective instinct of the three men working the case was that Gerry had played some type of role in Fahey's disappearance, probably a more active role than Louis had. For that reason, Connolly decided not to call Gerry before the grand jury. He needed to know more about the boat ride. There was no way he would even consider granting Gerry immunity until he knew what had happened out in the Atlantic that morning.

Alpert had a list of Gerry's friends. He and Donovan had been picking up street talk about their drug use. They decided to run the names past a detective who used to work undercover narcotics for the Wilmington Police Department but was now assigned to a special task force working for the Bureau of Alcohol, Tobacco and Firearms.

The names meant nothing to the detective. But during the course of a second conversation he and Alpert kicked around the idea of launching an undercover operation in which Gerry and his friends would be targeted.

The idea was to get close, get their confidence, and then just listen. It was a long shot, they both knew. There was no one available to make an introduction. The undercover would have to go in cold, but he was willing to give it a shot.

Connolly liked the idea and gave the go-ahead. And with that, working off the books, Richard "Doug" Iardella began the one phase of the Capano investigation that has never been fully reported. The role of the ATF and its undercover operatives—Iardella's wife, Diane, herself an ATF agent, and Frank Sullivan, a state police detective assigned to the ATF Task Force, would also work the investigation—was crucial to the case against Tom Capano. Without it, the feds might not have been able to "flip" Gerry. And without Gerry Capano's cooperation, his brother Tom might still be a free man.

At the end of August 1996, however, Gerry had no intention of cooperating. When he sat down with his own lawyer for the first time, he told him the story that he and Tom had agreed upon during their drive back to Wilmington after dumping the body.

Gerry, through his brother Tom and Tom's lawyer Charles Oberly, had retained a local criminal defense attorney named Dan Lyons. Tall and lanky, with an easygoing manner that belied a cut-to-the-chase intellect, Lyons had once been a federal prosecutor attached to the Organized Crime Strike Force in San Francisco. His father had been a prominent Wilmington attorney, a partner at one point in the law firm where Capano had worked back in the late 1970s and early 1980s. Lyons's father, in fact, had written a letter of recommendation for Capano to Boston College, his own alma mater, when Capano was still in high school.

But while Dan Lyons had come back to Wilmington to practice law after leaving the U.S. Attorney's Office, he was not part of anyone's old-boy network. Tom Capano had underestimated Lyons when he recommended him to his brother Gerry. Tom Capano thought Lyons would be a de facto member of the defense team, the Capano defense team.

Dan Lyons took the business of criminal law more seriously than that. He wasn't going to play the Wilmington political-legal game that Tom Capano had been playing for his entire career. Lyons, once he signed on to represent Gerry Capano, was only interested in his client's welfare.

Over the course of the next fifteen months, Lyons would have an inside and fairly accurate view of how the Fahey investigation was unfolding. From his client, he would learn—

months before Connolly, Donovan, and Alpert—the details of Anne Marie Fahey's horrible burial at sea. But at his first meeting with Gerry, Dan Lyons got the Capano family line.

The day after Louis Capano testified before the grand jury, Gerry Capano sat down to meet with his lawyer. During that session in Lyons's office in downtown Wilmington, Gerry outlined the alibi story he and Tom had agreed to, including the business about an early-morning meeting on June 28 to discuss an investment matter that Tom also planned to talk to Louis about that day. Gerry said both he and Tom met later in Stone Harbor, where they looked at a piece of real estate that Gerry was planning to buy. He said that when they got back to Wilmington, he helped his brother throw out an old sofa that had been in the Grant Avenue home.

That night, Gerry said, he went bar-hopping with a friend. His wife had taken their baby son and daughter to visit relatives in Ohio. The next morning, he said, he and three friends drove to Virginia, where they spent the weekend at a drag-racing rally. He said he was back in Wilmington late that Sunday afternoon, June 30.

"On Sunday evening about 7:00 (?) Charlie Oberly and Tommy showed up at Gerry's house and told Gerry that a girl Tommy had been dating—Anne Marie—was missing and that Tommy was the last person to have seen her," Lyons wrote in a memo that detailed what Gerry had told him during that first meeting.

"They counseled Gerry if the press showed up at his door or if the police appeared, to say nothing but to refer them to Charlie Oberly. They cautioned Gerry not to lose his temper and punch any newspapermen. Gerry was so freaked out by this that he went over to his friend's house again and spent the night.

"Gerry is adamant that he has no knowledge of where Anne Marie Fahey is at the present or whether any foul play was involved . . ."

It would be eight more months before Gerry would tell Lyons what he knew. By that point, Connolly had begun to bear down on him. And Gerry was haunted by a recurring nightmare, in which he heard a splash and saw a foot and ankle disappearing into the shark-infested waters.

10

In a follow-up interview with Lisa D'Amico on July 29, Donovan got the young hairdresser to expand on what she had told Lieutenant Daniels in the immediate aftermath of Fahey's disappearance.

D'Amico said that Fahey had told her "Capano was very controlling and determined what she could and could not do." Fahey said she and Capano had nearly come to blows during one angry confrontation while sitting in Capano's Jeep in front of her apartment. Anne Marie said she had again told Capano she wanted to end their relationship, that she just wanted his friendship. With that, she told D'Amico, "Capano started screaming and yelling at her," called her "a slut and bitch" and "grabbed her by the neck."

Fahey told D'Amico she jumped out of the car and ran into her apartment.

It was a troubling story on several levels, and one that Donovan and Alpert would eventually run past psychologists and psychiatrists familiar with the patterns of an abusive relationship. While D'Amico was the first to offer even a second-hand account of a physical confrontation, other friends of Fahey's who had begun opening up to Donovan and Alpert were clearly describing an emotionally abusive situation in which Capano would badger and harass Fahey. But the flip side of that equation, and the one that was even more disturbing to the investigators, was Fahey's reaction. She didn't walk away from Capano. Instead, she continued to see him. There were dinner dates in May and June. There were the notes about the money he had given her, and the thank-you notes she had sent in return. And there were dozens of e-mail messages between Capano and Fahey, several written in May and June. One, in fact, was sent on the night before their fateful dinner at Panorama.

What was the attraction? How was Capano able to abuse and dominate a woman, and still keep her interested in him? Was it his money and power? Was it his status in the community? His political connections? Or a combination of all of those things? The complicated answers to those questions said as much about Fahey as they did about Capano. Even more ominous was the fact that those same questions could be applied to other Capano relationships. They certainly fit his affair with Debby MacIntyre, the other "other woman" in Capano's life. And they were fundamental to another affair that dated all the way back to 1977, and that in many ways established the pattern of abusive and possessive behavior that led to Fahey's murder.

Tom Capano had done it before. He had threatened and harassed a woman who had spurned him, scared her so much that she fled Wilmington.

And he had gotten away with it.

Linda Marandola was a young legal secretary working for a lawyer who was a friend of Capano's back in 1977. She first met Capano at a staff party at the Attorney General's Office. Both Capano and her boss, James Green, were former deputy attorneys general. After the party, Capano started calling her at work, inviting her out to lunch. She was engaged and she knew he was married, but she saw nothing wrong with a lunch date.

Usually Jim Green would go along. Over a span of several months, she thought that she and Capano had become good friends.

"I thought he was a nice guy," Marandola said.

Later that year there was a bachelorette party for one of her girlfriends at Gallucio's, a local tavern. Capano was there that night. She had a little too much to drink. They started to flirt with one another. They ended up in his car in the parking lot, where they had sex.

In the weeks that followed Capano wanted more, but Marandola said she wasn't interested. She told him that what had happened at the party was a mistake, that she had had too much to drink, that "it was just one of those things." It wouldn't be happening again, she told him. She was engaged and had already set a wedding date.

"He would call every day," said Marandola. "Constantly. Sometimes a couple of times a day."

He wanted to take her to lunch. He wanted to take her to dinner. He wanted to see her again. He wanted to be with her. He needed her.

Capano could be kind and gentle and caring. But he also had a nasty streak that surfaced when he did not get what he wanted, and at those times he could be crude and abusive. It was during one of those occasions that he told an associate that Marandola "was the best cocksucker he ever had."

Despite her insistence that she was not interested in pursuing a relationship, Marandola had sex with Capano again. It happened about a year after their first encounter.

She and her husband-to-be had been having trouble finding an apartment in the Wilmington area. Her husband worked two jobs, one as a butcher and one at the DuPont Chamberworks Plant just across the river in Carneys Point, New Jersey. They wanted something close by. Capano's family owned the Cavalier Apartments, and he arranged to have their names moved to the top of a waiting list. She was grateful and thanked him, but she wasn't interested in having an affair with him.

Capano was invited to her bachelorette party. It was a few days before her wedding. Like some feudal lord, Capano decided he had to have her that night, that he was entitled. Again, she had been drinking. And again, she got into a car with him. But this time he drove her to a house on Seventeenth Street that he and his wife, Kay, had just purchased. The house, a sprawling home on a tree-lined corner surrounded by a high row of hedges, had once been the residence of the Catholic bishop of the Wilmington Diocese. Capano had paid $100,000 for the property, but he and his wife had not yet moved in. There was still renovation work being done.

Capano and Marandola had sex in the house that night. It was probably the first time he was intimate with anyone in the home he would share with his wife for the next eighteen years, the home where they would raise their children and build their life together. Then Capano drove Marandola back to the party, and he headed back to the condominium where he and Kay were living.

A few days later, Capano danced with Marandola at her wedding reception while his wife sat happily and obliviously at their table. While they danced, Capano whispered in Marandola's ear.

"He told me that he loved me and that he didn't want me to be married," Marandola recalled.

Eric Alpert interviewed Linda Marandola on September 30 and again on October 31, 1996. At that time, she was reluctant to discuss what had happened. A thin, dark-haired woman in her mid-forties who had lost a lot of the sultriness that first attracted Capano to her, Marandola told Alpert she was still afraid of what Capano might be able to do to her. As a result, when her relationship with Capano was first detailed in an FBI affidavit filed by Alpert, she was referred to as only as "VW," for "victim woman." Her name did not surface publicly in the case for several more months, and then it was the *News Journal* that identified her.

That authorities were able to find Marandola was another one of those quirks in the case and another example of the workings of small-town Wilmington. Capano liked being the big fish in a small pond. It was easy to dominate, to be a master of this small universe. But it also was more difficult to hide. There was not a lot of anonymity in Wilmington. In the summer of 1996, Capano and Fahey were, literally, the talk of the town. Everyone knew, or pretended to know, some inside information about the case. Rumors were rampant. Most were without foundation.

In fact, Celia Cohen, then a local political reporter, said that when she was covering the Republican National Convention in San Diego that summer, members of the Delaware delegation spent as much time gossiping about the Capano-Fahey story as they did talking up the GOP ticket for the fall. At one point, she said, she was standing on the convention floor talking with Congressman Mike Castle when Republican Party bigwig John Sununu walked up.

"One of the first things he did was ask about the investigation into Fahey's disappearance," Cohen recalled. "It seemed like everyone was asking about it and wanted to know what we heard and what the rumors were."

At that time there were only a handful of people who knew about the Capano-Marandola incident. One was her former boss, James Green, who in 1996 was working in the same law firm as David Weiss. Weiss had been hired by the Fahey family to represent them. He would eventually file a multimillion-dollar wrongful death suit on behalf of the Faheys against Tom Capano and his brothers.

In addition to Green, there were two other men who knew about the Marandola affair. One was a former FBI agent who died before Capano came to trial. The other was his sometime underworld snitch, a man named Joe Riley who, coincidentally, had also struck up a friendship with Jim Green.

In 1996, when Alpert first sat down to interview him, Riley was in his late seventies, hard of hearing, and walking with the aid of a cane. The short, once stocky, now overweight street hustler had a sandpaper voice right out of *Guys and Dolls* and a story to match. He told Alpert that Capano had solicited him in 1980 to harass Marandola, that Capano had even discussed having her assaulted. He said Capano was upset because Marandola refused to have a sexual affair with him. Capano said that he couldn't eat or sleep, that he was "crazy about her," but that she kept turning him down.

Alpert wrote it all down. He was now getting two versions of the same story, one from Riley and the other from Marandola. They were two pieces of the same puzzle—two views of an arrogant, obsessive, and potentially violent Tom Capano.

*   *   *

After she returned from her honeymoon in the summer of 1978, Marandola and her husband moved into their new apartment at the Cavalier. Unbeknownst to her, Capano had arranged to have the unit completely repainted, and had had new rugs installed. Marandola said she was upset because it appeared she was receiving "special treatment."

When she told that to Capano, he told her she was being "ungrateful."

Over the next several months, Capano continued to call and badger Marandola to go out with him.

"He told me he would divorce Kay if I would leave my husband," she said. Marandola said she wanted her marriage to work and had no intention of leaving her new husband. Then Capano changed his tack. He asked her to come to work for him as his legal secretary, promising her better pay and better working conditions. She turned down the offer. Again, Capano said she was being ungrateful.

But his phone calls persisted. And he once again started to pester her about going out. Sometimes, when she arrived for work in the morning or left in the afternoon, she would see him staring out his office window, watching her as she walked down the street. It was a strange feeling. There were times when she knew that he was watching even before she looked up and saw him in the window.

During the Christmas season in 1979, there was an office party at Gallucio's. Capano was there and was once again on the prowl. That night, he followed her back to her apartment and confronted her in the parking lot.

"He said he had to have me, that he couldn't stand being without me," Marandola recalled.

She said she wasn't interested.

A few months later, he sent a case of Asti Spumante to a wedding party for a member of Marandola's family. The party was being held in the Holiday Inn that the Capano family owned in Penns Grove, New Jersey. Marandola said she was embarrassed and hard-pressed to explain to her in-laws why Capano, whom none of them knew, had sent a case of sparkling wine to their party.

Finally, in the summer of 1980, she had had enough.

During one of his many phone calls, she lost her temper and told Capano never to call her again. That Wednesday, she and her husband left for a long weekend at the Jersey shore. When they returned to their apartment on Sunday night, there was an eviction notice waiting for them.

This was in August. They moved out in September. Before they left, Marandola received a long, rambling letter from Capano. His wife, Kay, had recently given birth to their first child, a daughter they named Christine. To all appearances Capano was a loving husband and cherished the idea of being a father to his brand-new baby girl. But in his letter to Marandola, he told a different story.

"He said he wished it was me giving birth to his child and not Kay," Marandola said. "And he said if he couldn't be with me, he didn't want me staying in his state. . . . He said this was his town and I couldn't stay in it."

He also told Marandola that if she didn't quit her job, she "would be sorry."

In words that echoed a confrontation he later had with Fahey, Capano threatened to go public with their affair and embarrass Marandola. He said he would tell the managers at the law firm where she was then working and anyone else in the Wilmington legal community who might consider hiring her "what kind of person she was" and how she had had a secret affair with him.

"I was upset and afraid," Marandola said. But she was also stubborn. While she and her husband left Wilmington and moved to southern New Jersey, she did not quit her job.

Two months later, the anonymous, threatening phone calls started.

Joe Riley said he met Capano by chance. He walked into his law office one day looking for representation in a landlord-tenant dispute. Capano took his case and lost it. When Riley asked what his fee would be, Capano told him not to worry about it. Then he began talking about "this problem" he had with a woman.

Riley said that Capano had told him he was "in love" with this woman, that he "couldn't live without her," but that she had told him off and as a result, he wanted someone to "hurt the bitch."

Capano then asked Riley if Riley could find someone who might be willing to beat her up or run her over with a car. He said he wanted her "hurt very bad."

Riley asked if Capano wanted her killed.

"No, I couldn't live with that," Capano said.

Riley said he told Capano that if his actions were ever discovered, Capano would have serious problems not only with the law, but also with the Delaware Bar Association. He could lose his license to practice law.

"I can handle that," Capano said confidently.

Riley said he played along with Capano, even made some anonymous threatening phone calls to Marandola's office and to her home and her in-laws' home in New Jersey. But he said he never planned to go through with any acts of violence. Instead, he said, he got in touch with his former FBI contact and, at his urging, tape-recorded not only the phone calls he made to harass Marandola, as Capano had requested, but also the phone conversations he had with Capano.

Riley told Alpert that the former agent had those tapes.

A short time later, the tapes were in Connolly's office and the Capano investigation was spinning in yet another direction.

Phone call from Joe Riley to Linda Marandola, December 1980:

Marandola: Mr. Green's office.
Riley: Hello?
Marandola: Hello?
Riley: Is this Linda?
Marandola: Yes.
Riley: Listen, Linda. I want to tell you something. We have a new, a friend. My name is Mr. Davison. Mr. Thomas Capano. He was telling me some things about you ... if you don't give me some money I'm gonna tell your husband ... about you and his activity. Are you there?
Marandola: Yes.
Riley: Thomas Capano, he told me the things that you did in his office.

Marandola: I'm not sure what you're referring to.

Riley: And at a hotel. And, he owes me money, that bum. And if you don't give me some money I'm gonna tell your husband who works over at DuPonts. Ya listening to me?

Marandola: Yes, I am.

Riley: Yeah, I just thought I'd tell ya about it 'cause I had a hard time getting money from him. You can go and tell him if you wanta but . . . you better come around and talk terms with me. What do ya say?

Marandola: I don't know what you're talking about, sir.

Riley: You don't want to talk about it? Well I'll talk to your husband over there, I got his telephone number, I got your telephone number too over there at Pennsville, New Jersey. I know where you live . . . I'll call you again and let you know. Alright? Linda?

Marandola: I don't think you should call me anymore.

Riley: I'm going over and tell you husband if I don't hear from you in a couple of days . . .

Linda Marandola had heard enough. She hung up the phone. Over the course of the next two weeks, there would be nearly a dozen more calls, to her office, to her house, and to her in-laws' home. Each time she hung up, and she told her family to do the same.

Riley also taped several conversations with Capano in which they discussed strategy, and in which Capano appeared to vacillate over whether he wanted Riley to proceed. Ultimately, he told Riley to continue and to make an effort to reach both Marandola's husband and her father-in-law.

Capano told Riley "this was his town, this was his state," and that no woman was going to turn him down and get away with it.

Riley also told Alpert that he met Capano's wife, Kay, and his mother, Marguerite, one night when Capano invited him home for dinner. Riley said he liked both women and asked Capano why he was willing to jeopardize his career and his family by harassing Marandola.

Capano said he couldn't get Marandola out of his mind and told Riley to keep the "pressure" on her. When Riley told him how Marandola had slammed down the receiver after hearing his voice, Capano said, "Oh, that's good. You ought to keep it up."

Saddest of all, however, were two phone conversations that Riley recorded with Kay Capano in late December 1980. Riley had called the Capano home in the evening trying to reach Tom. He wasn't home. Kay was there, however, with Christy, their six-month-old infant daughter.

The Capanos had been married for eight years. They had met at Boston College where Kay Ryan was a nursing student, and were married in 1972 after they both graduated. Tom went on to law school at BC, and she worked to help support him. They moved to Wilmington in 1974 after Tom graduated from law school. She went on to get a master's degree from the University of Pennsylvania. She worked as a public health nurse, and then as a nurse practitioner in a pediatric office. Described as strong-willed and independent, Kay Ryan Capano was designated the roles of wife and mother in Tom Capano's compartmentalized world.

It is hard to believe that over the course of their twenty-six-year marriage she was never aware of his darker side and of his other life with his other women, but in 1980 it is conceivable that she was completely unaware.

Capano's law practice and later his involvement in government were perfect covers for spending evenings away from home, for "working late," for attending dinners and political functions that would explain the smells of smoke and perfume and alcohol on his breath and his clothes. Maybe Kay Capano believed him at first. And maybe later there came a time where she simply wanted to believe. Finally, they may have reached a point in their marriage where she was so tied up with raising the girls and having her own career that it was no longer a question of believing. Maybe she just didn't care anymore. He was the provider; she was the wife and the mother. They each had their jobs. And their separate lives.

But in 1980, that wasn't the case. The betrayal of Kay Capano had begun long before she had a clue. When Joe Riley called her at home, she was the loving, caring, and faithful wife worried about a husband who was working too hard.

"You know he didn't come home till midnight last night and the night before," she said to Riley. "Isn't that awful?"

"What the hell," said Riley, laughing. "Does he want all the money in the world?"

"I don't know," said Kay Capano. "I don't know."

"No, I'm only kidding with you," said Riley reassuringly.

Kay Capano laughed into the phone as Riley praised her husband for his dedication. But he told her that she ought to get him to stop working so hard.

"Why don't ya talk to him?" Riley said.

"I—I do," said Kay Capano. "It doesn't make, it doesn't do any good."

The harassing phone calls to Linda Marandola stopped in January 1981.

By that point, Tom Capano had a new love interest. At a New Year's Eve Party he had made a pass at the wife of one of the other young lawyers in the law firm where he was working. Capano put Marandola out of his mind and focused instead on Debby MacIntyre Williams.

Riley took the tapes of the phone calls he had made to the FBI agent with whom he was working. The agent in turn took the tapes to a partner in Capano's law firm. The partner, who had also been a member of the Delaware State Bar's Censure Committee, later said that no action was taken against Capano because to him the tapes did not seem to indicate any criminal activity on Capano's part. Capano had harassed Marandola, literally driven her out of the city. He had discussed having her beaten up, assaulted, perhaps run over with a car. But no one had done a thing about it.

Later, prosecutors would argue that if some action had been taken at that time, Anne Marie Fahey might still be alive today. It was another one of the what-ifs to add to the growing and agonizing list being compiled by the Fahey family.

In 1980, however, the attitude of those involved was best reflected by what Jim Green told Alpert when the FBI agent interviewed him about the incident some sixteen years after the fact.

In an affidavit in which he never identified Green by name, Alpert wrote that the lawyer told him that "he did not approach Capano about [harassing Marandola] because he thought that

Capano had simply gotten carried away about Marandola's refusal to accept his job offer." Green said he "thought that Capano was the type of person who believed that he could have anything he wanted and that this characteristic explained his conduct towards [Marandola]." Finally, Alpert noted, Green said Marandola "was probably better off away from Capano and not in a position beholden to him."

Amazingly, Marandola told Alpert she had two other encounters with Capano.

In 1987, she said, he called her "out of the blue" at a law firm where she was then working and "acted as if nothing had ever happened." Marandola said she always suspected Capano had been behind the harassing phone calls, but was never entirely certain. The only reference he made to them in 1987 was a cryptic aside in which he told her, "You cost me a lot of money."

Marandola said she was divorced in 1987, but wasn't interested in renewing her friendship with Capano. But he persisted. There were several phone calls in which he told her how desperately he wanted to see her again. She said that wasn't a good idea. Finally, she agreed to meet him in the parking lot of the Ramada Inn. They talked and agreed to go out.

"I thought maybe he had changed," she said by way of explanation. "That maybe he deserved a second chance."

He suggested a trip to Atlantic City in April to celebrate her birthday. "He badgered me," she said. "He kept calling. He said he didn't think it was right for me to spend my birthday alone." Marandola agreed, and on April 22, 1987, they left Wilmington for a night in Atlantic City. Capano, she said, gave her a watch as a birthday gift and had it engraved with the date "4/22/87" and their initials "TC" and "LM."

But when they got to their hotel room that night, Capano asked if she had been seeing any other men since her marriage ended. She said she had.

"He freaked out," she recalled. "He called me a slut and a whore."

Those were the same words Fahey had told D'Amico Capano had used when he screamed at her after she told him she wanted to end their relationship.

Marandola said they never left their hotel room that night. They never went down to the casino to gamble, as they had intended, and, she added, they did not have sex. The next morning, he took her home. He told her to keep the watch.

Capano called again in 1989 and in 1992. Marandola refused to see him. Then, four years later—in the middle of his last blowup with Fahcy—Capano called again. And for a time, at least, Marandola considered renewing their relationship.

11

When it came to men, Anne Marie Fahey's life was a series of bad choices.

Thomas J. Capano was the last in a long line that began while she was in college. Her therapists would later offer a detailed explanation for her troubles, linking them to her problem-plagued childhood, to her lack of a solid father figure while growing up, to the uncertainty and chaos in her life, and to her low self-esteem.

Nick Halladay, Fahey's college roommate, saw it in simpler terms.

"She always seemed to put more into a relationship than she got back," Halladay said. Now married and running his family's florist shop in West Chester, Pennsylvania, Halladay had shared an apartment with Fahey for more than two years while they both were enrolled at Wesley College in Dover in the late 1980s.

Halladay said he and Fahey were never romantically involved, but often talked about each other's relationships. He said Fahey seemed to be attracted to two types: guys her own age who were selfish and needy and older men who she knew were off-limits. There were, he said, at least two professors who tried to develop romantic relationships with her. Halladay said he didn't know whether Fahey had encouraged their interest, but he remembered one incident that especially upset her.

One of her professors wrote her a long letter in which he expressed his nonacademic interest.

"She had hidden the letter under her mattress," Halladay said. "She showed it to me and said, 'What am I gonna do?'"

The professor had become something of a mentor for her, Halladay said, and had been instrumental in her decision to spend the 1990 spring semester at the University of Granada in Spain. She returned from that semester abroad, he said, much more self-confident and self-reliant. Halladay said he never knew if Fahey had pursued anything further with the professor. He was aware, however, of a relationship Fahey had had with a younger member of the faculty who, Halladay said, liked to hang out at keg parties where he would drink and occasionally smoke marijuana with his students. Both professors were married.

Fahey played basketball and field hockey during her first two years at Wesley, leaving in 1987 to attend the University of Delaware. Her one semester at the larger university was a flop both academically and emotionally, and a little more than two years later, after Wesley instituted a four-year program in political science, she was back in Dover. She graduated in 1991.

"She was a caring person, a true friend, and a lot of fun to be around," said Halladay. "She worked two or three jobs. We both worked at a restaurant. She also had a job at The Limited and she would work as a nanny."

Money was always a problem for her. Paying her bills was a continual struggle, made worse by her desire for the finer things in life. Anne Marie had champagne taste, and a shot-and-a-beer pocketbook.

"She knew how to dress," he said. "She knew what looked right on her."

And on occasion, when she couldn't afford that "perfect" dress for some special event, she wasn't above purchasing it with her credit card, wearing it, and then returning it, Halladay said, still somewhat embarrassed to be telling the story on his old roommate.

Anne Marie loved to be around people and was usually upbeat, he said. But she also had a "dark side" that would flare up unexpectedly. On those occasions, she would disappear into a moody depression and tell him she just wanted to be alone.

"Sometimes I'd hear her wake up in the middle of the night crying," Halladay said. "Once she got up at three A.M., put her Walkman on and went out. I screamed at her about that. We lived near campus in a decent neighborhood, but two or three blocks away Dover wasn't so nice. It was no place for a woman to be walking alone. But she just said she needed some time to think and to get herself together."

Halladay remembered one other relationship that ended badly.

"The guy was a student and he played in a rock band," he said. "Anne Marie dated him for a while, but then she ended it. But he kept pestering her. He'd come up to her in bars and restaurants. He'd come over to the apartment. He didn't want it to be over, but she did."

Halladay said he last spoke with Anne Marie at a Blue Rocks baseball game the summer before she disappeared. He said they had grown apart. She had moved out during her senior year because her then-boyfriend, Paul Columbus, didn't like him.

"I don't think he ever believed we were just friends," Halladay said. "But that's what we were. It was never anything other than platonic. And for a time, at least, I thought we were very good friends."

Halladay said he took part in the July 4, 1996 search for Fahey at Brandywine Park. It was a surreal experience.

"I had to be there," he said. "But I hoped we wouldn't find her. At that point everyone wanted to believe there was still a chance she was alive."

At Wesley College they have retired Anne Marie Fahey's uniform number and dedicated a small garden on campus to her memory. She had hoped, Halladay said, to do something with her life, something in politics or education, something, perhaps, that had to do with helping children. That's how she would have wanted to be remembered. But she never got the chance.

To her psychologist and her psychiatrist, Anne Marie Fahey was, among other things, an ACOA—adult child of an alcoholic.

This, they would say, went a long way toward explaining her lack of self-esteem, her emotional dependency, and her eating disorder.

To Donovan and Alpert, she was a victim. But eventually the two investigators would realize that their assessment and that of Fahey's therapists were remarkably similar. Donovan learned on the night Fahey was reported missing that she was being treated by a therapist named Michele Sullivan. In fact, he spoke with her that night and it was she who, in cryptic terms because she was still trying to guard her patient-client confidentiality, mentioned the potential problem with Capano— Anne Marie's desire to break off the relationship and her fear that he would not let her.

In the weeks that followed, both Donovan and Alpert learned that Anne Marie had told her counselors many things that were important to the investigation.

"She had a great deal of difficulty finding a healthy relationship with a man," said Gary Johnson, a clinical psychologist who treated Fahey from around July 1995 through January 1996. "And a great deal of difficulty understanding what makes a healthy relationship work."

Johnson told authorities that Fahey had mentioned problems she was having with "a man" she had been seeing. She refused to identify him, but said that he was a "prominent" individual and that he was married.

Fahey told Johnson she wanted to end the relationship, but he wouldn't let her. She felt guilt and shame over having an affair with a married man, and she also felt trapped and controlled by this individual. She talked about how he had harassed and threatened her, at one point telling her that he would expose their relationship to her family and friends, including Michael Scanlan.

Alpert heard Linda Marandola in the comments Johnson attributed to Fahey.

Johnson subsequently referred Fahey to Michele Sullivan, who specialized in eating disorders. She began treating Fahey in February 1996 and last saw her on June 26, the day before she disappeared. After her initial conversation with Donovan, Sullivan spoke to investigators at length about her client; after the Fahey family waived Anne Marie's privacy rights, she testified at Capano's trial.

She described Fahey as a classic anorexic, someone who had trouble controlling almost every aspect of her life and as a result transferred her focus to her body and her food intake. The amount of food she ate was one of the few things Fahey felt she could control. It was her way of coping with the stress and chaos she felt all around her.

Anorexia tends to intensify when things in life get out of control, Sullivan said. Donovan and Alpert knew that for the last year, perhaps even the last eighteen months, of her life, Anne Marie Fahey was under terrific stress, living on emotional tenterhooks. She was juggling the affair with Capano and her relationship with Scanlan, questioning her future in the governor's office, wondering whether she wouldn't be happier pursuing a career as a teacher, and agonizing over how to afford the career change. And all the while, she was trying to keep a smile on her face and her family in the dark about her romantic, emotional, and financial problems.

She had also reduced her diet to a bagel and a pretzel a day, she told Sullivan during their first session at the end of February 1996. And she said she was constantly struggling with thoughts that she was "unattractive, unacceptable, unworthy and just not a good person."

Part of this anxiety and low self-esteem, Sullivan said, stemmed from her troubled childhood and her upbringing in a home where her father was an alcoholic. It was not unusual for a child in those circumstances to look for reasons and to blame herself for the irrational, abusive, and demeaning behavior of an alcoholic parent.

Fahey told Sullivan how she used to hide under the kitchen table when her father went on a rant, beating and cursing her older brothers. When she got older and he directed his anger at her, she would hide or run away. But on at least one occasion she had used her field hockey stick to fend off her father, keeping him at bay as he screamed and threatened to beat her.

While a part of her realized she was a victim of abuse, neglect, and poverty, there was another part of Anne Marie that somehow believed she was to blame for her own troubles.

"Anne Marie Fahey was desperately afraid of losing the love of people that she loved," Sullivan said. "She felt profound shame about her background. . . . She talked about having to have the school provide lunch for her . . . and felt that she was responsible for it."

Her eating disorder was both an attempt to control the chaos in her life and a way to punish herself, to focus and express the anger she still felt over what she had experienced growing up. The anger showed up in other compulsive behavior as well: When Anne Marie jogged, she would run until she felt like dropping. When she took laxatives, she couldn't stop at one or two. Often she took more than a dozen over the course of a day.

One of Sullivan's first notes about Fahey was that she had "difficulty hanging on to her own reality." Another was that she had survived by "putting on a happy face."

"Anne Marie was terrified of being rejected, of being abandoned," she said.

The explanation helped explain the early part of the Capano relationship. Donovan, Alpert, and Connolly had gone over Fahey's diary several times and had been struck by the fact that while Capano's obsession for Fahey was the reason she was dead, Fahey's obsession for Capano was the reason the relationship had not ended a year earlier.

Part of Fahey's problem was that Tom Capano filled a void in her life, a void probably left by her father. She had searched for other substitutes; certainly her brother Robert had been a father figure. But once he had children of his own, Anne Marie knew that it wasn't fair for her to continue to depend on him in that way. Bob Connor, the therapist who had treated her before Johnson and Sullivan, was another substitute father and a man whom she deeply admired. Some people, Capano included, told her that she was secretly in love with Connor.

On January 24, 1995, as he drove home from work, Connor was killed in an automobile accident. The driver of the vehicle that struck him was drunk. In a poignantly characteristic reaction, Anne Marie felt a sense of responsibility for Connor's death; at his request, she had canceled her own appointment with him that day so that he could see another patient. If he had seen her instead, she thought, the rest of his day would have gone differently. He might have left work sooner or later. And he might not have been on the road at the precise moment when he was struck and killed. Of course, that line of thinking made little sense; Connor's death was a random and unforeseeable accident. But that was the way Fahey thought. She was full of self-doubt and quick to blame herself for anything that went wrong. Connor's passing left her emotionally distraught and vulnerable. Alcoholism, which had consumed her father and was destroying one of her brothers, had taken another key man from her life.

In an early diary note, she had described Connor as "one of the few whom I know beyond a shadow of a doubt that will never judge me. That is a pretty great feeling." A month after his death, she wrote that Connor "was the only person who knew everything (even a little bit about Tommy—not much) about me and it felt great to get all this shit inside of me—out . . . He believed in me and actually liked me for me. Not many people know the real Annie. Bob was, and probably (will) be the only person who really knew me and understood me and my insecurities. . . . I miss him terribly and my life is a bit less fulfilling w/out him."

With Connor's death, Tom Capano became the most important man in Anne Marie Fahey's life. Mature, interested, and full of empathy, Capano was everything Connor had been—and more, for he was also her lover. He was everything Fahey wanted in a man. And she was desperately afraid of losing him.

On a Saturday night in the middle of February 1995, Capano, his wife, Kay, and several of his political cronies, including Bud Freel, were at a bar in Wilmington when Anne Marie walked in with Ginny Columbus and Jill Morrison. Annie knew Capano was going to be there that night. He had planned a party for Freel and had told her about it. But he hadn't invited her. And he was not happy to see her. Anne Marie Fahey was not welcome in that part of his life.

"He was furious because I was there," she later wrote in her diary.

She and Ginny and Jill stayed on the other side of the bar, drinking beer and shots of vodka with twists of lemon. But the alcohol didn't have the effect Fahey was after.

"I was sad and very sick in my stomach," she wrote of that night. "I am madly in love with him and did not truly realize just how deeply I felt until that night when I could not be near him, and I then realized the fact that he . . . never will be mine!"

Fahey seemed to enjoy the pathos. Her diary notes over the next nine days read like the script from a junior high romance novel. It was the most intense and consistent writing that investigators would discover as they read and reread her words in the months following her disappearance.

On Monday she called Capano at work. "He was cold and seemed disinterested," she wrote.

"What's up?" Fahey said, trying to sound carefree.

"Nothing, Ana Maria," he said, using the Spanish version of her name, which he knew she liked. "My life sucks."

She became concerned and asked if he was upset with her, if her showing up at the bar on Saturday had made him angry.

"No, just everything in my life is wrong and sucks," he said again. Then he told her that he was busy and had to get back to work. And he hung up the phone.

From Anne Marie Fahey's diary, Tuesday, February 21, 1995:

> I called Tomas but he never returned my call. What the fuck is going on? Why won't he talk to me? What did I do? God please tell me what the fuck is going on!!!
>
> I spent Tuesday night lying on my couch and falling asleep. By 9:00 I woke up only to take 2 laxatives and climb into my bed. Tomas, please talk to me! I love you.

From Anne Marie Fahey's diary, Wednesday, February 22, 1995:

> I woke up feeling sad and depressed. I need to talk to Tommy. If it's over between us—I need to have some closure. Tomas why don't you talk to me? Jesus, how and why

did I allow myself to fall in love w/a married man???? I know exactly why: Tomas is kind, caring, responsive, loving, has a beautiful heart, extremely handsome and was kind and gentle to me. If he loves me like he used to say (which I still believe he does) then why is he treating me like this???

Fahey had called Capano at the office that day. She was shocked by the way he spoke to her. He was cold and indifferent. He had never raised his voice to her before.

"Why are you furious with me?" she asked. "Why aren't you talking to me?"

"Drop it, Annie," Capano said condescendingly. "And quit fucking talking like this in the office. We'll talk later."

She wanted to cry. She asked if she would ever hear from him again.

"Do you want to?" he said.

What kind of question was that? He knew she wanted to hear from him. He knew she loved him. She didn't understand. Was he playing a game? He said he would call her later, at home.

From Anne Marie Fahey's diary, Wednesday, February 22, 1995, continued:

When T. asked me how I would like to spend my last day on earth—I told him by playing hooky from work and making marinara sauce together, making love while it was cooking, drinking red wine, eating bread and watching all the movies we have talked about watching together. He said he did not believe anything I just said. Where has this . . . come from? Did somebody say something to him? What has he heard? I wish I knew . . .

I often fantasize about T. and me, and how I would love to spend the remaining yrs. of my life w/him: wake up in his arms in my bed, lay next to him and read books together, travel w/him, love him, hold him, taste him, etc . . . Will any of this ever happen? I am madly in love w/T.!

They spoke on the phone the next day, but the conversation was "superficial." They talked about work and their individual plans for the weekend. Fahey had been dumped enough in her life to read the signs. Capano was letting her down easy, but he was getting out. She wanted to say more, to tell him how she felt, but she was afraid he would fly off the handle again, get nasty and sarcastic, or worst of all, hang up on her. She wanted to hear his voice. She needed to hear it, even if she didn't like what he was saying. As they spoke, offering innocuous and meaningless comments about things that didn't matter, tears were streaming down Fahey's cheeks. She wanted to tell him he was breaking her heart, wanted to ask him to stop. But she couldn't.

That night, when she got home from work, she crawled into bed and cried herself to sleep.

Capano stopped by the governor's office in Wilmington the next afternoon on business. He was cool, but friendly. He said hello to Anne Marie and the other women who worked in the front office. And he told Anne Marie that he thought she had left the high beams on in her car. Then he went into Carper's office for the meeting that had been scheduled.

Fahey didn't know how to react, so she said and did nothing. Later, she called his office and left a message on his answering machine, asking him to call her over the weekend so that they could "work this mess out."

From Anne Marie Fahey's diary, Friday, February 24, 1995:

> I have shared my soul w/T. I gave him my whole world, body and love. What I have not shared w/T. is my fear of abandonment. I will w/hold thoughts, info, etc ... about myself if I think that it may steer one away from me. If I ever have the opportunity to speak to T. again—I will share everything (even my soul) and let him know exactly the way I feel. If I'm rejected,—at least I know that I told him about me, and let him into my world.
>
> I love you, T.

Anne Marie Fahey spent the entire weekend thinking about Capano. She waited around her apartment almost all day Saturday, hoping he would call. Then she went out to run an errand. When she got back, there was a message on her machine. It was him. He sounded sad, almost suicidal, she thought. It was frustrating. She couldn't call him back because he was at home with his wife and his daughters. The next day at Mass she prayed for her married secret lover, asking God to "give him the strength that he needs."

From Anne Marie Fahey's diary, Sunday, February 26, 1995:

> Maybe tomorrow I will know what is troubling my boyfriend. I miss his voice, words, hugs and smile . . . I will continue to pray. I love you, Tomas.
> Now—I have problems with my body because I am continuing to take two laxatives each night before I go to bed. I know because I want to be thin and now I think that I am a little bit fat. I want to weigh 130, and now I weight 137! Yuck—Fat.

Whatever game Tom Capano was playing with Anne Marie Fahey's emotions reached its climax the next day. He called her at work late in the afternoon and told her they needed to talk. He said he had "very strong" feelings for her and was jealous whenever other men looked at her or talked with her. But he said that she needed to think about her future without him, that she would be better off with someone else, someone younger and someone able to give her the time and attention that she needed.

The words were not unexpected. Capano had said similar things the first time he tried to break it off with her. But she didn't want to hear it. She could not think of her life without him. She had no future if it did not include Tom Capano.

"You need to find your own Patrick Hosey," he said of the handsome young man her sister, Kathleen, had married.

"I don't want my own Patrick Hosey," she had replied. "I want you."

When she hung up the phone, she was crying. She left the office a few minutes later and drove to her apartment on Washington Street. When she got out of her car, she saw Capano walking toward her.

Fahey's version of what happened next was like a scene out of one of those romantic movies that she loved so much: A bittersweet, May-September version of *When Harry Met Sally*.

They ran toward one another and began hugging and kissing and talking all at once. He was on his way to his daughter's basketball game, but he said he had to see her first. She was crying and laughing at the same time and kissing him and squeezing him. She never wanted to let him go.

"Please don't leave me," she said. "My life doesn't exist without you."

She wanted him to come in. She wanted him to take her up to her apartment and make love to her. But he said he couldn't, that his daughter was expecting him.

"Ana Maria, no," he said. "I need to go."

When he left, she walked into her apartment and broke down in tears, tears of both joy and sadness. She had him back, but she would never have him completely. Now she wanted him more than ever.

From Anne Marie Fahey's diary, Tuesday, February 28, 1995:

I felt a lot better today,—because I have talked to Tomas. But I was still sad. But, I am not letting go. Love is so infrequent (True love) and I am not giving up. I love to make him smile, laugh, hug him, make love, etc . . .

He deserves happiness—he does not deserve to be miserable! I'll wait 4-ever.

He's a wonderful, kind, caring, generous, sensitive man who deserves to be showered w/the same kind of generosity he gives.

I want to be that person! I love you.

12

They wanted to visit the house on Grant Avenue.

They had closed up the apartment on Washington Street in August, packing away all of Anne Marie's clothing and belongings in boxes and carting them over to Kathleen's house, where they were stored in the basement. They made an inventory of it all for Chancery Court, which had appointed Kathleen as the guardian for her sister's "estate," such as it was. There was her car, the green 1993 Volkswagen Jetta, and her membership in the local YMCA where she worked out regularly. She had less than a thousand dollars in her checking account. No savings account to speak of. There was some jewelry, and she had a few savings bonds. That was Anne Marie Fahey's estate.

Her bank account grew in the first month after her disappearance. The governor's office continued to pay her salary, a direct deposit of $843 every two weeks. The only withdrawals were automatic. There was $116 for her car insurance and $35 for her membership to the Y. Kathleen, once she was appointed guardian, would stop those payments and freeze the account.

The Faheys no longer believed their sister was coming home. They knew—they were certain—that she was dead. And they needed some way to acknowledge that. The visit to the house on Grant Avenue was an attempt to do that.

"It was like going to a junkyard to look at the car after a

horrible accident," Robert Fahey said in trying to explain why he, his brothers, and his sister wanted to visit Capano's former home. "It was our way of trying to see where Anne Marie's last resting place was. We knew in our hearts she had died in that room. The only way we could say goodbye to Anne Marie was by going to the place where she was brutally murdered."

"That room" was the combination den/dining room Capano called the great room. Donovan and Alpert had already spent hours with Connolly going over possible scenarios. The information provided by Ruth Boylan, the housekeeper, and by Shaw Taylor left little doubt that blood had been splattered in the room on the night Fahey disappeared. The investigators, certain that Capano wouldn't have had the guts to face Fahey as he shot her, speculated that he had fired a bullet into the back of her head. Given the layout of the room and the position of the furniture, they were not surprised when, during the July 31 raid, the two specks of blood that were found were on the baseboard of the wall opposite the couch.

"We had talked about blood splatter," Donovan said. "We figured that's where it would be."

They also figured that Capano had spent hours in an exhaustive attempt to clean up the crime scene, and they felt lucky to have located even those small dots of blood.

By the time the Faheys visited, early in October 1996, the crime scene was a large, empty room.

Capano had moved out after the raid. He was on a month-to-month lease at the time and gave the required sixty days' notice in August, giving up $4,800, two months' rent. At the time of the Fahey visit, the place was being prepared for the next tenant. David Weiss, the Faheys' attorney, had arranged through the real estate agency that was handling the property to allow them to walk through. Weiss accompanied the family; so did a private investigator he had hired, along with a videographer who made a film of the interior.

Soft-spoken but self-assured, Weiss was a former federal prosecutor who had worked in the U.S. Attorney's Office in Wilmington from 1986 until 1989. He did not know Connolly, but he knew the ways of the Justice Department. That was the reason the Faheys hired him. Originally, he said, there hadn't been any discussion about a wrongful death suit. That would come later.

"They just wanted someone who could help them understand the way the process worked," he said.

Weiss first met with the Fahey family on July 2, just two days after Anne Marie was reported missing. He was referred to them by one of his law partners who happened to be a neighbor of Robert Fahey's. From that day through the conviction and sentencing of Thomas J. Capano, David Weiss was with the Faheys, counseling them through the entire ordeal. But he will tell anyone who asks that he got more from the family than he was able to give. He taught them about the way the criminal justice system works. They taught him about grace and courage and fortitude.

"They are a remarkable family," he says. "I feel bad that we were brought together by a horrible set of circumstances. But I am happy to be their friend."

Weiss already knew a little bit about the Capano family when he was first contacted by the Faheys. He was the federal prosecutor who worked the political corruption and bribery case against the New Castle County councilman convicted of soliciting an illegal payoff from Louis Capano Jr. back in 1989.

"I got to know Louie very well," Weiss said sardonically as he recalled that investigation. "Tom was his advisor. Louie had other defense attorneys, but Tom was always there in the background. He was the quiet Capano. He was supposed to be the sane one in the bunch."

During the Fahey investigation, Weiss also spoke several times with Jim Green. Weiss and Green worked for the same law firm. Green had been a close friend of Tom Capano's, and had ended up in the middle of the Marandola-Riley investigation that Alpert revisited as he dug into Capano's past.

"All these intersections were amazing," Weiss said. Green had been Capano's friend, he had been Marandola's boss, and in 1993 he had struck up an acquaintance with Riley that allowed him to put Alpert in touch with the low-level wiseguy Capano had used to harass and threaten Marandola in 1980.

Weiss said he spoke to Green from time to time about Tom Capano's "dark side." A part of Capano that simmered just beneath the surface, it was a subtle shading to his character. But it was there. Tom Capano had to have things his way. He knew best.

Green told Weiss about a trip Capano had planned one time for a group of his friends and their spouses back in the late 1970s or early 1980s. Green and his wife were part of the group. "Tom planned the entire outing," Weiss said, "and when some of the couples decided they didn't want to do everything exactly the way he had set it up, he sulked and ruined the trip for everyone."

Robert Fahey said packing away Anne Marie's things and closing up her apartment was "torture."

"It was like a funeral without a body," he said.

Not knowing what had happened to Anne Marie was like being trapped in a "deep, dark hole," he said.

"It's a black hole without boundaries and it's as deep as it gets," he said. "And you never know how deep it is and you never know when, or if, you're going to get out of it."

The Faheys went to the house on Grant Avenue in an effort to dig themselves out, but in many ways it only made things worse. They looked at the great room and imagined what had happened, where Anne Marie had been sitting, what she might have seen, what she might have been thinking.

Part of the horror is not knowing. Even now, they can only speculate.

"When you know nothing, anything is possible," Brian Fahey said.

"We will never know the final ten percent of the story," Robert Fahey believes. "It's a difficult thing to sleep with. Did she die without knowing she was dying?"

Or was she afraid, hurt, in agony, Brian wonders.

Was there a confrontation? Did Capano go into a rage, ranting and yelling in one final attempt to bully Fahey into resuming their affair? Was she adamant in refusing? Did she have the courage to stand up to him? Or did she set him off by being sullen and silent, by slipping into an emotional shell? Theirs was a complex relationship. There was no doubt about that. They knew how to push each other's buttons.

All of that hung in the air as the Faheys walked quietly through the Grant Avenue home. They spent most of the forty-five-minute visit in the great room, picturing the couch and Anne Marie sitting on it, looking at the baseboard across the room where the blood specks had been found, and wondering what their sister's last moments had been like.

"It was like visiting the scene of an accident," Weiss said. "We didn't say very much. I think the same thing was going through everyone's mind. Everyone was thinking about what might have happened or how it happened."

It was quiet in the house. No one said very much. The sounds of their footsteps echoed through the empty rooms. It was eerie. One thing that everyone noticed was the narrowness of the stairway leading to the recreation room and the garage. The assumption was that Capano had carried Anne Marie's body, or dragged it, down those steps, probably wrapped in the rug. No one knew about the cooler at that time. There wasn't a lot of room on those steps to maneuver. It was a tight squeeze for all of them. They each thought about how much more diffi-cult it would have been to carry or drag a body down those steps.

And they each thought about the body of their sister.

Once of the first signs that the pressure Connolly hoped to apply on the Capano family was working came around the same time the Faheys visited the Grant Avenue home. On October 8, 1996, Louis J. Capano Jr. went back before the grand jury. The appearance came at his request; he said he wanted to clarify and correct some earlier misstatements.

Part of the strategy Connolly had devised hinged on getting Louis Capano Jr. locked into a version of events that investiga-tors would be able to show was untrue. Perjury was a heavy club to wave over Louis's head; he already knew the power of the federal government, and when he was pushed into a corner in the 1989 bribery case he had willingly rolled over and coop-erated.

Connolly knew it would be more difficult to get Louis to give up his own brother, but he also believed that a potential perjury charge could be a first step in that direction.

Louis Capano Jr. spent about forty-five minutes testifying under oath during his second grand jury appearance. He lied again, insisting that he had met with his brother on the morning of June 28. And he again withheld what he believed was the true version of events, the story of Anne Marie attempting to slit her wrists. He "clarified" part of his earlier testimony by claiming that on Sunday, June 30, he met with his brother once that morning, but not a second time later that day at Kay Capano's home. Instead, he said, he was certain he and his wife, Lauri, had gone to a movie that night. It was his recollection that he spoke with his brother Tom several other times that Sunday, but did not meet with him face-to-face.

On another, more important matter, Louis Capano admitted that he was not in his home on the night of June 27, 1996. The feds already knew this. They had phone records indicating that Louis had used his cell phone early on the morning of June 28, around 4:30 A.M., to call his home and check his answering machine. (His wife was in a golf tournament in Atlantic City at the time.)

Louis had earlier testified that he met his brother at his home on the morning of June 28 somewhere between 7:30 A.M. and 9:00 A.M. This, he had said, was after he had gotten up and gone jogging.

During his second grand jury appearance, Louis continued to insist that he and Tom had met at his home that morning, but admitted that he had not slept there that night.

Connolly pressed him on the issue.

"Where did you sleep that night?" the prosecutor inquired.

"I slept at a person named Kristie Pepper's house," Louis replied.

Louis said he left Pepper's house on Harvey Road at about 7:00 A.M. that morning. He also confirmed what the feds already knew—that he had called to check his answering machine a few hours earlier. First, he said, he tried his portable cell phone, but the batteries were dead. So he had had to go out to his car and use the other cell phone.

Capano said that Pepper and her two children were home that night. He admitted that he had been seeing her for several months, that they were more than friends. But ever the stickler for the truth, Louis Capano told Connolly he was wrong when he implied that, among other things, Capano had bought Pepper a car.

"No, I paid—some people would think it was that, but I paid up a lease for her," Louis Capano explained. "I made substantial payments on a lease for her for a car and did not—there is a difference. She doesn't own the car."

"She leases the car?" Connolly asked.

"She leases it," said Louis.

"And you have paid the lease for her," Connolly said.

Louis Capano said he had. When Connolly asked if Pepper worked for him, Capano said she did not. When he asked if she worked for any of his companies, he replied that she had done some "consulting" work, she was in real estate, but was not an employee.

"You have a social relationship with her?" Connolly asked.

"I *had* a social relationship with her," Capano said, correcting the prosecutor.

"When did it end?"

"I don't know," Louis Capano said. "A month or so ago."

Pepper would eventually be called before the same grand jury. She would also agree to record telephone conversations with Louis Capano. None proved significant to the investigation, but Louis Capano's attempt to influence her grand jury testimony became another legal wedge for the prosecution as it continued to pressure the Capano brothers.

Connolly could not resist asking a few more questions about the phone call home early on the morning of June 28. Louis Capano called home to find out if his wife had been looking for him. Connolly wanted to make sure that was clear to the grand jurors.

"Do you often check your voice mail at four-thirty in the morning?" he asked Capano.

"I only check my voice mail when I wasn't supposed to be somewhere at four-thirty in the morning," Capano replied candidly.

Louis Capano Jr. was a realist. He knew how the system worked, and he was a master at playing the game on the edge.

It was his guile and gumption and foresight—some would also argue his willingness to play fast and loose with the rules—that had turned the successful company his father had left the family into an even more successful multimillion-dollar development and real estate enterprise.

Louis had spent a year at Wentworth Institute outside of Boston and another two at the University of Delaware, but he had never graduated from college. Still, he was a shrewd businessman—savvier, in fact, than Tom. And in the business community, at least, he was more willing to take chances.

But Louis had also been burned in the bribery-kickback case. He knew there was a thin line between being a victim and being a coconspirator. As the pressure continued to mount in the Fahey case, he worried that he was on the other side of that line. Louis Capano Jr. realized that both he and his brother Gerry were viewed by Connolly, Donovan, and Alpert as possible coconspirators in a murder-kidnapping investigation. The stakes were extremely high. And he didn't like the odds.

He decided he needed to talk to Gerry.

They met outside Gerry's house on Emma Court in one of the more exclusive neighborhoods in North Wilmington. Gerry lived there with his wife, Michelle, and their two young children. They also had a home in Stone Harbor and a condo in Boca Raton. It was all part of the good life, the rich and carefree existence, that his family's wealth had bought him.

Now all of that was in jeopardy.

It didn't take much to get Gerry to open up. Louis talked about the grand jury and where he thought the investigation was going. He insisted that he believed in Tom's innocence, but told Gerry that he needed to know what, if anything, had happened. He pressed Gerry for the story.

And Gerry, who had kept it bottled up for nearly four months, let it all spill out. They walked up and down Emma Court that afternoon talking at length. Gerry cried several times, told Louis he had been having nightmares, said he had been drinking heavily and taking drugs in an attempt to forget, or at least to block out the horror.

It had all started right there on Emma Court, he said.

At a little before 6:00 A.M. on Friday morning, June 28, Gerry had walked out of his house to get the morning paper and saw Tom sitting in his black Jeep Cherokee in the driveway. Gerry walked over to the passenger-side window.

Tom looked up and said, "I need to use your boat."

"Did you do it?" Gerry asked.

Tom nodded and said, "Can you help me?"

Gerry then explained the background to Louis. Earlier in the year, back in February, Tom had told Gerry that he was being extorted by a couple, a man and a woman, who wanted money and who were threatening to harm Tom's daughters. Tom had borrowed $8,000 from Gerry, money he quickly repaid. But he implied that the money was for the extortionists. He asked if Gerry knew anyone he could hire who would be good at "breaking legs," a line he had used with Riley sixteen years earlier. And he also briefly borrowed one of Gerry's guns. Gerry had suggested a shotgun after Tom said he needed it for protection.

"A shotgun is best," he said. "You just point it and shoot."

But Tom had insisted on a handgun, and Gerry gave him a pistol in a case. A few weeks later Tom returned the gun. As best Gerry could tell, he had never taken it out of the case. It had never been fired. But Tom continued to talk about the extortionists and about how he might have to kill them if they tried to hurt his kids.

If he did, he told Gerry, he might need to use Gerry's boat to dispose of the body.

On the morning of June 28, when Tom asked to go for a boat ride, Gerry knew what it meant.

Louis couldn't believe what he was hearing, but Gerry continued to unload the story he had been carrying around inside for months.

At first, he said, he told Tom he didn't want to get involved.

"I've got a good life," Gerry told his brother at he stood next to the Jeep that morning. "I don't want to ruin it."

"You're all I've got," Tom said. "Don't let me down, bro. I need you."

Gerry then told Louis about meeting Tom at Grant Avenue later that morning, about how he helped load an ice chest into the Suburban Tom had borrowed from his wife Kay and about driving down to Stone Harbor.

Gerry insisted he did not look inside the chest, which was wrapped in a large chain secured with a padlock. But he said it was heavy and difficult for even the two of them to lift. He said he thought he heard ice sloshing around inside the cooler as they carried it.

He was crying and sobbing and walking up and down the street as he told Louis the story, finishing with the boat ride, the shotgun blast, the burial at sea, and his haunting vision of a foot and part of a calf disappearing in the shark-infested waters.

Now there were three Capano brothers aware of what had happened. It is unclear if Joe, the fourth brother, ever heard the full story.

That night, after meeting with Gerry on Emma Court, Louis Capano returned home. Tom was still living at the house. He knew Louis had spoken with Gerry.

"Are you happy now?" he asked sarcastically. "You've got Gerry all strung out. Are you satisfied?"

Louis said he just wanted to know what was going on, what was at stake. He believed in Tom's innocence, he said. He was even willing to lie to a grand jury to protect him. But he had to know what had happened.

"Just leave Gerry alone," Tom Capano said angrily.

Over the next several months, however, Louis and Gerry continued to talk—sometimes with Tom, sometimes between themselves. They wanted to believe there was a logical explanation for what had happened, that Tom hadn't killed Anne Marie Fahey. But they wanted him to talk to the authorities, to tell what had happened, to clear everything up, and to end the pressure that was building and that was tearing their family apart.

Once the three brothers met in Oberly's office. Alone in the conference room, Louis and Gerry pressed Tom to turn himself in. If not, they said, they were going to the authorities with what they knew. Tom convinced them not to.

"He told me if the situation were reversed, he would do this for me," Louis said of his brother's insistence that he and Gerry remain silent. "He said it wasn't time. He talked about the impact this would have on his children . . . He told us he would protect us."

Louis argued for himself and also for his brother. He said Tom had put Gerry in a terrible position, that Gerry was having trouble coping with it all, that the pressure was tremendous.

"I told him both of us were upset," Louis said.

Later, when he was alone with Gerry, Tom looked disdainfully at his youngest brother.

"Be a man," he said. "Grow up and be a man."

13

Deborah MacIntyre was Tom Capano's Wednesday-night girl. That was all she was ever going to be. For nearly seventeen years she was there whenever he needed her, did whatever he asked her to do. She was his friend, his lover, his confidante. And until she realized how she was being used, she nearly helped him get away with murder.

Anne Marie Fahey was the woman for whom Capano left his wife. She was the one he would have married. Another girlfriend, Susan Louth, was a fling, a beautiful younger woman who was a willing sexual partner and an impressive ornament. Fahey and Louth got to go to the fancy restaurants. Capano liked being seen in their company.

Debby MacIntyre got to stay home and share takeout, got to watch movies they rented from the video store or pornographic films from her private stash. Porn videos that Capano said had come from her late father's collection and that she kept wound to the best spots—scenes that turned them both on, scenes of three-way sex in which a woman is ravaged by two men or a man is pleasured by two women who then turn to one another as the sated man looks on.

They had met in the late 1970s, when Capano went to work for Morris, James, Hitchens and Williams, an old and well-connected Wilmington law firm. David Williams, the son of one of the partners, was also a young attorney in the firm at that time. His wife was the former Debby MacIntyre, the oldest daughter of a millionaire industrialist who had earned his fortune running one of the city's old mills. There were, in fact, several young lawyers, all recently married, all about to start families, who worked at Morris, James. They became part of a social set. Most lived in Wilmington. Products of the 1960s, they at least mouthed the words of social consciousness that were the mark of that generation. And, among other things, they joined with other urban homesteaders who were rediscovering the city. Dan Frawley, a young lawyer working for the DuPont Company at the time, was one of the first. He bought a house, renovated it, and moved in with his family. Others followed. For the most part, however, these were older homes in safe, stable neighborhoods. Homesteading in this case meant taking a property in need of repair and modernizing it. The Capanos, for example, bought the $100,000 former bishop's residence at 2500 Seventeenth Street. A large, sprawling home on a corner lot surrounded by a hedgerow, the property was worth close to $250,000 when Capano was arrested twenty years later.

These were yuppie lawyers and their wives and kids. They talked about their commitment to the city, but most had enough disposable income to ensure that their own taste of urban life would not be too gritty. Private schools for their sons and daughters. Summer camps. Vacations in Florida. Beach homes at the South Jersey or Delaware shore. Occasional trips to Europe. And an extramarital affair whenever it fit into their busy schedules.

"Of all the women in our group, Debby was by far *not* the most attractive," Tom Capano said later, implying that she had pursued him, and that if he were the pursuer, he would have gone after one of the other married women in the group.

"She made all the advances and I didn't control myself," he said. "I didn't push her away, but I did say this was not a good idea."

MacIntyre, of course, insisted that Capano made the first move. The truth is probably somewhere in the middle. They were part of a group of married men and women who were constantly and, for the most part, harmlessly flirting with one another at parties, in restaurants, at wedding receptions and other social settings.

Capano, however, was different. Capano always had his antennae up. He had an ability to pick out the one woman in a crowd who would be receptive, who was needy, who was lonely. Debby MacIntyre was all of those things.

It was at a New Year's Eve party, the last night of 1980. Capano was still smarting from the Marandola escapade. Although he felt some sense of satisfaction over the way Riley had been able to harass her, he knew that he was not going to get Marandola back into his arms anytime soon. The "best cocksucker" he had ever had was no longer sexually available to him. So he started to look elsewhere.

That night, the couples from the law firm had all gone out to dinner together. Then they went to a private home for a party to welcome in 1981. Sometime late in the evening, Tom Capano got Debby MacIntyre alone in one of the bathrooms. He said he needed to speak with her. He said he was in love with her.

"This is crazy," MacIntyre said. "You're married. I'm married."

Capano kept her in the bathroom for fifteen minutes, explaining how he felt, working her emotions, playing to her insecurities.

MacIntyre was flattered and flustered. Kay Capano was her friend. They both were young mothers with baby daughters. Both were married to young lawyers who had their careers in front of them. Still, there was something intriguing about Capano: his intensity, his sensitivity, his ability to make you feel as if you were the only person in the room, the only person who understood what he was saying, the only person who mattered.

The dance had begun.

They started to talk on the phone. Nothing serious, a continuation of the flirtation that was common to their social group, but which Capano had moved up a notch with his New Year's Eve declaration. That spring, he asked Debby to help him plan a surprise birthday party for his wife, Kay. This gave them another reason to keep in contact. Debby willingly agreed. Both she and Capano knew where this was going.

Once she stopped by the law office to visit her husband, then said she had to stop in and see Tom about the party. Capano's office was at the opposite end of the building from her husband's. She walked down the hall and knocked. He told her to come in, closing the door behind her.

She walked over to his desk. He came up behind her, kissed her, lifted her onto the desk and began to pet and paw at her. It was a makeout session, like two high school kids cheating on their steadies, but with the added danger and excitement of the locale. This was a law office. The door was closed, but it wasn't locked. There were people all around. Debby's husband was just down the hall.

"Stop," Debby said. "Somebody might walk in."

Capano said he didn't care, that he needed her, had to have her, couldn't live without her. Debby left the office that afternoon with a smile on her face and with the unspoken expectation that the next time, wherever that might be, they wouldn't stop.

"I enjoyed it because it made me feel good," she said, "but I was afraid someone would walk in."

Over the Memorial Day weekend that year, Tom Capano was home alone. Kay had taken their daughter to visit friends out of state. He was outside mowing the lawn when Debby rode up on a moped. They both knew why she was there. He took her inside and they made love for the first time. On the floor. In the den. Then she got on her moped and rode back home to her husband and baby daughter. At that point, Tom Capano had been living in the house on Seventeenth Street for about three years. And he had made love there to at least three women—his wife, Linda Marandola, and now Debby MacIntyre Williams.

The affair that started that spring afternoon would last for seventeen years. In retrospect, several friends now say, they always suspected that something was going on between Capano and MacIntyre. A few even claim that they always knew. There is even a story that Capano's mother, Marguerite, sensed it. There was a summer, early in the 1980s, when Debby was staying in Stone Harbor. She would make a point to walk down the beach to "visit" the Capanos whenever Tom was in town.

"Why doesn't she stay with her own family?" Marguerite Capano asked pointedly.

"Her interest was obvious," Capano said smugly when he was asked about the affair years later.

After the love set in the den, Capano and MacIntyre began to meet regularly one night a week, usually Wednesday. She was taking night classes at the University of Delaware at the time and told her husband Wednesday night was one of the nights the class met. Instead, she would meet Capano at a Motel Six out on Route 9 near the Delaware Memorial Bridge. It was a fitting location for the start of their affair: Debby MacIntyre never got the champagne treatment from Capano.

Tom would just tell Kay he had to work—business with the law firm, or later, when he went to work for Frawley at City Hall, meetings and politics. There was always a reason for Tom Capano to be away from home. Kay never doubted him, or if she did she kept her thoughts to herself.

They would have three more daughters. The last, Alex, was born in 1985.

Debby MacIntyre would have one other child, a son, Michael, born in 1982. In one of the seamier asides that came out during the murder trial, Capano implied in a letter written to Michael from prison that he might have been the boy's father. It was another attempt at manipulation; according to everyone else involved, there was no basis—other than the timing of his affair with MacIntyre—for Capano to make such a claim.

MacIntyre separated from her husband, David Williams, in the fall of 1983. They divorced a short time later. Independently wealthy from money left her by her father and later by a rich aunt, Debby MacIntyre never wanted financially. That was one string Capano couldn't pull.

He laughed about it. Other than some piece of jewelry that might have some romantic significance, he admitted, there was nothing that he could give MacIntyre to win her love. On the other hand, he said that while she was clearly rich and Fahey was certainly poor, they both had come out of dysfunctional family backgrounds. Friends and acquaintances say that

MacIntyre, the second-oldest of four children, grew up in a household where alcohol was a problem. Like Fahey, she was an ACOA. And like Fahey's, her insecurities were exploited by Capano.

A few years after her divorce, in the fall of 1985, MacIntyre moved with her two young children into a large home at 2425 Delaware Avenue, just a few blocks from Capano's home on Seventeenth Street. Now Capano would visit her there, usually on Wednesday nights when her husband had the kids, and occasionally on weekends when he was able to slip away from Kay.

MacIntyre went to work at the Tatnall School, an exclusive prep school in Wilmington from which she herself had graduated. She worked in the administration offices, eventually heading up the before- and after-school and summer day camp programs.

In 1985—the year Anne Marie Fahey graduated from high school—Debby MacIntyre was deeply in love with Thomas J. Capano, although she knew he had no intention of leaving his wife and children for her.

"He cared for me, he listened to me, he respected me," MacIntyre said as she tried to explain to a jury the relationship that had nearly led to her arrest as an accessory to murder. "He enjoyed my company. He made me feel good about myself.

"I wanted to spend my whole time with him. I would have loved for him to leave his wife for me, but I knew he wouldn't. I developed low expectations. The relationship was making me feel so good, it was like a compromise. I learned to live with that."

Sexually, the affair was gratifying for both of them. Each tapped into the other's needs. Capano claimed that MacIntyre introduced him to pornography; she also had some "sex toys" that they would use to enhance their lovemaking. Tom Capano liked to watch. Among other things, Debby had a large, nearly floor-to-ceiling mirror in her bedroom, a second-floor suite of rooms in the Delaware Avenue house. The mirror was positioned so that she and Tom could look at each other as they were having sex. Sometimes they'd have one of her porn videos playing in the bedroom. Pictures of three-way sex always got them both excited.

On at least two occasions, they took their video visions and tried to turn them into reality. The first occurred around 1988, when Debby went to a high school reunion with a plan to seduce a former boyfriend who had moved to Boston. Tom encouraged her. All he wanted, he said, was the chance to see it.

The reunion occurred over a weekend, with parties on Friday and Saturday nights. After the Saturday-night function, Debby brought her old boyfriend home to Delaware Avenue. They had drinks and got comfortable. She excused herself to make a phone call, then joined him again in the living room, where they both began to undress.

The phone call was to Capano at his home on Seventeenth Street.

His kids and his wife were asleep.

"Kay's a morning person," Capano said in explaining the circumstances that night.

Capano slipped out of the house and drove the two blocks to MacIntyre's home. He crept up to the living room window and peered in, enjoying the sight of MacIntyre having sex with her old high school flame. The guy had no idea Capano was there or that he was taking part in a prearranged show.

"It was like watching a live pornographic movie," Capano said.

After the old boyfriend left, Capano and MacIntyre made love. Then he drove home and went to bed.

"I'm not the jealous type," he said of his reaction to seeing a woman with whom he was involved engage in sex with another man. "I have a very liberal attitude toward sex."

Capano claimed MacIntyre did as well, that she was a willing participant in what the *Philadelphia Daily News* would later call their kinky "sexcapades." MacIntyre said she did it because she loved Capano and because he asked her to. She said she was afraid to say no, afraid that he might leave her.

A few years after the reunion tryst, Capano showed up one afternoon at MacIntyre's home after a game of golf with a fellow worker. At the time, Capano was chief counsel to Governor Mike Castle. He and his golf partner stopped over for a drink after playing eighteen holes at the Wilmington Country Club, where Capano was a member. By prearrangement, MacIntyre was wearing a tiny two-piece bathing suit under her shirt and shorts. While sharing drinks with the two men, she began to strip. While not a stunning beauty, MacIntyre had a taut, well-proportioned body. Those who were watching her weren't focusing on her face. Capano loved it. Eventually they all ended up naked and in the bedroom with a porno film playing on the VCR. Capano made love to MacIntyre, then watched while she performed oral sex on the other man.

Capano's golf partner would testify that he was an unwilling and unwitting participant in the three-way sexual encounter, that in fact he was unable to get an erection. He denied a defense attorney's allegation that he, in turn, had performed oral sex on MacIntyre. He said he was ashamed and embarrassed by the entire affair, and by the pain and agony its subsequent disclosure had brought to his wife, his children, and his parents.

The other man in the bedroom that day with Capano and MacIntyre was Keith Brady, who in 1992 worked with Capano in Governor Castle's office, and who in 1996 was the First Deputy Attorney General for the state of Delaware. Brady was the state's second most powerful law enforcement figure. He was the man Capano called on June 28 and again on July 2. Capano, it was clear, was counting on the state or the city to run the Fahey investigation.

As a former city solicitor and city hall chief of staff, Capano had several lines into the highest levels of the police department. And if the Attorney General's office took over the probe, Capano felt he could count on his old golf buddy, Keith Brady, to keep him abreast of the investigation.

That, of course, is not the way things played out. Within days of Fahey's disappearance, Brady recused himself from the investigation. He wanted nothing to do with it, perhaps surmising that Capano might try to play on their past ties. Brady had had one unexpected encounter with Capano's dark side. He didn't want another.

More important, of course, was that the feds took over the case. Connolly, not a state prosecutor, started directing the investigation. And while Donovan was the lead detective on the case, he was beyond Capano's reach. He reported directly to Connolly and worked almost exclusively with Alpert. Those three were the only ones who knew all the details of the investigation.

"If I was at my office, I couldn't talk about what I was doing," Donovan said of the seventeen long months that he worked the Capano case.

State prosecutor Ferris Wharton, who would later join Connolly in prosecuting Capano, was kept out of the loop once it became a federal investigation. Wharton could not legally be apprised of what was taking place before a federal grand jury.

Only Connolly's boss, U.S. Attorney Greg Sleet, and Assistant U.S. Attorney Richard Andrews, who headed the office's criminal division, were kept abreast of the investigation.

Donovan first interviewed MacIntyre on July 23, 1996. He was less than impressed.

"She didn't strike me as a very smart person," Donovan said.

Alpert talked to her a week later. Donovan spoke with her again early in September, and then, on September 10, 1996, she testified before the grand jury.

During those interviews and in several others that followed, MacIntyre lied repeatedly. She said she had been a longtime friend of Tom and Kay Capano's, but she insisted that she and Tom hadn't started going out together until the fall of 1995, which would have been after Capano separated from his wife and moved into the Grant Avenue home.

At first, Donovan and Alpert had no reason to suspect that MacIntyre wasn't telling the truth. Over time, however, they began to hear rumors about the affair between the two and about how it had begun long before Tom and Kay Capano split up. Eventually there would be reasons to question MacIntyre's statements and to challenge her blind loyalty to Capano. But not at first.

It would be eighteen more months before investigators asked MacIntyre the question that she dreaded, the question that she knew hung over the case and over her then-blossoming relationship with Tom Capano.

Every time she was questioned by authorities, Debby MacIntyre expected to hear someone say, "What about the gun?"

*   *   *

In November 1996 the FBI executed a search warrant and seized a file Capano had stored in the office of one of his partners at Saul, Ewing in Wilmington. The file included several handwritten notes that Capano said he had prepared for his defense lawyers and that, he argued, should have been off-limits to prosecutors. A judge eventually ruled otherwise, and the file became part of the case.

Included in the notes was a "time line" in which Capano detailed his whereabouts on June 28, 1996. The notes confirmed that he and Gerry went to Stone Harbor that day, but made no mention of the boat ride. Instead, he said, he met with Gerry there for lunch, and to look at the piece of real estate Gerry was considering buying.

There were also more than a dozen pages on which Capano had scribbled notes and observations about his relationship with Fahey. Connolly, Alpert, and Donovan spent hours going over the information. They already had Fahey's diary notes and dozens of e-mail messages exchanged by Capano and Fahey. Now they had Capano's own jottings, which would surely be self-serving, but which would also add to the picture of the troubled relationship that was at the heart of the case.

Connolly, ever the prosecutor preparing for trial, also looked at the notes for hints about how Capano might try to spin his defense—how he would take facts that were not in contention and try to use them to his advantage. In a largely circumstantial case it was not the evidence, but what the evidence meant, that was important.

Capano wrote at length about Fahey's emotional problems and her eating disorder. He referred to a dispute they had because he had described her as "high maintenance" and "materialistic." He said her weight had dropped to 117 pounds, that her hair was falling out, and that they fought over his attempts to force her into a residential treatment center for her eating disorder.

He said that he frequently lent her money, that he helped pay her bills for the psychological counseling she was receiving, and that she was amazed that the amount he paid in income tax was larger than her annual salary. He said they had gone to din-

ner five times during the month leading up to her disappearance—an indication that she was not afraid of him and was not
trying to end their relationship—and that he had "credit card
receipts to prove it."

He said Fahey confided in him about her problems and
that he "tried to help her when her family and other friends
were either unwilling or unable to."

On another page of a legal pad he had listed all the gifts he
had given her. There was the cash for her trip to Ireland, a television, pots and pans, clothes, books (*The Prince of Tides, Congo,
Gold Coast*), a clock, a heating pad, Mace for her key ring, a
watch, a *Jeopardy!* game, a fajita pan, a spatula, and several
videos, including *Only You, Belle Epoque, Doctor Zhivago, West
Side Story, The Godfather, My Cousin Vinny,* and *Moonstruck.*

On one note, Capano wrote that on "6/27 [Fahey] was troubled by lots of things; relationships, family, jobs, friends." On
another in which he again made reference to the night she disappeared, he wrote that "she chooses Panorama" instead of a
political function to which they had tickets. He made the dinner reservation for 7:00 P.M. and called her from his office at 6:25
P.M. "to advise on way." Fahey, he wrote, was "very depressed."

The notes were full of mentions of Capano's care and concern, and directly and indirectly described ways in which he
was trying to help her. Reading between the lines, though,
Connolly saw another theme emerging. If prosecutors were
going to contend that Fahey was afraid of Capano and had
been trying to end their relationship, Capano was prepared to
show that up to the night she disappeared, he was her friend
and confidant and was trying to do all he could to keep her
from harming herself.

Obsession or concern?

The case could turn on a jury's decision to choose one over
the other.

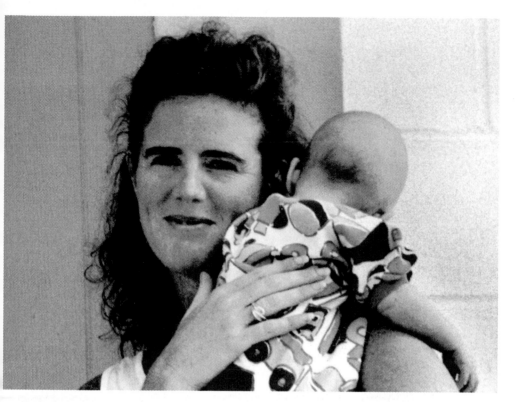

Anne Marie Fahey holding her infant nephew Sean, August 1995 (above), and during her last Christmas season later that year. *(Courtesy of the Fahey family)*

Kathleen Fahey-Hosey (center), the victim's sister, talks with Delaware state troopers during a volunteer search of Brandywine Park soon after Anne Marie's disappearance. *(Tim Shaffer)*

As soon as Anne Marie was officially designated a missing person in early July 1996, the Delaware State Police began publicizing its search across the state. The billboard shown here was erected along Interstate 95 south of Wilmington, the missing-persons poster on a utility pole across the street from Thomas Capano's rented residence in town. (*Tim Shaffer*)

Wilmington police officer Thomas Lisckiewicz, left, looks on as fellow officer Fred Filippone uses a metal detector to search the yard of Capano's rented home in Wilmington: July 31, 1996. *(Tim Shaffer)*

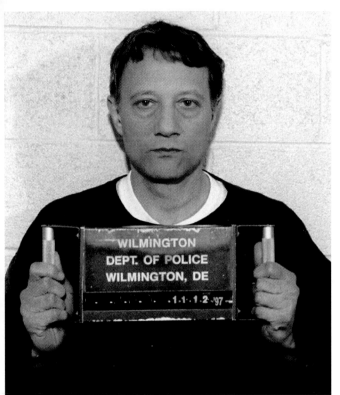

Wilmington attorney Thomas Capano, booked in November 1997 for the murder of Anne Marie Fahey. *(Fred Filippone/ Wilmington Police Dept.)*

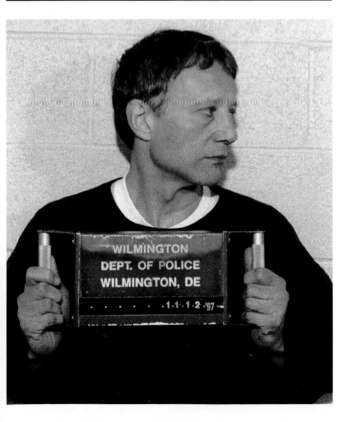

Joseph Capano, brandishing the umbrella he swung at reporters after his brother Tom's arraignment in January 1998. *(Tim Shaffer)*

Colm Connolly, the assistant U.S. attorney who prosecuted Thomas Capano. *(Tim Shaffer)*

Kay Ryan—Thomas Capano's ex-wife—enters the courthouse with her daughters Alex, Katie, and Jenny during the trial. *(Tim Shaffer)*

Marguerite Capano, Thomas's mother, with his daughter Christine during Capano's bail hearing in February. *(Tim Shaffer)*

Thomas Capano entering the courthouse for his fourth day on trial: October 29, 1998.
(Tim Shaffer)

Gerard (near left, with attorney Dan Lyons) and Louis Capano (below, with attorney Catherine Recker), whose testimony was central to the state's case. In the penalty phase of the trial, both returned to testify for the defense. *(Tim Shaffer)*

Two other Capano mistresses: Deborah McIntyre (left), whom Capano tried to finger for the murder, and Susan Louth (above), who testified for both the prosecution and, in the penalty phaser, the defense. *(Tim Shaffer)*

FBI special agent Eric Alpert, left, with detective Robert Donovan of the Wilmington Police during the Capano trial. *(Tim Shaffer)*

Anne Marie Fahey's boyfriend Michael Scanlan, leaving the courthouse after testifying for the prosecution. *(Tim Shaffer)*

Judge William Swain Lee entering the courthouse, early January 1999. *(Tim Shaffer)*

Lead defense attorney Joseph Oteri leaves the courthouse with defense team members (from left) Charles Oberly III, John O'Donnell, and Eugene Maurer Jr. on December 7, 1998, after a dispute with Capano on the first day of his defense. *(Tim Shaffer)*

The cooler that held the body of Anne Marie Fahey, introduced as evidence late in the trial. *(Tim Shaffer)*

Joseph Capano wheels his mother Marguerite into the courthouse after the conviction; the trial had taken its toll. *(Tim Shaffer)*

Thomas Capano leaves the courthouse after the jury voted 10 to 2 in favor of death by lethal injection: January 28, 1999. *(Tim Shaffer)*

14

Anne Marie Fahey had succinctly and graphically described Tom Capano's obsession in her last diary entry. But investigators continued to get other versions of the "controlling, manipulative, insecure jealous maniac" from interviews with her closest friends, Kim Horstmann and Jackie Vinnersley Steinhoff.

Both had seen Capano in action.

Over the course of the investigation, the two young women—arguably Anne Marie's best friends—provided the best insights into the relationship between Capano and Fahey and were the first to provide firsthand information about his obsession.

Horstmann, of all Fahey's friends and family members, knew the most about the affair. She had watched it all unfold. She was Anne Marie's sounding board and confidante. And she played a limited but similar role for Capano. Capano used Horstmann to stay close to Fahey, and later tried to use her to manipulate and control the investigation into Anne Marie's disappearance.

By the summer of 1995, Fahey was no longer bemoaning the indifference of her married "boyfriend." Instead, she was complaining to Horstmann about his attempts to control every aspect of her life. That summer she and Horstmann arranged to rent space in a beach house in Avalon, sharing a room in a home that several other young people, including some young men, had rented for the season. The renters needed two more boarders to cut down on the overall cost. Anne Marie heard about the opportunity at work; neither she nor Kim knew any of the people who would be living in the house, but they had friends who would be at the shore, so they decided to sign up.

From the first, there were problems with Capano. On the surface, he complained that they were living with people they did not know, that it was a potentially dangerous situation. In fact, he was livid over the thought of other men sharing living space with Anne Marie—particularly young men her own age whom she might find attractive and who, he was certain, would attempt to hit on her.

Horstmann said she and Fahey had discussed the situation, that they had been a little concerned about living with strangers. But they'd decided to take advantage of the opportunity anyway. They'd be together. They both enjoyed spending summer weekends at the Jersey shore. And they'd be content to put up with less-than-ideal living arrangements in exchange for a chance for some sun and fun each weekend.

Fahey's other concern, she said, was with Capano.

"She knew Tom would have a fit if he thought that she was going to be in a house with a bunch of guys that he didn't know," Horstmann said. "She was concerned about his reaction to it. . . . He was jealous of any attention she got from any other guys. He was always jealous of that. He didn't like her, you know, going to Dover because she would get in the Dover office and apparently there were guys there that would pay attention to her. And he almost forbade her to go to Dover anymore because he didn't like that. So she knew if we were living in a house with a bunch of guys that would upset him very much."

Fahey's decision to take space in the beach house over Capano's objections was the first indication that she was considering making a break, or at least trying to put some space between herself and her secret lover. Annoyance, and the first hints of indifference, had replaced the angst and pathos that had colored those passionate diary notes in February. "Tomas" was starting to wear thin. Still, while she had rented space at the Jersey shore that summer, Fahey seldom took advantage of it.

"We actually only stayed in that house for three nights," Horstmann recalled. "Three nights for the entire summer."

Every time they made plans, she said, Capano would intervene. Sometimes he would beg. Sometimes he would cajole. Sometimes he would pick a fight and simply wear Fahey down.

Since Horstmann lived in Philadelphia and Fahey lived in Wilmington, they usually planned to meet at the shore rather than drive there together. But their plans seldom worked out. Horstmann grew to expect, even anticipate, Fahey's call to cancel out on another weekend. "Tom is having a fit," Fahey would say. "I can't make it this week."

He would make dinner plans for a Saturday night. Or he would complain or start to question her about the sleeping arrangements in the house. While Capano would boast about his liberal sexual attitude when it came to MacIntyre and her other lovers, he was apparently much more conservative when it came to Fahey.

"Don't go," he would say. "I don't want you to go to the shore."

Horstmann remembered one Saturday that summer when she was supposed to meet Fahey at noon at the home of a friend in Avalon. From there, they planned to go over to their own beach house together. She called Fahey for nearly three hours that afternoon, repeatedly leaving messages on Fahey's answering machine.

"Finally, she called me back at maybe four or five o'clock," Horstmann said. "Tom had just left and she was exhausted because they were fighting because he did not want her to go to the shore. He had brought over salmon and shrimp and wine and all kinds of things, groceries to her apartment and had been there for a couple of hours. And they were arguing and fighting, that he did not want her to go to the shore under any circumstances."

Fahey told Horstmann she wouldn't be able to drive down that night.

"I'm too exhausted," Fahey said. "I'm drained from this fight we just had. I'm not coming. It's just too much for me. . . . "

It was a summer of emotional conflict for Fahey and one that ultimately drove her to make the fatal decision to break with Capano.

On one hand, she told Horstmann that she still cared for Capano, and that she didn't know if she would ever meet anyone else who could take care of her the way he could. "The guys that she had dated were just boys compared to Tom, who she thought was a real man," Horstmann said. Capano was someone to whom Fahey had told the intimate details of her life. They had a relationship. And even though it was sometimes twisted and even though his obsession was often exhausting, Fahey knew a part of her would always love him.

On the other hand, she told Horstmann she was becoming more and more concerned about his attempts to control her life, to keep her isolated and all to himself. In February Capano had told Fahey she would be better off with someone her own age, someone she could relate to. Back then she had cried and said he was all she wanted. Six months later, in the summer of 1995, Fahey was starting to believe Capano might have been right. But at that point, he was no longer willing to step aside.

"She didn't think he would fit into her social life," Horstmann recalled Fahey telling her. "He wouldn't be able to be a part of our group because he was older and would have nothing in common with us."

Fahey didn't want to give up that part of herself. She liked that Anne Marie. And she began to realize that with Capano she had to be someone else.

Finally, Fahey lived in fear of two other things. She worried incessantly that someone in her family would find out about her relationship with Capano. And she agonized over the thought that Capano might leave his wife and children for her. They had had several discussions, and Fahey was adamant about how she felt. "If you want to leave your wife, that's one thing," she told Capano, "but it has to have nothing to do with me." Fahey told Horstmann she didn't want to be responsible for the breakup of Capano's marriage. She couldn't live with the guilt, the anguish, and the shame she would feel.

In August, Fahey agreed to go away with Capano for a weekend to the Homestead, a fancy resort in Virginia. He pitched it as a chance for the two of them to iron out their difficulties, to figure out their relationship alone and away from all the distractions that were ever-present in Wilmington. Capano later described the trip as one of the fonder moments of their affair.

Fahey told Horstmann a different story.

She said it was a "disaster." Their relationship, at least from Fahey's point of view, ended a few weeks later.

In September, she agreed to a blind date arranged by the governor. Carper had been trying for months to set her up with a young executive named Mike Scanlan from MBNA. Scanlan headed up the company's community affairs department, and was involved in charitable and social service operations, many funded by his office. Soft-spoken and somewhat shy, Scanlan was considered a solid individual with a bright future. Carper thought he and Anne Marie might hit it off.

They met on a Friday night in the middle of September at O'Friel's—too crowded, too noisy, not a good place for a first date. They could hardly hold a proper conversation, let alone get to know one another. Both Scanlan and Fahey were conscious of the eyes that were watching them, all the friends and acquaintances who wanted to see if they would hit it off.

"It didn't go very well," he said.

But when they got together a second time for dinner, they found they had a lot in common. Both cared about many of the same social issues, particularly issues involving children. Anne Marie had been an after-school mentor for needy children, and talked frequently about becoming a teacher.

Scanlan, who went to work for MBNA after graduating from Georgetown University, left the company after just two years to work as a counselor and administrator for social service agencies in Maryland and then in Florida that provided rehabilitation programs for teenagers convicted of crimes. Scanlan, a varsity swimmer at Georgetown, liked the programs because they used oceanography, marine biology, aquatics, and seamanship as ways to teach discipline, self-esteem, and self-control.

MBNA lured him back by offering him the post of vice president in charge of community relations. The six-figure salary and the chance to dole out large charitable contributions to causes he considered important brought Scanlan back to Wilmington. His new job brought him in contact with the city's and the state's power elite.

Carper had been talking to him about Fahey for months before he finally agreed to the blind date. Like Fahey, he came from a large Irish Catholic family; he was one of seven children. Like Capano, he had attended a private Catholic prep school and a prestigious Catholic university. Georgetown, like Boston College, is part of America's Catholic Ivy League; as Notre Dame is to Harvard, so Georgetown and BC are to Princeton and Yale.

Scanlan, who grew up in Rhode Island, owned a house in Sharpley, an upper-middle-class Wilmington suburb just off Concord Pike. He drove a Jeep and a Mercedes 560 convertible. Cynics would say that Fahey was trading up when she moved from Capano to Scanlan; he had the income and potential to provide her with the good life she had been seeking, but none of the emotional or marital baggage that Capano carried with him.

But others said that Fahey was genuinely taken with Scanlan. He was quiet and reserved, which surprised several of her friends. He was not her type. He didn't need to be the center of attention, didn't much care if anyone knew who he was. Scanlan had self-assurance without arrogance. Too many of Anne Marie's other relationships had been with guys who showed plenty of arrogance, but too little substance.

The relationship grew steadily over the next several months. Fahey confided to several friends that Scanlan was the kind of guy with whom you would want to build a future. Her daybook at work was filled with notations that marked the progress of their relationship. They had first met on September 15. Periodic notes on her calendar marked the "anniversaries." She referred to him as "Miguel" and kept a box with mementos—a program from an opera, holiday cards, concert ticket stubs—in her bedroom dresser drawer. His picture was on the bureau in her bedroom along with those of her brothers and sister and her nephews.

There was, however, no sex.

Scanlan said they had both agreed to wait. Others, however, said that Fahey was a little frustrated by Scanlan's failure to force the issue. But because she wanted the relationship to work and because it was clearly unlike any other she had ever been involved in, she was willing to let things evolve slowly.

Capano, of course, would later point to their lack of sexual activity as a clear indication that she and Scanlan were not serious. In conversations with Horstmann he described Scanlan as a "geek," questioned his sexuality, and implied that Scanlan and Fahey were using each other in a relationship that was all about appearance and image.

Capano separated from his wife on Labor Day that September. He moved into the house on Grant Avenue and, for a brief period at least, ignored Fahey. Perhaps it was the trauma of the breakup of his twenty-three-year marriage and his concern over its impact on his four daughters. Perhaps he was busy putting his affair with MacIntyre in place, letting her know that he still did not want to go public with their relationship despite the fact that he and Kay were living apart.

Whatever the reason, there was a "quiet time" early in the fall of 1995. But then Capano turned his full attention to Anne Marie, and for the first time, she was frightened.

"She was very upset because he was completely obsessed and kind of crazy," Horstmann said. "He would leave fifteen messages in a two-hour time frame on her answering machine. At night he would be e-mailing her constantly to the point that she was afraid to read his e-mails anymore because she didn't want him to know that she had read them because then she would have to respond to them."

There was an angry confrontation in November, when Capano showed up unexpectedly at Fahey's apartment house, insisting that he wanted to talk. Once inside, he began to rant about her dating Scanlan, and, in a rage, started to gather up all the gifts he had given her, taking clothes and shoes out of her closet, grabbing the television set and books and cooking utensils.

"No other man is going to see you in the dress I bought you," he said. "No man is going to sit here and watch the television I gave you."

Fahey told friends Capano took away the gifts, but later returned them. Capano acknowledged that there had been a blowup, but said nothing ever left Fahey's apartment. He said Anne Marie "gave as good as she got" during the heated argument, in which items were thrown into a pile on her living room floor. But he said the argument ended in tears and hugs after Fahey threw one last item on the pile—a heating pad he had given her because of the stomach cramps she got whenever she had her period. When Fahey threw the heating pad on the pile, Capano said, "We looked at one another and started to laugh."

Horstmann, however, said Fahey had little to laugh about when it came to Capano.

"I was one of the only people she could talk to about it," Horstmann recalled. "So we would talk about it constantly. And . . . we would say, 'What is he? I don't understand why he can't accept that you don't want to be with him anymore. Doesn't he have any pride? Why is he continually trying to get you to be with him when you don't want to be with him?'

"We didn't understand it, so we talked about it constantly."

Fahey was concerned about Capano's obsession, but at first didn't seem to think he would harm her. She told Horstmann that the solution might be for her to leave the Wilmington area, to move out of state. Fifteen years earlier, Linda Marandola had reached the same conclusion.

"She felt like she was never going to be able to break free of him, but I don't think she was afraid," Horstmann said of Fahey's emotional state at the end of 1995. Still, she also acknowledged that Anne Marie was full of self-doubt, plagued by a host of insecurities that Capano seized on and attempted to manipulate.

People meeting Anne Marie for the first time would be fooled by her laugh, by her outgoing nature, by her ability to put strangers at ease with her brash personality and her apparent zest for life. But inside, underneath that shell, Horstmann knew there was a worried, insecure, and often lonely person who constantly questioned her own self-worth.

"She was very insecure as far as her appearance and, actually, anything about her," Horstmann said. "She . . . seemed like the most confident person in the world, but she was actually not at all. She was very vulnerable."

Capano pushed all her buttons in an attempt to keep their relationship alive. Sometimes he would belittle her, picking at the wounds of her poor and troubled childhood.

THE SUMMER WIND   157

"You're nothing but white trash," he would say. "You should be lucky that I'm even interested in you. I could give you the world."

At other times he would appeal to her sympathy, repeating what he had told her back in February—that his life "sucked," that he was terribly unhappy and didn't want to go on living.

In one frantic series of phone messages in the fall of 1995, Capano told Fahey, "I have to see you. I have to see you. I'm going to kill myself. I swear I can't live without you. I have to see you. Please see me. Please see me."

Fahey was afraid to check her e-mail, afraid to dial in for her voice mail. Capano would be there. Again and again and again.

"It was just constant obsessiveness," said Horstmann. "It was him threatening to kill himself. . . . I was in shock. . . . He didn't sound like a stable adult."

In contrast, Fahey told Horstmann, her relationship with Scanlan was progressing, and she was excited about their future together. Even as she tried to keep Capano at bay, Anne Marie saw the chance for a better life with Scanlan. They were seeing each other regularly. It was understood that they were dating, that they would be with each other on weekends and for special events. Scanlan had asked Anne Marie to help him redecorate his kitchen.

"She was excited at the prospects of where it was going," said Horstmann. "It was kind of the first guy she had dated since Paul [Columbus] that she thought that there might be, that there was marriage potential here."

Desperate to stay in Fahey's life, Capano made two other overtures at the end of 1995. For Christmas he sent her an airline ticket to Spain. He knew she and Kim had talked about taking a trip there, perhaps visiting the family with whom Anne Marie had lived during her semester abroad while in college. The open-ended, round-trip ticket cost about $1,300. Fahey sent it back to Capano.

Scanlan gave her a sweater for their first Christmas together. She loved it.

Capano also began to work on Jackie Steinhoff, Anne Marie's other close friend. He would stop by her coffee shop in downtown Wilmington and bemoan his plight in life. He looked terrible. He had lost weight and his skin was sallow. His suits hung on his frame like clothes on a wire hanger.

"I can't eat or sleep," he told Steinhoff. "Sometimes I feel like killing myself."

Steinhoff called Fahey, as Capano knew she would. "What's wrong with Tom?" she asked.

Fahey was less than forthcoming. She had never told Steinhoff about their affair, so she answered in oblique terms.

"He'll be okay," she said. "He just has some problems."

Capano began to press Steinhoff to arrange a dinner date for the three of them. Just three friends getting together, for old time's sake. Steinhoff, who hadn't seen Anne Marie much once her coffee shop opened and the holiday season made everyone's life hectic, thought it was a good idea. She pressed Anne Marie, who at first looked for excuses, but eventually agreed.

"Call Anne Marie," Capano would say when he stopped in the coffee shop. "My schedule is flexible. Book something with her."

"Do we have to go?" Fahey would ask when Steinhoff brought up the topic again.

"He's really depressed," Steinhoff replied. "He needs a friend. Let's just go out to dinner."

Early in January 1996, Steinhoff recalled, Anne Marie finally agreed. But her tone carried a note of weariness, of "Let's just go so he leaves us alone." They went to La Famiglia, another upscale Italian restaurant in center-city Philadelphia. Located on Front Street, about a block from Panorama, it was owned and operated by the same family and offered a similar high-priced, mouth-watering menu.

Fahey picked up Steinhoff that night and they drove together to Capano's home on Grant Avenue. Steinhoff brought a pasta maker as a housewarming gift. Capano took pride in showing her through the house—particularly the rooms he had set up for his daughters, who, he said, usually spent one night each weekend with him.

Capano then drove the three of them to Philadelphia. Earlier, Anne Marie had asked Jackie not to mention Mike Scanlan to Capano.

"They don't work well together," she said, implying that the two had had some work-related problems. In fact, the two had never done any business together; they didn't even know each other.

Steinhoff remembers the night as fairly uneventful. Anne Marie was not her usual, outgoing, life-of-the-party self, but she was cordial and friendly with Capano. The one thing that Steinhoff thought was unusual was a brief conversation she had with Capano when Anne Marie left to use the ladies' room.

"Why does she hate me?" Capano asked.

"What do you mean?" said Steinhoff; the question had come out of the blue. "Why would Anne Marie hate you?"

"Oh, she hates me," he said. "She hates me."

Steinhoff thought that Capano might have had too many glasses of wine that night, that the question might have come from his depression.

"She doesn't hate you," she said reassuringly. "Why would she be here if she hated you?"

They stopped by Capano's house on the way home that night to pick up Fahey's car. It was a little before midnight. He wanted them to stay and watch a movie on the VCR. But they said it was late and they'd be going. So Capano let Steinhoff borrow the video, telling her he thought she would like it. It was *Amadeus*, the story of Mozart, the libidinous, misunderstood, and unappreciated genius.

15

Later, when it all fell apart, when Gerry Capano went to the feds and told them the story of what he had seen and done on the morning of June 28, 1996, people talked about the betrayal. Gerry, they said, had caved in to the tremendous pressure federal authorities had brought to bear in the high-profile case. Faced with the possibility of being arrested on federal drug and weapons possession charges, he had given up his older brother Tom to save his own neck.

But in the end it was Tom who had betrayed Gerry, just as he had betrayed or would betray everyone else close to him. Before it was over, Tom Capano would use his mother, his sister and brothers, his ex-lovers, his wife, his daughters, his pastor, his Jesuit professors at Boston College, his former colleagues in the legal profession, and even the memory of his father in an attempt to protect himself from prosecution and conviction. He would show little or no remorse for the death of Anne Marie Fahey, but would rant and rave about how he was being made a scapegoat, unjustly targeted and vilified by both the prosecution and the news media.

Gerry Capano was just the first in a long list of friends and family members to be used by Tom Capano. More important, he was the first to crack.

By April 1997, the kid gloves had come off. The unsealing of the search warrant affidavit earlier in the year had outlined the government's case and its suspicions. The game of cat-and-mouse had escalated. To anyone paying attention—and most of the time it seemed that the entire city was—it was obvious that Colm Connolly and Tom Capano were heading for a showdown. There was no longer any doubt that Capano was the target of a kidnapping-murder investigation. Most people had stopped wondering if Capano would be charged and arrested. The question now was when.

Capano had ducked a grand jury subpoena in January by declaring, through his lawyers, that he would refuse to answer any questions, citing his Fifth Amendment right against self-incrimination. It was the smart move legally, but it reinforced the perception that he had something to hide.

Privately, Tom kept insisting that the government didn't have a case. Gerry Capano, less sophisticated but with more street experience, wasn't as sure. Gerry knew the government could do just about anything it wanted. He and Louis had talked about the way the investigation would play out, and they were both convinced that everyone in the Capano family was being watched. Louis sensed the presence of the IRS. Gerry, even more paranoid, was concerned about undercover narcs.

Both brothers were constantly looking over their shoulders, and their paranoia was justified. Gerry's lifestyle, in particular, had already been compromised. Although Gerry didn't know it, the ATF had planted Doug and Diane Iardella inside his social circle, working the case at a level that amazed even Connolly, Donovan, and Alpert.

On a Sunday early in April, Gerry called his lawyer, Dan Lyons, at home. He said he needed to talk with him, but didn't want to do it over the phone. Lyons told Gerry to meet him at his office the next day, Monday, April 7. The ex-prosecutor was savvy enough to suspect what was troubling his client, but wanted to let him tell the story in his own way and in his own time.

Lyons had several court appearances that day, so he arranged to meet Gerry late in the afternoon. His office at that time was located in the 800 block of Market Street, two blocks from the state courthouse.

Gerry began by telling Lyons that he was a wreck, that he hadn't been able to sleep, that the case was tearing him and his entire family apart. In fact, Gerry had become more and more dependent on cocaine. He was using the drug more often, and using more of it. It was one of the only ways he could cope with the guilt and the fear and the anger.

Lyons had already laid out the ground rules for his client. He had told Gerry during their first meeting back in August that he had two choices: Gerry could either tell the truth or keep quiet. Lyons also told him that as an attorney, he could not knowingly help his client present false testimony to investigators or a grand jury.

That Monday afternoon, he repeated what he had said earlier.

"You don't have to tell me anything at all," Lyons said as Gerry sat nervously in a chair across from him, "but without accurate information it's difficult for me to help you decide what to do."

Gerry said the only people who knew he was there that afternoon were his brother Louis and his wife, Michelle. Louis, he said, had urged him to come in and "tell the truth." Michelle knew that he had been upset for months, but had no idea what he was about to tell Lyons. Tom was not even aware that Gerry had called.

At some point early in the conversation, Gerry mentioned the possibility of obtaining "immunity." Lyons said that was certainly something he would explore if Gerry authorized him to do so. But Lyons knew that would also depend on two other things: what Gerry had done, and what investigators already knew and could prove without his assistance.

"I haven't told you the whole truth," Gerry said.

For the next hour, as Lyons took notes, Gerry recounted the story of how he had helped his brother dispose of a body in the Atlantic Ocean. He told Lyons that in the months preceding that fateful morning, Tom had told him about a "crazy woman" he had been dating and about how she and her boyfriend were "extorting" him and threatening his children. He told Lyons how he had lent his brother $8,000 and a handgun, both of which had been returned. And he described how Tom had shown up at his house on Emma Court unexpectedly shortly before 6:00 A.M. on June 28, 1996.

"He looked like hell," Gerry said, "like he had been up all night."

Lyons would interrupt occasionally with a question, but for the most part he let Gerry tell the story. Unlike the account that Gerry had provided back in August, this one had the ring of truth. Gerry didn't try to embellish, nor did he try to explain away his role in the horrible events of that morning. He was ashamed of what he had done. But he held very little back. Shooting the cooler with a deer slug, for example, made Gerry look almost as heartless and callous as his brother Tom. In addition, it was a detail that only he and Tom were aware of. Yet Gerry volunteered that information, first to Lyons and later to investigators.

When Lyons asked Gerry what he thought had happened to the cooler after he and Tom threw it overboard, Gerry, like nearly everyone else, assumed it was long gone.

"It's probably washed up on a beach in Cuba," he said.

Gerry insisted he never saw a body that day, that he only had a glimpse of a foot and an ankle as they disappeared into the ocean. And he said Tom never mentioned the name Anne Marie Fahey until after she was reported missing.

Lyons was fascinated by the story, and immediately realized the impact it could have on the case. If Gerry was telling the truth, there were only two people with firsthand knowledge of what had happened that morning. One was Tom Capano, the target of an all-out federal investigation. The other was his client.

And while investigators had clearly been speculating about Gerry's involvement in the disposal of Fahey's body—the reports about the missing anchor and the sale of the *Summer Wind* made that obvious—no one had made any mention of an ice chest. Now Gerry was telling Lyons things only he and Tom knew.

Gerry insisted he had never seen the cooler before that morning when he walked into Tom's garage on Grant Avenue. Lyons wanted to be sure that his client had not provided it to his brother; Gerry, after all, was the only Capano brother who would have had a legitimate use for a "fish box."

Gerry used his arms to show Lyons how big the cooler was. He estimated that it was about five feet long, two and a half feet wide, and two and a half feet tall.

"Gerry said the box was big enough for a person to be in it," Lyons wrote in his memo of that meeting. "Tommy had no reason to own a fish cooler. . . . He doesn't know where Tommy got it. . . . Gerry and Tommy lifted the cooler and put it in the back of Kay's Suburban. Gerry did not look in the cooler, but it was heavy, consistent with the weight it would have had if it contained a body. Gerry could hear some ice sloshing around in the cooler. Gerry said he didn't want to know what was in the cooler."

The next day, Lyons had his first discussion with the two Philadelphia lawyers, Robert Welsh and Catherine Recker, who were representing Louis Capano Jr. Over the next seven months, the lawyers for the two brothers would keep in contact as their clients agonized over what to do. Lyons met with Gerry on three other occasions in April, and each time they discussed his options.

They had several discussions about Lyons approaching Colm Connolly and trying to make a deal. Gerry had no doubt, nor did Lyons, that Louis would be happy to follow his younger brother into Connolly's office.

"We discussed going to the prosecutor several times," Lyons said later. "Gerry would go back and forth. . . . He told me that both he and Louie were falling apart, that they couldn't sleep, that they couldn't take it anymore, this burden."

Lyons, whose angular features and thick shock of sandy brown hair gave him the look of a gritty Michael Douglas, had become more than just a lawyer for Gerry. He was in many ways the only person Gerry could depend on, the only one looking out for Gerry's best interest and welfare. That certainly couldn't be said for Tom; nor was it the case with most other members of the Capano family—even Gerry's mother, Marguerite.

Tom Capano kept insisting that the prosecution didn't have a case, that Connolly was bluffing, that the grand jury subpoenas were a charade, that if Gerry and Louie would just keep their mouths shut, nothing would happen.

"I won't let anything happen to either of you," he promised during a meeting they had outside a delicatessen north of Wilmington one afternoon that spring. He insisted that if things took a turn for the worst, he would come forward and tell prosecutors the whole story. But he pleaded with his brothers to let him do it on his own terms. If not for him, he said, then for his children.

"I wanted to believe him," Louis Capano Jr. said later. "He was my brother."

At the end of April, under mounting pressure from his former employers, Thomas J. Capano resigned as a partner at Saul, Ewing, Remick & Saul. His career as a high-powered, high-priced rainmaker was over. Capano had been on leave from his job for months; now he was living with his mother in the sprawling stone colonial on Weldin Road where he grew up.

He spent a lot of time puttering around the house, helping his mother organize and straighten out years of memories, files, documents, and old clothes. Remarkably, a friend said, in the seventeen years since her husband had died Marguerite Capano had done very little to put Louis Sr.'s personal affairs in order. Tom helped rearrange things in the house. He organized her checkbook and bill-paying schedule, packed up some of his father's clothes and donated them to a charitable organization, set up a schedule for his mother's daily medication, and rearranged and organized several of the storage closets in the house.

When a friend complimented him on the concern and dedication he was showing his seventy-four-year-old mother, he replied, "What else have I got to do?"

While Capano watched and waited, Connolly, Donovan, and Alpert continued to build their case. They were working nonstop now, ten, twelve, fourteen hours a day, sometimes seven days a week.

They would meet each day in Connolly's office on the eleventh floor of the U.S. Attorney's Office in downtown Wilmington or in a conference room down the hall. Several times a week they would also debrief the Iardellas, adding the information they brought in to the ever-expanding file that was the Capano case.

Gerry's life was clearly built around drugs, sex, and rock and roll. He partied hard and often, sometimes spending thousands of dollars on drugs, hotel rooms, and the tips he would stuff into the g-strings of the topless go-go dancers at the "gentlemen's cabarets" he and his cronies frequented in Philadelphia.

Thee Doll House and Delilah's Den were two of his favorites. Lap dances started at $20 and, depending on the length of time and degree of intimacy, went up from there. Gerry had season tickets to the Philadelphia Eagles football games, but sometimes he would slip away at halftime—particularly during Monday-night games—in order to make the scene at the cabarets, where he was well known and where he often referred to himself as "the Big G."

Sometimes the parties would move from there to the Four Seasons, one of the more expensive hotels in Philadelphia. But when Gerry slipped into party mode, money was not an issue.

All of this would be used as leverage when Connolly finally closed the net on him. It was a vicious circle. The mounting pressure of the investigation drove Gerry to even more reckless behavior, and allowed the undercovers even greater access. The more intensely he partied—the more he drank and did drugs—the more he would open up to those he considered his close friends.

Once the undercovers had gotten inside, they and Connolly plotted to manipulate the situation. They used the media to generate stories that they knew would get Gerry and his friends talking. A document would be unsealed, a subpoena would be issued, a covert and obvious surveillance would be set in place. All were designed to get a reaction from Gerry or those around him.

"He wasn't the kind of guy you could ask a question," said Doug Iardella. "If you did, he would clam up or get suspicious. So the idea was just to be in the right place, to be out with him and his friends, when he started to talk."

It didn't always work out. Tom Capano had been harping on Gerry for months about keeping a low profile. He knew the feds would target his younger brother, and told him so. In fact, for several months after Fahey's disappearance, Gerry "didn't come out to play," Iardella recalled. But by the fall of 1996, with the football season going strong and the lap dancers gyrating at full throttle, the Big G was back. And by 1997, his private parties had gone public. On any given night, he would be at a bar in and around Wilmington or at one of the clubs in Philadelphia. Sometimes the party would move on to a hotel.

But there also would be days or weeks when Gerry would just disappear. He'd head for the shore, where he moved in a different social set, or for Boca Raton, where he had a condo.

"You never knew where he was going to be," Iardella said.

On May 13, 1997, Connolly brought Kim Horstmann, Jackie Steinhoff, and Jill Morrison, another Fahey friend and coworker, in front of the grand jury. And for the first time the anonymous panel that had been tracking the disappearance and suspected kidnapping and murder of Anne Marie Fahey got a detailed account of her relationship with Capano. By that point, Donovan, Alpert, and Connolly had tracked the relationship through Fahey's diary notes, through interviews with her friends, and through the more than fifty e-mail messages Capano and Fahey had exchanged between January and June of 1996.

Like her diary notes, Anne Marie Fahey's e-mail messages were a voice from the grave. And, balanced against the corresponding e-mail messages from Capano, they provided an eerie yet spellbinding account of a complicated relationship that investigators were now certain had ended in murder. To read the messages and to place them in the historic context of what was happening at the time they were written and what investigators knew was going to happen was a surreal experience for those working the case.

Rarely do a victim and a suspect leave such a detailed written record behind. But both Fahey and Capano were compulsive in that way—Capano even more so than his victim. Much to the consternation of his defense team, he would continue to "memorialize" his thoughts in notes, letters, and correspondence following his arrest. Perhaps it was his legal training at work; more likely, it was his ego. Ultimately, his own words, spoken directly from the witness stand and taken from his correspondence and taped telephone conversations, would bury him.

"The fucking guy has to write everything down," said one of his defense lawyers in the middle of the trial. "I've never seen anything like it."

For investigators, of course, it was an unexpected windfall.

"You have to remember," Connolly said on more than one occasion, "Tom Capano always believes he's the smartest person in the room."

Tom Capano had taken Anne Marie Fahey out to dinner for her birthday in 1994—the night they first made love—and again in 1995. In January 1996, after trying (and failing) to use Jackie Steinhoff to get back in Fahey's favor, he attempted to use the birthday gambit again.

Fahey wasn't interested.

One of the first e-mails recovered by investigators was a January 17, 1996, message in which Fahey made reference to an angry shouting match that had occurred the night before. Fahey apologized profusely to Capano in the e-mail, in a gesture that was typical of the relationship. She was under a lot of stress, she said. Her therapy sessions with Gary Johnson were not going well. But she was not willing to consider checking herself into a clinic for her anorexia, a move Capano had been suggesting.

Author: afahey@state.de.us
Date: 1/17/96 11:23 A.M.

Good Morning Tommy:
I want to apologize for my "outbreak" last night. I'm sure it must have scared (amongst other feelings) you. Quite honestly, I scared myself last night . . . Right now I need a friend more than anything else. There was a part of me that just

wanted to be alone to think things out clearly. So, when I asked you not to rub my stomach, and you responded by saying how much I hurt you, I couldn't take feeling guilty about what had happened along w/everything else that I am feeling. It is my fault because I was not communicating with you, and you didn't know how to respond. I am sorry for my behavior. Please try to understand that right now I have some things that I need to "work out" but I'm not sure where or how to start. I know that I am not ready to check into a Clinic, and confront my family, friends and co-workers about my situation. Blah, Blah, Blah. I am not making any sense (as usual) so I am going to sign off. Annie.

The e-mail was one of Fahey's first attempts to articulate her feelings and draw some lines in her relationship with Capano. But while Tom Capano listened and said he understood, he continued to pursue the relationship that he wanted.

"Hey, Honeybunny," Capano wrote on January 24, a Wednesday three days before her birthday. The message, sent from his law office to Fahey's desk at the governor's office, rambled through several topics, including Capano's meeting the day before with the new Catholic bishop of the Wilmington and his plans to chaperone a party for his daughter Katie at his Grant Avenue home early in February. Capano also discussed a possible birthday dinner date and closed with the words, "Te amo. Sempre."

Fahey replied a few minutes later. She talked about the bishop, noted that January 24 was the first anniversary of the death of her therapist Bob Connor, and included her concern for the health and mental well-being of her brother Mark. Making no mention of a birthday date with Capano, she closed with the words, "Have a good day, Annie."

Fahey's birthday, January 27, fell on a Saturday that year. She was turning thirty. Her family planned a surprise party to mark the milestone. The party was scheduled for Friday night, January 26, at Kathleen's house. Annie knew about it, but promised Kim Horstmann she would act surprised. But she wanted Horstmann to be sure of one thing: that Tom Capano, whom her family considered one of her friends, was not on the guest list.

Horstmann checked with Ginny Columbus, who was helping Kathleen put together the invitations. Capano had not been invited. When she heard that, Fahey breathed a sigh of relief.

"She was afraid to death of Michael Scanlan finding out about her relationship with Tom because Michael is . . . such a devout Catholic," Horstmann said. "And she thought that if he found out that she had been involved with a married man that that would be horrible in his eyes; he would judge her and it would definitely effect their relationship. So she was very afraid of him finding out. . . ."

Scanlan was not supposed to be at the party. He was away on business in Colombia. But he came back a day early so that he could surprise Annie. More important, he and Anne Marie had a date the next night for the Grand Gala. It was a coming-out of sorts for them as a couple; all the city's movers and shakers would be at the black-tie fundraiser, which attracts a capacity crowd every year. Anne Marie had never attended.

Capano, obviously, could snare an invitation, but it would have been impossible for him to escort her to such an event. Scanlan, on the other hand, couldn't wait to take her. Later, Anne Marie would tell friends that the Grand Gala was one of the happiest nights of her life. She and Scanlan sat through a stellar performance at the Opera House that featured a concert by Mel Tormé. They laughed and hobnobbed the rest of the night away at the Hotel duPont on Rodney Square, where all the guests from the Gala repaired after the performance. Waiters in starched white jackets served champagne and hot hors d'oeuvres from silver trays as the tuxedo-clad and jewel-bedecked guests glided from one lavish ballroom to another.

For Anne Marie Fahey the Grand Gala was a wonderland. She may have been the only guest there who had grown up in a house where heat and hot water were not always available, where the refrigerator was often empty, where money for a new pair of shoes or a first-day-of-school outfit was impossible to come by. For Anne Marie Fahey, this was the end of the rainbow. And Michael Scanlan was the guy who had brought her there.

It was a beautiful and memorable ending to a night that had started badly.

Capano had called repeatedly while Annie was getting ready for her date. Jill Morrison, who helped her get dressed that night, said Fahey was beside herself with worry.

"We had gone shopping for shoes and a dress, and I went over that day because it was her birthday and to help her get ready," said Morrison, who lived a few blocks from Fahey's Washington Street apartment. "When I got there, she was upset and angry."

Capano had been calling Fahey all day, and six more calls came in while Morrison was at Fahey's apartment that night. Capano was angry that Fahey had blown off a chance to go to dinner with him on her birthday and instead chose to go to the Grand Gala with Scanlan. He said he might get a date of his own and show up at the Gala.

"Anne Marie was terrified that he would expose their relationship not just to Michael, but to everyone," Morrison said. "She said it was the thing that she was most ashamed of and most regretted in her life."

Morrison said she spent half her time helping Fahey get dressed and the other half trying to calm her down. Fahey talked about canceling out on Scanlan and not going anywhere that night. Morrison told her not to be silly, to go and enjoy herself. Capano was bluffing, she said. He wouldn't do anything.

After Fahey and Scanlan left for the Gala, Morrison drove around Wilmington looking for Capano's home on Grant Avenue. She wanted to make sure his car was in the driveway, that he had not gone to the Gala.

"But I couldn't find the house," Morrison said.

Instead, around 9:30 that night, she called Capano at his home. She had the number from work. When he answered the phone, Morrison hung up.

"I figured if he answered the phone, he wasn't going to the Grand Gala," she said.

Capano did not show up at the Grand Gala. He did not make any attempt to publicly embarrass Fahey. But he flooded her voice mail with messages about the pain and hurt she had caused him.

Later he would claim that it wasn't the fact that she had gone out with Scanlan that upset him, but the fact that she had been dishonest about it. He said Fahey kept putting him off about a birthday date, claiming that she might have to babysit her nephews. When he finally realized she was stringing him along, Capano said he blew up and lost his temper. Tom Capano, the master manipulator, could not stand being manipulated.

Fahey, as Capano had hoped, responded to his weekend of bombast and self-pity by attempting to smooth things over. Once again, she apologized.

Author: afahey@gov.state.de.us
Date: 1/29/96 7:50 A.M.
Tom:
First let me start off by saying that I'm sorry for the pain I have caused you over the weekend. I am afraid and I do not know where to begin. I spent a good part of yesterday morning/afternoon at Valley Green Park thinking about a lot of stuff: Us, Girls, Eating disorder, my family, etc. I desperately want to talk to you, but I'm too afraid to place the call. I do love you Tommy and no matter what happens—I will always love you. Annie.

From: tcapano@saul.com
On: 1/30/96 10:59 AM
Annie:
Our system was down yesterday so I just got your email. I only wish I had seen it yesterday. I desperately want to talk to you, too, and I'll go out of my mind if I don't soon. Please don't be afraid to place the call. I need to hear your voice . . . Please call me. Not hearing from you since Saturday afternoon is making me crazy. And you know how much I love you and need you. I'll wait for your call. Te amo.

Fahey was telling friends that she wanted nothing to do with Capano. But her e-mail messages seemed to be saying something else. There was still a relationship of some sort there: twisted and contorted, no longer sexual, but still very much a part of both of them. Fahey would tell friends she wanted to break away, but in private conversions and in messages to Capano, she at least hinted at a desire to keep a line open. Later his lawyers would use several of the e-mail messages—particularly the ones in which she spoke fondly of her continuing feelings for him—to refute the allegations that Capano had forced himself on her, that he was stalking her, that she was trying to break away but that he wouldn't let her.

The reality was that Anne Marie Fahey didn't know what she wanted. Her relationship with Scanlan seemed to be moving forward, but it scared her. In many ways, he was too nice. There was a part of her that felt she didn't deserve the happiness, that she wasn't entitled to a normal relationship. There was another part of her that was afraid to break completely with Capano, not because she feared him but because she was afraid of losing the attention and the financial support he so readily provided. If nothing else, Tom Capano was Annie's Thursday-night date, a dependable weekly escort to a fine restaurant. He was someone who would always listen to her complaints, someone who would buy her gifts, someone who would treat her like a princess. And she wasn't ready to give that up.

There was a series of short, chatty e-mails over the next week in which Fahey and Capano discussed their jobs, their families, and plans for a lunch date. "Buenas Dias Señor Capano" Fahey wrote in a February 1 message in which she asked how his dental appointment had gone that day and talked about an impending snowstorm. From the references in the e-mails it was clear that Capano and Fahey were talking on a regular basis on the phone. In one, Capano made reference to their habit of calling each other and watching their favorite show, *NYPD Blue*, over the phone together. Like a lovestruck teenager, Capano was using whatever he could to stay close to Fahey, to remain a part of her life.

Fahey sounded cool but cordial in most of her messages. Capano, often repeating his "te amo sempre" line, was more impassioned and clearly trying to stoke the fires of their relationship.

A week after the Grand Gala blowup, Fahey tried again to draw some lines and define their relationship. And Capano again said he would go along with whatever she wanted.

*   *   *

Author: afahey@gov.state.de.us
Date: 2/7/96 7:51 A.M.
To: Thomas Capano at SERS-Wilmington
Good Morning Tommy:
. . . Sorry I did not call you back last night . . . wanted to see the last part of NYPD Blue and of course I fell asleep and woke up around 1:30. Typical Annie. This week is not going to work for me for dinner . . . I am supposed to have nachos/beer w/ a couple of my running partners from the gym on Thurs. nite after we work out. We set this up on Tuesday nite, so I am not sure if we are still on or not. If not, I would be happy to have dinner w/you on Thursday . . .
Tommy, I meant what I said on Sunday night about right now only being able to offer you my friendship, and if you cannot deal with that then I understand. I'm still very much confused, and I am trying to work out a lot of personal things on my own. I would like to talk to you about what happened yesterday in Phila., but again it is up to you. Annie.

From: tcapano@saul.com
On: 2/7/96 9:50 A.M.
Good morning Annie,
Thank you for the email . . . I also watched NYPD Blue and wanted to call you at the end like last week but thought you might be asleep. How about that Puerto Rican chick's interview with Greg about her brother Sal . . . Turns out that I'm now free on Saturday night instead of Friday anyway. The kids changed plans last night for a bunch of reasons. I'd like to have dinner with you on Saturday night. I need to talk to you about work and I think you need to talk about Gary Johnson, etc. I understand that you're confused and want to limit our relationship now to friendship. I love you enough to accept that and ask only that we treat each other kindly and honestly. I don't want to lose you. I also think we shouldn't lose the closeness we've developed. If nothing else, you know you can tell me your fears and hopes and rely on me to support you. I still want to be there for you, which, I guess, is the surest sign that I still

love you with all my heart. You cannot do all of this on your own, Annie—no one can. Let me help. Please call me when it's convenient or send me an email . . . You look like you could use a good meal! And you have to admit I've always fed you well. Te Amo.

Anne Marie's anorexia was flaring up again. She had begun to lose weight. Capano, as his e-mail message indicated, had noticed. So had Jill Morrison. "We would go to lunch almost every day," Morrison said. "I would order a sandwich. Annie would order a pretzel."

Morrison said she confronted Fahey about the problem, pleading with her to get some help. Fahey said she was seeing a new therapist, Michele Sullivan, and was going to take care of herself. She also complained to Morrison about Capano.

"Doesn't he realize I'm the way I am because of him?" Fahey told Morrison. "I can't control him, but I can control what I put in my body."

Morrison, like Horstmann and Steinhoff, saw a part of the relationship. Several months earlier she had been taken aback by Capano when he complained about her and Fahey carousing in Washington, D.C., while on political business for the governor's office. They had gone out to several bars after the business day had ended, and only made it back to Wilmington early the next morning. When Capano heard about it, he said they were "acting like whores."

Morrison was also one of the few people who knew about the calls that preceded the Grand Gala. That same night Fahey told her that she thought Capano was spying on her, that in their conversations he would mention times when he had seen her car parked in front of Scanlan's house. He wanted to know if they were having sex. She told Morrison about the time Capano drove her back to his home on Grant Avenue and locked her in his car in the garage while they argued about their relationship.

"She had a fear of being locked in small, dark places," Morrison said.

Capano knew it. And he used it. He couldn't stop himself.

Author: afahey@gov.state.de.us
Date: 2/12/96 7:34 A.M.

To: Thomas Capano at SERS-Wilmington
. . . Tommy, you scared me this weekend. Starting with
Friday, and all the calls you placed. It really freaks me out
when you call every half hour. I truly understand how fragile
you are these days, and I feel the same way. But . . . when
you keep calling that way, it makes me turn the other way,
and quite frankly, shut down. My weekend was not a good
one. Believe it or not, I no longer sleep. When I got home
from Kevin's (8:30) I once again made a mistake and was in
bed by 9:15. I woke up at 3:00 and never went back to sleep.
I arrived here at 7:00, because I was getting tired of hanging
out at home . . . I'm sorry that I am nothing but a constant
disappointment to you these days. It is not fair to you. I have
an idea of what I need to do, I just cannot bring myself to
start the process. I apologize for being such a horrible person
to you. You are the last person on this earth I want to
hurt!!! . . . Anyway, I know we have to talk today, but I wanted
to start off with this email. Let me know your schedule for
today. Annie.

Two short e-mails followed the next day. Both were follow-
ups on phone conversations. In one, Fahey joked about "the
most intelligent, superior, handsome nationality—The Irish."
In the other, Capano made a passing reference to yet another
therapist who might be able to help with Fahey's anorexia and
boyishly told Fahey that "I wanted to ask you out on a date."
He closed with the lines, "Ciao. Te amo. God knows why."

Fahey and Capano would not exchange another e-mail
message for the next two and a half months. Capano claimed
Anne Marie wanted to distance herself from him because he
had begun insisting that she check into a clinic to deal with her
anorexia.

Fahey's friends say she was aware of her eating disorder
and trying, through Michele Sullivan, to come to grips with it.
In that scenario, Capano was not part of the solution, he was
the problem.

On Valentine's Day, a large bouquet of red roses arrived at the governor's office in Wilmington for Annie Marie. They were from Scanlan. She smiled and placed them on her desk for everyone to see. A short time later, another bouquet of roses arrived for her. They were from Capano.

She threw them in the trash.

16

As he tried to piece together the last months of Anne Marie Fahey's life, Colm Connolly was struck again and again by what had taken place between Valentine's Day, when Fahey threw Capano's roses in the trash, and June 27, when she sat across from him at a table in Ristorante Panorama.

Tracking Capano and Fahey for those four months would prove to be the key to the investigation. It was all there. The e-mails provided a road map of sorts, but as always when it came to Fahey, there were gaps in the written correspondence. There was no record of any e-mail between Fahey and Capano from February 13 until April 24, when the messages picked up again as if nothing had happened.

Kim Horstmann said this had been a "quiet" time, when Capano had backed off. When the correspondence resumed in April, Fahey believed she and Tom had reached an understanding: They were going to be friends.

Capano, of course, had other things in mind. Connolly, Donovan, and Alpert were convinced that by that point, Capano had set a definite course of action. Either he would have Fahey, or no one would.

Gerry Capano got a call from his brother sometime early in February 1996. Tom asked him if he could meet him outside his law office in downtown Wilmington. There was something he needed to talk to him about, but not over the phone.

Around lunchtime that day, Gerry's pickup truck was double-parked outside the high-rise office building in the 200 block of Delaware Avenue where Saul, Ewing was headquartered. Tom sauntered out of the building and got in the passenger side of the truck. After some brief small talk, he told Gerry he needed a favor. He had to borrow $8,000. He needed it in cash. Then he told Gerry about the extortion and the "crazy woman" he had been dating and about her boyfriend. He also told Gerry he needed to borrow a gun. He said he was afraid, living alone on Grant Avenue, and needed it for protection.

Though Gerry suggested a shotgun, Tom insisted he needed a handgun. He also asked Gerry if he knew anyone who could "break someone's legs." Gerry said he might. He asked his brother if he was in trouble. Tom again mentioned the "crazy girl" and her "boyfriend." He said in addition to demanding money, they were threatening his children.

"If they hurt my kids, I'll kill them," Tom said.

A few days later, Gerry cashed a personal check for $8,300. He kept three hundred for himself—pocket money—and gave his brother the eight grand. He also brought him a pistol, a ten-millimeter Colt still in its original gun case.

The day before and the day after Gerry cashed his check, Tom Capano cashed two checks of his own, one for $8,000 and the other for $9,000.

"Why did he need twenty-five thousand dollars in cash?" Connolly asked Alpert and Donovan during one of their many brainstorming sessions.

And why did part of the money come from Gerry?

In tracking Capano's finances, the investigators discovered that within a week of generating the cash, Capano had written an $8,000 check *to* Gerry. He had paid his brother back almost immediately.

Connolly had worked enough financial cases to surmise that Capano was trying to get around the banking laws that required disclosure of withdrawals and deposits in excess of $10,000—a technique called structuring. Capano thought that by writing two checks and borrowing cash from Gerry, he would avoid raising any questions at his bank. In retrospect, given what happened, the moves looked even more suspicious than if he had simply withdrawn $25,000 from his own account.

Capano later admitted that he didn't want anyone to know about the money. He said he used the cash—a stack of large bills—to confront Anne Marie. It was, he said, part of a desperate attempt on his part to force her to sign herself into a treatment center to deal with her anorexia. In fact, he said, it was his harping on her—his insistence that she deal with her problem—that had caused the split that occurred in February and lasted until April. Capano said he confronted Annie with the money, which he said was enough to cover one month in a treatment facility. He said he threw the cash on the table in front of her during an argument in her apartment. This, he said, was done for dramatic effect. Throwing a check on the table, he argued, would not have made the point as well.

Fahey looked at the money, Capano claimed, then scooped it up and threw it back in his face.

Capano said he took the cash back and hid it in his home on Grant Avenue. Eventually, he said, he lent some of the money—about $500—to Fahey to pay for her therapy sessions. He also gave her money to have the crack in her windshield fixed and another $30 in cash one week when she was broke.

When investigators raided the home on Grant Avenue on July 31, 1996, there was still about $20,000 on hand. Capano said he had been using the cash for household expenses. He never explained why he didn't put the money back in the bank.

The investigators, of course, have a different view of what Capano intended to do with the money. They point to the Marandola incident back in 1980 and the discussions with Riley at that time about finding someone to break her legs or run her over with a car. And they compare it to his discussions with Gerry in February about finding someone who could "break legs." Tom Capano, they believe, had a different and much more sinister reason for generating $25,000 in what he thought would be untraceable cash.

"We think he was going to take a hit out on her," Donovan said.

"Given his state of mind at that time," added one of the undercover investigators, "I think he was going to kill somebody. It was just a question of who."

Capano's bizarre games with large amounts of cash constituted just one of the many strange developments that had occurred that winter and spring, as Capano mounted a desperate effort to win Fahey back even as he plotted her murder.

Fahey, meanwhile, had begun seeing Michele Sullivan, and for the first time since her treatment by Bob Connor she seemed confident that someone would be able to help her.

For Fahey, therapy was something like confession—but without the comfort of absolution. Instead, she imposed her own penance: anxiety, depression, and anorexia. Sullivan's goal was to reduce, if not eliminate, the feelings of self-doubt and help Fahey assert herself. Over the next four months they would discuss those goals, and go into greater detail about her feelings and about her relationship with Capano, whom Fahey eventually identified by name to Sullivan.

"Her fears kept her frozen a lot," Sullivan said of Fahey. "The closer she got to someone, the more she would obsess over the disappointments and betrayals of the past."

This affected her relationship with Scanlan, and may have been one of the reasons their relationship had progressed in such an uneven manner. While she told friends she wanted to marry him, there was a part of her that was certain he was going to dump her. It had always happened in the past, she reasoned. Eventually, like the other men with whom she had been in love, Michael would bolt.

Capano, of course, was another matter.

During a therapy session on April 3, Fahey told Sullivan she felt as if he were "haunting" her, that he was "trapping" her with the gifts he was always giving. Four days later she wrote the diary note about bringing "closure" to the "controlling, manipulative, insecure, jealous maniac."

But at a later session, when Fahey complained about Capano's harassment and Sullivan suggested that she contact either the police or the Attorney General's office, Fahey said such a thing was out of the question. She worried about the public exposure such a complaint might generate because of her job and because of who Capano was. She just couldn't do it.

On Saturday, April 20, almost two weeks after Fahey made what would prove to be her last diary entry, Tom Capano drove out to the Sports Authority on Route 202 just north of Wilmington. He walked around the large sporting goods store for several minutes before stopping in the hunting and fishing section and spotting the item that he wanted.

At 3:15 P.M., according to a MasterCard receipt he signed, Tom Capano paid $179.96 for a 162-quart white Igloo marine cooler.

Four days later, the e-mails started again between Capano and Fahey. The messages were light and breezy, their tone seeming to confirm the friendship Fahey believed now existed between the two of them. How the rapprochement came about is unclear; Fahey and Capano had begun communicating over the phone sometime during the period between February and April, and at some point her fears and concerns were trumped by her desire to please Capano and be his friend.

These e-mails were filled with light banter and a kind of casual, teenage-style flirtation. Sometimes they would write to each other three or four times a day, their messages usually short and touching on issues of little importance. It was almost as if they were trying to get to know one another again. From Fahey's standpoint, at least, they were establishing new boundaries for their relationship. In one message, Capano joked about having seen "her Lexus" on the street that day. The Lexus 300 was a car she loved. He had offered several times to buy her one, but she had always refused. Among other things, she didn't know how she would explain a $35,000 car to her family.

But she played along with the e-mail reference.

"Where did you see my car?" she wrote. "Please let me know because my Lexus was stolen last night right out in front of my estate."

In another he posed a trivia question—"Who owns Coach Leather?"–and asked about the cost of repairing the crack in her windshield. Her response was vintage Anne Marie.

*   *   *

Subject: re: Trivia
Author: afahey@gov.state.de.us
Date: 4/29/96 2:26 P.M.
Well look here Mr. Smartie Pants. The owner of COACH
Leather is SARA LEE!!! How do you like them apples? What
do I get for this discovery? As for the windshield, 3 separate
places quoted me 460.55. Exactly. I will call you later this
afternoon. I enjoyed our chat this morning. Thanks for mak-
ing me laugh and getting my mind off my financial problems.
Call you later, Annie.
P.S.–Nobody does it like Sara Lee!!!

They began going to dinner again, usually on Thursday
night. They would go to The Saloon ("think mussels in a white
sauce," Capano wrote in one e-mail), the Dilworthtown Inn,
Panorama, and La Famiglia—all their old haunts. He sent over
money, cash, to help pay for the windshield repair. She thanked
him, joked about the new twenty-dollar bills—"Monopoly
money," she called it—and insisted she would pay him back.

"She was comfortable that things had gotten to a normal
level with Tom," Kim Horstmann said of that time in Fahey's
life. "She didn't think he was a threat . . . as far as telling
Michael or exposing her. She thought that they had come to a
mutual agreement and they were good friends. . . . He wasn't
quite as obsessed anymore. There was a period of time where
he was very quiet and she felt a great sense of relief that maybe
now he's finally accepted this . . . that he was comfortable with
the fact that it was over between them."

If it was over, it would be on Capano's terms, not Fahey's.
That was what struck the investigators as they read the e-mails
and fit the messages into the puzzle. It was frightening to
watch it all unfold, even after the fact. Capano was clearly trying to be cute and charming in his electronic notes to Fahey.
He joked about the "Eyetalians" at St. Anthony of Padua, the
Catholic Church that they both attended. He referred to the
parish as "Saint Antnees." He tried to strike another ethnic
chord with an e-mail about *Riverdance*, the Irish folk-dance per-

formance that was all the rage that spring. He had seen one of the dancers interviewed on television and wrote to Fahey about the dancer's bright red hair and "incredible wheels."

He opened another front by claiming that his daughter Katie—who Anne Marie knew was his favorite—needed brain surgery, a topic he returned to for several weeks with both Fahey and Horstmann. On the surface such concern may sound understandable, but Capano was exaggerating wildly in a bid for sympathy; Katie Capano had fainted twice at basketball practice at school, but a medical workup showed no serious problems.

Capano also tried to use Fahey's anorexia as a wedge, a way to force his way back into her life. During a business trip to Philadelphia in May he called Horstmann, who worked for Smith Barney, the financial investment firm. Capano said he was in town and asked her to dinner. They met at the Ritz-Carlton off Rittenhouse Square.

"The main gist of the entire dinner was his complete concern for Annie," Horstmann said of that evening.

Capano told Horstmann that Fahey had lost an unbelievable amount of weight, and that she was going to be shocked when she saw her. He said he wanted to get her into a treatment program, and talked about an intervention where he and Horstmann and some of Annie's friends and family members might force her to sign into a clinic. When Horstmann suggested she call Robert Fahey to discuss the problem, Capano backed away. He suggested they hold off on that until they had had more time to think about the problem. He implied that neither Robert nor any other members of the Fahey family were really that aware or concerned about Anne Marie's eating disorder.

Then he told Horstmann how frustrated he was. He said he was still deeply in love with Anne Marie, but that she was sending him mixed signals. He said he had left his wife and daughters for her, that he thought she should support him in that just as he had always supported her when she had problems. Instead, Anne Marie was keeping him at a distance.

Capano said he could have any woman he wanted, that lots of woman would jump at the chance to be with him. He couldn't understand Anne Marie's indifference.

"Look where she comes from and I can offer her the entire world," he told Horstmann over dinner that night. "I could buy her anything she wanted. I have more money than I can spend in a lifetime. Am I crazy to want her? Am I crazy to be going after her?"

Horstmann didn't know how to answer the question. She had thought—Fahey had told her—that Capano was comfortable with the new relationship, content to be Annie's friend. Obviously, that was not the case. The obsession that Horstmann had seen several months earlier and that had frightened both her and Anne Marie was still very much a part of Capano's makeup.

"Do you think I should back away?" he asked. "Am I putting too much pressure on her?"

Horstmann jumped at the chance to respond.

"Yes," she said emphatically, trying to sound sympathetic, but in fact relieved that Capano had provided her with an opening. "I think you definitely should back away and leave her alone."

Capano, however, had other plans.

In the middle of all this maneuvering, while he was trying to worm his way back into Fahey's bed—and woo Marandola back into his life at the same time—Capano went on a business trip to Washington, D.C., with Debby MacIntyre. It was a two-day legal seminar like the one they had attended in Montreal two years earlier.

MacIntyre, ever the loyal and oblivious mistress, knew nothing of Fahey, the woman for whom Capano had left his wife and children; nor was she aware of Marandola, who preceded her on Capano's long list of extramarital conquests. She was just happy to be with the man she loved, even if it was on his terms.

That spring, however, he told her he needed her to do him a "really big favor" and that he would "really appreciate" her help. He said he needed her to buy him a gun. He said he was being extorted and needed some protection.

MacIntyre said she asked Capano why she needed to buy the gun, why he couldn't buy it himself. He told her he "didn't want to," that he only needed the gun for a little while, that he would eventually give it to her and that she could keep it in her home for personal protection.

It didn't make sense, but MacIntyre was in no position to question or challenge Capano once he had taken a position on an issue. In retrospect, there was only one question that needed to be asked, and it was the one that Connolly, Donovan, and Alpert came back to again and again once they finally learned of the gun: Why couldn't Capano, a law-abiding citizen, a member of the bar, a man without any criminal history, buy the weapon for himself?

MacIntyre's first attempt to make the purchase ended in failure. She went, as Tom had instructed her, to the Sports Authority, the same store where he had purchased the cooler. But she naively told the salesman there that she wanted to buy a gun for a friend. He quickly informed her that that was illegal. So-called "straw purchases," he said, were a federal violation. The law stipulates that you can only buy a gun for yourself and in your own name.

Embarrassed and afraid, MacIntrye left the store without making a purchase. But on Monday, May 13, the day after she and Capano came back home following their weekend in Washington, she tried again. This time Capano went with her. He picked her up during her lunch break, and the two drove out to Miller's Gun Center off Route 13 near the New Castle County Airport.

The gun shop, located about ten minutes from downtown Wilmington, is a squat brick building situated on the corner of Jackson Avenue and Route 13, a six-lane highway lined with stores, gas stations, restaurants, and, in the middle of it all, Our Lady of Fatima Grammar School. A red and white sign on the side of Miller's includes a drawing of a revolver and a long-barreled pump-action shotgun. On a chain-link fence next to the building is a sign for BERETTA USA and the company's slo-gan, NOBODY ELSE GIVES YOU MORE WAYS TO WIN.

With Capano waiting outside in his Jeep, MacIntyre went inside and bought a twenty-two-caliber Beretta pistol and a box of bullets. She paid cash ($181.99), filled out the required fed-eral forms, and walked out with her gun and ammo. She and Capano then drove about two hundred yards up Route 13 to

Arner's Restaurant, a popular area diner, where they had lunch. While eating a BLT and sipping her iced tea, MacIntyre asked Capano about the gun laws and whether she could get in trouble. He told her not to worry; there wouldn't be any problems. It was just between the two of them.

"People do this all the time," he said.

Capano drove MacIntyre back to the Tatnall School. Then he headed to his law office. He had to finish some work and get ready for that evening. He was taking Fahey to The Saloon. The date that night—the very day he got the gun he would eventually use to kill her—went very well. They had lobster and crab, and the next day joked about how fantastic the food had been.

Author: THOMAS CAPANO at Sers-Wilmington
Date: 5/14/96 11:04 A.M.
Good morning Annie Fannie,
Called you but Virginia said you're on the phone . . . Sorry I missed you. Are you tired? I am. Couldn't sleep after I got home so watched Letterman. Very funny . . . I called you at 6:45 this morning but got your machine. The message is that I forgot the carrots, spinach and bananas I got for you that were in the refrigerator. I was going to drop them off this morning on my way to the girls. Let me know when I can do that. Please don't waste all that delicious lobster. I gotta get it again and next time I'll eat it all. Talk to you later . . . Also, let me know about making pasta on Saturday.

Author: afahey@gov.state.de.us
Date: 5/15/96 7:43 A.M.
Muy buenas!
I received both messages this morning, but I have no idea what time they actually arrived over this way of the hood. Anyway, I did not see a lick of NYPD Blue last night. How was it? I can tell you that the lobster and crab was fan-fucking-tastic! I ate the whole thing. Well, I am going to try to get a good hours worth of work in before I leave (8:40) to go to Michelle. Have a Good day, Annie.

*   *   *

Author: THOMAS CAPANO at Sers-Wilmington
Date: 5/15/96 10:17 A.M.
Thanks for the email and for the call last night. I sent you a package so be on the lookout for it. Glad the lobster and crab were "fan-fucking-tastic." Creep, you coulda saved me some. Oh, well, I guess we gotta go back soon. I think maybe we're becoming regulars there . . . So, NYPD Blue was also fan-fucking-tastic and I'll tell you about it later. I'll mention now that Simone still wears that purple coat; Andy had a rough night (among other memorable lines he told Father Kirifides that God could kiss his ass); Donna's replacement is a ditzy black chick with a skirt up to her googy; lots of people used the word "asshole;" etc. Talk to you later.

17

They didn't look happy.

That's what the waitress said when she was interviewed by the FBI about a week later.

They had come in around 7:00 P.M. on Thursday night, June 27, 1996. Anne Marie Fahey wore a light-colored print dress and a frown. Tom Capano was unremarkable. The waitress struggled for the word, finally settling on "unfashionable"—not the kind of customer she was used to seeing in Ristorante Panorama, which rightfully prides itself on being one of the best in Philadelphia.

Located at Front and Market streets in the Old City section of town, the restaurant occupies the first floor of a five-story brick building that also houses the quaint, forty-room Penn's View Hotel. The restaurant itself is divided into two well-appointed dining rooms. In each, the walls are covered with murals depicting the rolling hills, lush countryside, and fertile vineyards of Tuscany. The second room includes a lavish, forty-foot-long wine bar constructed from highly polished mahogany taken from the pews of an old church. The bar boasts 120 different wines, each of which can be ordered by the glass.

Panorama is where the city's most powerful players meet for lunch, and where its lovers—married and otherwise—come for a romantic dinner. It is a piece of Rome set down in the heart of the City of Brotherly Love, a taste of Italy captured not only in the fine menu, but also in the ambiance of the setting. Panorama is not for those who like to eat and run. The food is to be savored, one course at a time, each washed down with a different type of wine. Ideally, the night should be long and filled with good conversation—conversation that picks up again over breakfast the next morning.

Anne Marie Fahey and Tom Capano were memorable, the waitress said, because she couldn't fit them into any niche. When an FBI agent showed her a picture of Fahey she recognized her right away, but she said the picture made Fahey look "much healthier" than she appeared at dinner with Capano. That night, the waitress said, Fahey looked "frail, sallow and washed out." Her hair looked "disheveled and flyaway."

Fahey, she said, seemed "sad and uncomfortable."

They had started with cocktails—a vodka Sea Breeze for Fahey, a rum and tonic for Capano—and then a bottle of white wine. The waitress recommended the fish, which Anne Marie ordered. Capano asked for one of the chicken entrées. They also shared two appetizers, the grilled calamari and the bruschetta. Neither ate much, and when the waitress asked if everything was all right, Capano shooed her away.

That was one of the reasons she remembered the couple. The other was Capano himself. His look wasn't right for the restaurant, the young waitress said. Black-on-black New York chic was the dinner style of most of the customers; Capano, with his large, horn-rimmed glasses, his barbershop haircut, his conservative sports jacket, and nondescript tie, "seemed outdated compared to the regular clientele."

Fahey seemed "extremely solemn" that night. She didn't say very much during dinner, which lasted nearly two hours; "barely touched her food"; spent much of the night toying with her wine glass. Capano was "definitely dominating"; Fahey was "very meek."

They passed on dessert, but Capano ordered a "very cold" glass of white wine for Fahey and a Sambuca for himself. When the waitress brought the check, Capano took out a credit card and slid it and the bill across the table to Fahey. The waitress said they left a few minutes later without saying much else. She remembered that Fahey, who had tabulated the bill and signed Capano's name to the credit card receipt, "left a very good tip."

Usually, she said, she is able to tell whether a couple is having a business meeting or is out on a date. But she could not figure out "why this couple was there." There was "absolutely no joviality or conversation," she said.

Fahey and Capano left Panorama around 9:15 that night.

The waitress, a young woman named Jackie Dansak who later testified at the murder trial, may have been the last person, other than Tom Capano, to see Anne Marie Fahey alive.

The specifics of what actually happened in Capano's home that night after they got back from dinner at Panorama will probably never be known. Only Capano is in a position to tell the story, and he has opted thus far to provide only half-truths and tiny pieces of the puzzle.

What led up to that night, however, is fairly well documented. Both Capano and Fahey had been on emotional rollercoasters through the months of May and June in 1996—rollercoasters that eventually collided.

One question observers have asked repeatedly is, Why couldn't Tom Capano just walk away? Why couldn't he accept Fahey's rejection? In the spring of 1996, Capano had MacIntyre. He was working on reestablishing his relationship with Linda Marandola, who despite her misgivings was once again seeing him. And waiting just off stage was Susan Louth, a sexy and attractive young Sharon Stone look-alike with whom he would soon begin an affair. Why did he have to have Fahey?

There are also several other questions—unanswerable questions—that continue to hang over the case. What did Anne Marie Fahey want? And what was she willing to give up to get it? A handwritten note she sent to Capano sometime in May underscored the conflicting messages and signals she was putting out at this time. If Capano was stalking her, as she complained, and if he was preying on her anxieties and emotions, then why was she continuing not only to communicate with him, but to offer him encouragement?

"Hola Amigo," she wrote.

> I wanted to drop you a wee note to let you know how much I appreciate all you've done and continue to do for me. You're a very genuine person.
>
> We've been through a lot the past couple of years and have managed (through hard work, determination and perhaps a bit of stubborn Irishness and Italian tempers) to prevail. You'll always own a special piece of my heart.
>
> Love you–Annie (Me)

A week after their May 13 dinner at The Saloon, Capano had pitched another trip to Philadelphia to Fahey. He wanted to take her to Victor's, a quaint Italian restaurant in the heart of South Philadelphia where the waiters and waitresses fill the gaps between the antipasto, the pasta, and the espresso by singing arias from famous operas. Fahey begged off. She said she was leaving for a trip to Cape Cod on Thursday, which was the night Capano wanted to go to dinner. She also said she hadn't been feeling well.

"My weight has dropped six pounds," she said in an e-mail to Capano that she sent on Monday, May 20, "and I nearly fainted in Church yesterday. I am starting to get scared."

While Fahey was telling friends that she was trying to break away from Capano—that his e-mails were annoying, that his attention was unwanted—she confided in him (and no one else) about her medical problems. And he, as she no doubt knew he would, jumped at the chance to play the role of the concerned and caring friend. In two different messages that followed, he wrote about how worried he was. He urged her to call Michele Sullivan to arrange an emergency therapy session. And since they couldn't get together for dinner on Thursday that week, he suggested a Tuesday-night date.

"It would be good for me and, at the risk of sounding pompous, I think you might get something out of it too under the circumstances," he said. "Please call when you can and let me know when I can call you. I'll wait to hear from you."

*   *   *

Author: afahey@gov.state.de.us
Date: 5/21/96 12:33 P.M.
Hey Capano,
. . . Please do not worry about me. Hey, I'm scared to death
that I am killing myself, and that's a positive thing, because I
am forced to do something to make myself better. It's kind of
a bitter sweet device, if you know what I mean. Tommy, I
know you want to feed me, but believe it or not, it's not the
right answer. I have learned through Michele and a lot of
reading that the more someone tries to get you to eat, the
less interested and more determined you become to do just
the opposite. I almost sent myself to St. Francis [a local
hospital] yesterday morning because of how weak I felt.
Believe me Tommy when I tell you that all of this is good for
me, because for the first time I am afraid that I am killing
myself . . . I'm ready to tackle this problem I have—whereas
before I did not see it that way. I know all you want to do is
help, and believe me it's greatly appreciated, but I also need
some time alone to work out a lot of stuff. I hope you can
understand all this mumbo. Anne Marie.

Fahey also told Capano that she had made plans to visit with
her brother Robert on one night and her sister, Kathleen, on the
other, and that it would be impossible for them to get together
for dinner before she left for Cape Cod. What she did not tell
Capano was that she was going to the Cape that Memorial Day
weekend with Michael Scanlan to meet his parents.

Over the next two days there were more e-mails and phone
calls between the two. In one, Capano mentioned the Cézanne
exhibit that was opening at the Philadelphia Museum of Art
and how he wanted to invite Robert and his wife, Susan, along
with Anne Marie and Kim Horstmann, to a gala private showing arranged through his law office. He also reminded Fahey of
a dinner date they had scheduled for the following Thursday,
May 30, at La Famiglia, and asked if Fahey wanted him to
invite Horstmann along as well.

On May 23, the day she was to leave for the Cape with
Scanlan, Fahey dropped off a book on anorexia and a note at

Capano's law office. She told him the book "may help you understand my disease a little better." In an earlier e-mail she had said
she was sorry for always crying on his shoulder. "Don't be sorry,"
he said in reply, "that's what it's there for. I want to help."

In another e-mail sent to Capano late that afternoon, just a
few hours before she was to leave with Scanlan, she told
Capano not to invite Horstmann to join them at dinner the following week. "I don't feel like sharing," she said.

"Smile, Capano," she wrote in closing, "I will get better. I
promise."

Fahey was being eaten alive by the contradictions and
conflicts that were now so much a part of her life. There was
no doubt that her relationship with Capano and her fear that
Scanlan and her family might learn about it were at the heart
of what was now a full-blown battle with her eating disorder,
a struggle that was tearing her apart physically. But other
than her therapist, the only other person Fahey was dis-
cussing the problem with was Capano—the very man who
was responsible for it. She was like a heroin addict seeking
help from a drug dealer whose only response was to offer
more drugs.

Capano's care and concern gave way to obsession once
Fahey had left for New England. In the middle of the holiday
weekend he paged Siobhan Sullivan, a Delaware state trooper
assigned to the governor's office. Sullivan, who worked closely
with Anne Marie, knew a little about their relationship. Fahey
had complained about Capano's unwanted attention, but never
told Sullivan they had been lovers.

When Sullivan returned Capano's page that Memorial Day
weekend, she was surprised by what he asked her.

"Have you heard from Anne Marie?" he said. "Do you
know where she is?"

Sullivan knew Fahey had gone away with Scanlan, but she
was not about to tell Capano.

"No, I don't," she said.

Capano hung up the phone, frustrated and angry. It had not
been a good weekend. Fahey had taken off without telling him

where she was going, and his plans to get Marandola to come to work for him had blown up in his face. He was losing control over the women he wanted in his life.

Early in 1996, Linda Marandola got a phone call from Tom Capano—the first she'd heard from him in nearly four years. He told her he'd had a rough Christmas, his first since separating from Kay, and needed someone to talk to. To Linda he sounded sad and tired.

Marandola was in a tight financial situation, working part-time as a waitress and collecting unemployment. Over the next three months Capano began to call her regularly. Eventually they went out to dinner, first to Panorama and later to La Veranda. In April she agreed to apply for a job at Saul, Ewing as his secretary. To sweeten the offer, he agreed to lend her $3,000 to help her cover some bills. She could pay him back once she began collecting a pay check, he said.

Early in May she went for a second interview and was offered the job of Capano's legal secretary. She accepted and was scheduled to begin on Tuesday, May 28, the first day after the Memorial Day weekend.

But on Thursday night, May 23—the night that Fahey left for Cape Cod—Marandola got a phone call from Capano that changed everything.

Marandola had an answering machine at home and had recorded a greeting that reflected her personality. "I'm not home right now," it said. "Leave a message and *maybe* I'll get back to you."

When she returned from her part-time waitressing job that night, she had an angry message from Capano. He told her that the greeting on her answering machine was "immature" and "unprofessional" and that she would have to change it or "the job offer would be withdrawn."

"I thought he was kidding," Marandola said.

In a series of phone calls that followed, Marandola learned that Capano was serious. And she decided she wanted no part of him. Capano told her she was being immature and "childish," that it was stupid to give up a $34,000-a-year salary over an answering machine greeting. Marandola refused to budge. She later told Alpert that Capano's behavior convinced her that she was better off not getting involved with him again.

"I told him what he could do with his job," she recalled. "I wasn't going to change my message."

She did not show up for work at Saul, Ewing on Tuesday. In the days that followed she was bombarded with a series of angry phone messages from her erstwhile boss.

"He left tons of messages," she said. "He said I had used him and that I was going to be sorry that I hadn't taken the job."

Two weeks later, Capano filed a suit in Wilmington small claims court seeking to recover the $3,000 he had lent Marandola. He said he was going to "fix her ass," according to a secretary who helped him draw up the complaint. A judgment was eventually entered against Marandola for the money. But by that point, Capano had more pressing concerns and did not pursue the issue.

When Fahey returned from the trip to Cape Cod on Monday night, May 27, she called Capano. At work the next day, however, after Siobhan Sullivan told her about being paged by Capano and questioned about her whereabouts, Fahey was livid.

"He's fucking stalking me," she said.

"You know that's a crime and there are laws against that," Sullivan said.

Fahey didn't want to hear it. She had been down that road before. It just wasn't an option. The publicity would be a huge embarrassment both to her and to the governor. What was more, any legal action would guarantee that both her family and Michael Scanlan would learn about her affair with Capano.

"I can handle it," Fahey replied. "I just have to end it."

"We can protect you," said Sullivan, offering an alternative that could have saved Fahey's life.

"She was ashamed because she had gotten involved with a married man," Robert Fahey said months later as he tried to analyze his sister's actions in the weeks leading up to her death.

"He held that over her head, threatening to expose it. And that prevented her from exercising her options.

"She feared this guy," Robert said, despite the tone and tenor of some of the notes and e-mails at that time. "He had political connections. He was a manipulator. She was worried about the impact on the governor's election. And she was ashamed and frightened."

Three days after returning from the Cape, Fahey had her weekly therapy session with Michele Sullivan. Sullivan was concerned with both her weight loss and her emotional state. She ordered a battery of blood tests and suggested that Fahey go back on medication to control her anxiety and depression.

"I told her to give me a week to think about the idea," Fahey said in a message to Capano after her session. "It's not one of my favorite subjects."

That night, Capano and Fahey dined at La Famiglia in Philadelphia, and the next morning his e-mail was full of the charm and warmth. He sounded, in fact, very much like a man on the make.

From: tcapano@saul.com
Date: 5/31/96 10:07 A.M.
Good Morning Sleepyhead,
I'm sure you're tired this morning but you gotta admit it was a great dinner. Thanks again for making time for me. Speaking of which, here's a thought: if you come home early Sunday . . . please consider making pasta with me Sunday afternoon or, if you prefer, dinner at Villa D'Roma Sunday evening.
Trivia: I assume you've seen the new Mercedes Benz commercials with the driving dream and the cascade of water (how 'bout that sexual symbolism!) Anyway, what's the song you hear and who sings it? Two hints: the name of the song is one of the lyrics you hear; the singer is dead, from Philly, Italian (there's a surprise), and starred in the movie about Enrico Caruso (don't you dare ask me who Caruso was and no, Ms. Smartass, he was not some bricklayer).
A friend called about playing golf this afternoon and I'm thinking about it . . . Please call when you get a chance.

*   *   *

Author: afahey@gov.state.de.us
Date: 5/31/96 10:19 A.M.
Sleepyhead is right! I got up at my usual time, but it was difficult. As for the commercial, I have not seen that specific one.
Sorry, cannot play on this one. You best get your ass on the
course! It's a beautiful day and you should consider taking
some time for yourself . . . My apartment smelled great this
morning. It was like being in a traditional Italian cocina [sic].
Thanks again for everything. Talk to ya later, Annie.

On Saturday, June 8, Fahey and Kim Horstmann attended
the wedding of two mutual friends of theirs.

Horstmann, who hadn't seen Fahey for several weeks, was
shocked when she saw her friend. She couldn't believe how
much weight she had lost.

"She was ghastly skinny," Horstmann said. "She did not
look healthy to me at all."

The next week at work, Anne Marie fainted.

And she called Capano for help.

He drove over to the governor's office and took her home.
He also bought a new air conditioner—hers hadn't been working properly—and installed it in her bedroom window.

Later, Fahey told Horstmann what had happened.

"It was because she wasn't eating at all and she wasn't taking care of herself at all," Horstmann said.

Still, the question remained: Why had Anne Marie chosen
to call Capano rather than Scanlan?

Horstmann said Fahey "was afraid to death of Michael ever
finding out that she had this problem. She didn't want him to
think that she was weak. She was aware that she was taking too
many laxatives at night and she wasn't eating, but she did not want
Michael to know because it would make her look weak in his eyes."

Capano, on the other hand, already knew all about it. He
was, Horstmann said, "more like a father figure to her."

Over Capano's objections, Fahey returned to work later
that afternoon. She said she felt better. Shortly before leaving
for the day, she e-mailed him a one-line message: "Thanks. I
will get better. Annie."

"You're welcome," Capano said in reply. "Sleep well now and for the rest of the summer. I know you'll get better. I just wish you'd let me help. Kind of like a coach, know what I mean?"

The Saint Anthony's Festival is one of the biggest events of the year in Wilmington. It is a weeklong celebration built around the June 13 feast day of the patron saint of the Italian parish in the center of Little Italy. The festival is an ethnic and earthy grand gala. A carnival of food, games, lights, music, and entertainment, it attracts busloads of visitors from up and down the East Coast.

As the celebration approached that June, Tom Capano swung into Italian overload. His e-mails included references to Liza Minnelli, Luciano Pavarotti, and Frank Sinatra. He wrote about his heritage and how his father and grandfather had literally helped build the parish. He said he was looking forward, as he did each year, to taking his daughters to the feast and showing them the handiwork of their forebears.

"I like to remind them of their roots," Capano said.

He also told Fahey that he was looking forward to seeing both her and Kim Horstmann at the festival on Friday night, and at the Cézanne Exhibit at the Philadelphia Museum of Art on Saturday.

Fahey stiffed Capano on both occasions.

She and Horstmann went on a double date to the festival that Friday with Scanlan and one of his friends. While walking through the crowded park area, they spotted Capano and his children.

"There he is," Fahey hissed at Horstmann before she quickly turned away and steered Scanlan in the opposite direction. Horstmann was sure Capano had seen them, but he made no attempt to pursue them through the crowd.

The next night he wore a look of disappointment when Robert and Susan Fahey showed up for the special private showing of the Cézanne Exhibit at the Philadelphia Museum of Art without Anne Marie. She sent word that she was sick. Susan Fahey picked up on Capano's disappointment, and later mentioned it to her husband. It seemed, she said, as if Capano was hurt by Anne Marie's absence.

The Faheys, Robert and Susan, were blown away by the evening. Still totally unaware of Tom Capano's relationship with Anne Marie, they were grateful for the good fortune and privilege Capano had bestowed on them. Tickets to the Cézanne exhibit, which had opened on May 30, were almost impossible to come by, yet they were taking part in a private showing that was one of the cultural events of the year in Philadelphia. Butlers served hot and cold hors d'oeuvres at the start of the evening, followed by a buffet "provençale." There were baskets of olive fougasse, pain de campagne, and baguettes; artichokes filled with chevre cheese; petit farcis eggplant; red snapper roasted with fennel, lemon, and anise; and herb-crusted tenderloin of beef with horseradish cream and cognac sauce. The dessert tables included madeleines au chocolate, poached pears in red wine, and gâteau à l'orange.

Capano was using every available tool to manipulate the situation and stay close to Anne Marie. He was sure the evening would place him in good standing with Robert and Susan, and that they, in turn, would mention that to Annie. In the days following, he and Robert would exchange phone messages concerning possible business deals and plans to get together to golf.

Both Robert and Susan thanked him profusely for the tickets to the exhibit.

That night Capano bought some prints, a t-shirt, and a few other souvenirs, which he dropped off at Fahey's apartment on Thursday, June 20, before taking her to dinner at the Dilworthtown Inn. On Saturday, June 22, Anne Marie went windowshopping with her sister Kathleen at the Christiana Mall outside of Wilmington and tried on the taupe pantsuit at Talbots. The next day she told Capano about the argument she had had; according to Capano, she said the only reason Cass was upset was because she couldn't fit into the size four that Anne Marie had tried on that day.

Capano called Talbots the next day and arranged to buy the suit. He wanted to surprise Anne Marie when they went to dinner that week. He also had ordered two tickets to a Jackson Browne concert in Philadelphia on August 5, and intended to surprise her with an invitation to the performance. A commitment to attend the concert together would be likely to keep their relationship going through the summer. Capano was now looking ahead, trying to make sure Fahey stayed close.

Anne Marie had a difficult session with Michele Sullivan on June 26. Her relationship with Capano and her need to end it were two of the things they discussed at length that day. Sullivan told the authorities that she believed Fahey intended to break off with Capano; that, she said, would have been the only reason she agreed to go to dinner with him. Finally, in what became one of the linchpins of the kidnapping investigation that allowed the feds to take over the case, Sullivan said she doubted that Fahey would have gone back to Capano's home willingly after having dinner with him in Philadelphia. If Capano had forced Fahey to go from the restaurant to his home, then Connolly would have the basis for a federal kidnapping case, for the couple would have crossed the Pennsylvania–Delaware state line on their return.

Anne Marie Fahey ended her last day of work by preparing the governor's schedule for the next day—Friday, June 28, 1996. Then she e-mailed the governor's staff, reminding everyone that she would be taking that Friday off; she would be back at work, she said, Monday morning.

As the evening of June 27, 1996, approached, Capano had the pantsuit in hand and the concert tickets on order. He also had the gun and the ice chest. It is impossible to determine if he planned to kill Anne Marie Fahey that night, or if something happened to set him off. But the last two significant e-mail messages exchanged by Fahey and Capano hint at a problem.

Author: afahey@gov.state.de.us
Date: 6/26/96 4:24 P.M.
Hey Tommy,
I would like to apologize for being such a downer today. I realize that your day has not been so great either, and I was not much help. I feel like some days I can handle my anorexia and other days I feel overwhelmed by the whole thing. Today has obviously been an overwhelming day. My appointment with Michelle was hard and in depth today, and quite frankly it drained all my energy . . . right now I am going to focus on

trying to get better. Sorry for being such a Doggy Downer today. Take Care, Annie.

Author: Thomas Capano at Sers-Wilmington
Date: 6/26/96 6:19 P.M.
I didn't get a chance to read this until after 6:00 and I assume you're gone and won't see this 'til tomorrow. I hope your sister went easy on you last night. I appreciate the apology but you don't need to worry about it. I just hope you know that all I want to do is help in any way I can. I promise to make you laugh tonight at Panorama, to order calamari and to surprise you with something that will make you smile. Please call when you get a chance.

Twenty-four hours later, Tom Capano and Anne Marie Fahey were sitting across from one another at Panorama.

18

What Capano said and did in the days immediately following dinner at Panorama were examined from as many angles as possible by those tracking the case. And Kim Horstmann again offered some of the best information.

She had had a series of phone conversations with Capano through late June and July of 1996, and at the urging of Robert Fahey, she had kept notes of what Capano said. In one conversation, Capano had repeatedly gone over what happened on the night of June 27, claiming again that he had dropped Annie off at her apartment on Washington Street at a little before 10:00 P.M. He told Horstmann he was sure of the hour because he got home in time to see the television show *ER* that night.

He also talked about a "turf war" among the various law enforcement agencies and how they were "screwing up the investigation." He predicted that he would become the scapegoat when they couldn't solve the case.

"I'm going to be the fall guy," he said. "All of a sudden it's all going to be my fault because they're going to be under pressure to come up with somebody."

Capano quizzed Horstmann on what she had told the police, and told her about "all kinds of rumors flying around," including one that Annie had had an affair with Carper when they both worked in Washington.

In another conversation, Capano tried to get Horstmann to

re-create what they had said to each other over the phone when she first called him on June 29 to tell him Anne Marie was missing. "My mind is playing games about the conversation we had on Saturday," Capano said. But Horstmann had the impression that he was just trying to get his story straight, to make sure that what she told investigators would jibe with whatever he would eventually say. "I felt like he was reading from a script," Horstmann said of that conversation. "I felt it was completely scripted. He went into such exacting detail it was almost ridiculous."

While Capano thought he was controlling the conversation, Horstmann cleverly managed to turn the tables on him during one critical moment, and by the time he realized what had happened it was too late. Capano had been going on about what a good friend he was to Anne Marie, about how they—he and Horstmann—were probably the two people closest to her. He told Horstmann about their e-mails and about their daily phone conversations. He mentioned all the things he had given her, and how close they had become. He thought he was Annie's "best friend."

"Do you talk to Annie every day?" Horstmann asked Capano innocently.

"Yes, I talk to her every single day," Capano replied.

"Did you talk to her on Friday?" meaning the day after their date at Panorama.

Capano became flustered and started to stammer.

"No, no, no, no," he said. "Ah, I was going to call her on Friday, but I went out for my morning walk and by the time I got back, I never got around to calling her. So, no, I didn't talk to her on Friday."

Horstmann was chilled by Capano's response. Capano didn't call Fahey that Friday because he, and only he, knew at that time that she was dead.

In the end, Gerry Capano was the key to the case.

As they marked the first anniversary of Fahey's disappearance, Connolly, Alpert, and Donovan kept coming back to that. Gerry was going to lead them to Tom. And while they were unaware of what Gerry had already told Dan Lyons, they were receiving a steady stream of information from Doug and Diane Iardella, who were now deeply entrenched in Gerry Capano's social set.

Connolly, with a sly smile, likened the undercover operation to the classic Paul Newman/Robert Redford movie *The Sting*.

"In the best con, the mark doesn't even know he's been conned," Connolly said several months after the trial had ended. "The people who were targeted didn't even know they were being swept up in this."

Friends of Gerry Capano's introduced him to the undercover agents who worked the case against him. But those friends were totally unaware of who they were dealing with. And so was Gerry.

By the summer of 1997, Connolly was fairly certain of what had happened to Anne Marie Fahey. In the broadest terms, he believed that Capano had killed her after bringing her home from Panorama. The murder weapon was probably a gun, and she was most likely shot in the back of the head. They also were fairly certain that Fahey's body had been dumped in the Atlantic Ocean. Gerry had said as much during one drunken, coked-up conversation as he partied with his friends.

"We knew as early as February that her body had been dumped at sea," Doug Iardella said.

In September 1997 Eric Alpert filed a revised affidavit in the Capano case, expanding on the allegations contained in the affidavit used to obtain the search warrant for Capano's Grant Avenue home back in July 1996. It was all part of the game of cat-and-mouse that Capano and his pursuers were playing.

Connolly was adamant about not leaking any information to the media. Not only were such leaks illegal; he also didn't want to tip his hand to Capano about where the case was headed.

But there were times when it was important to generate conversation and discussion in the Capano camp, particularly when the undercovers were out and about with Gerry and his wife and their friends. And there were also times when Connolly wanted Tom Capano to know the feds were all over him. Any time a new document was filed or unsealed, it created a buzz all over town. There were newspaper headlines and breathless television reports. Everyone started talking about the case, including Gerry and his friends.

Over the course of the investigation, Connolly's office would use that public filing system—a perfectly legitimate and legal procedure—to put information on the record. Alpert would revise his affidavit twice, each time adding more about the case.

In September 1997, for example, the affidavit was filed in conjunction with a request for a search warrant at Saul, Ewing, Remick & Saul. Connolly wanted access to the law firm's computer backup file in order to obtain any additional e-mail or telephone voice mail messages between Capano and Fahey, and to determine whether there had been any phone messages between Louis and Tom Capano around June 28, 1996.

In fact, Saul, Ewing was already cooperating fully with the U.S. Attorney's Office, and would have willingly provided that information without a subpoena. But by taking that route, Alpert was able to add new information about the investigation for public consumption. While hardly relevant to the request for computer information, the affidavit filed in September outlined the entire Marandola affair. While not mentioning her by name, it nevertheless provided a detailed account of the harassment that began in 1978 and extended through May 1996.

If nothing else, the gesture sent a message to Tom Capano about how thoroughly he was being pursued. There wasn't anything he had done that Connolly, Alpert, and Donovan wouldn't find out about. The affidavit, as Connolly had hoped, also sparked more talk among Gerry and his friends. And the undercovers were there listening. The time to draw the net closed on Gerry Capano was now fast approaching. Connolly's office was getting ready to make its move. It was of utmost importance to know where and when to strike. There would only be one chance. If they blew it, Gerry would run to deep cover. His brother Tom would make sure of that.

On a rainy Sunday afternoon that September a group of close friends and family members of Anne Marie's gathered in a tree-shaded alcove in Brandywine Park, the same park where fifteen months earlier they had searched in vain for any trace of her.

They stood around a new wooden bench nestled at the bottom of a sloping hill not far from Brandywine Creek. The creek dropped slightly at that point, and in the background there was the constant and pleasant sound of water running over rocks.

Those who knew Anne Marie best said it was the kind of place she would come to when she wanted to be alone to read or to "sort things out," as she often did. The bench had been placed there and dedicated to her memory by the friends and family members who had gathered there that day. A plaque fastened to it reads: ANNE MARIE SINEAD FAHEY, IN OUR HEARTS FOREVER, TE QUEREMOS, GOD BLESS, FAMILY & FRIENDS, 1997.

Jackie Steinhoff and her sister were two of the originators of the idea. They, like members of the Fahey family, were sadly convinced by the fall of 1997 that they would never be able to bury Anne Marie, that there would never be a cemetery plot they could visit. And so they created their own memorial.

"It's a nice place to kind of go and be with her," Steinhoff said a few weeks after the bench was dedicated.

The Faheys were touched.

"Nothing can ever make up for what we lost," Robert Fahey said of the memorial. "There are days when it's debilitating. . . . It's horrible that she has died, but not having the opportunity to say goodbye and bury her, that's been the hardest thing."

Most of the Faheys were seeing therapists of their own by then, in an attempt to deal with the trauma—the lack of "closure," in the parlance of the 1990s—and to cope with the unresolved and in many ways unresolvable feelings of anger and guilt and depression.

"You have this strong need and desire to have some kind of impact," Robert Fahey said of the feelings of helplessness that overwhelmed him during the long and at times tedious investigation. "You want to do the right thing for your sister. But at the end of the day, when the question is, 'Did I have an impact?' the answer is, 'Not a lot.'"

So it was the little things—like the memorial bench, like a special Mass celebrated on her birthday or the anniversary of her disappearance, like raising money for two children's charities that were her favorites—that got the Faheys through the days and the nights.

"It wasn't much," Robert Fahey said sadly. "But it helped us get up in the morning and go to sleep at night."

The raid came out of the blue and signaled the beginning of the end of the investigation. At around 7:30 P.M. on Wednesday, October 8, 1997, agents with the FBI and Bureau of Alcohol, Tobacco and Firearms hit Gerry Capano's house on Emma Court. Fifteen to twenty federal officers swept through the house while Bob Donovan, relishing the moment, held Gerry at gunpoint in his garage. The raid had been coordinated by Doug and Diane Iardella. Doug sat in a car with Connolly outside the house. Diane was poised to take possession of the firearms, which authorities knew they would be confiscating that night. They also scooped up small quantities of cocaine and marijuana, which they expected to find.

"Gerry was planning a little party," Doug Iardella said.

Gerry Capano would later admit that at that time he was using between two and four grams of cocaine a week, a habit that could cost him anywhere from $600 to $800 a month. Throw in the cost for the booze, the broads, the hotel rooms, and the lavish parties, and Gerry was dropping a few grand each month to live the good life.

On the night of the raid, Gerry was livid. The feds took twenty-one weapons out of his house—pistols, rifles, shotguns. Some of them were antiques that had been given to him by his father. All were registered. He was, after all, an avid hunter. But possession of firearms by a drug user was a federal offense, one that could carry a penalty of up to ten years in prison.

And Connolly was prepared to prove that Gerry was a notorious drug user.

The net had begun to tighten.

During the raid, authorities let Gerry's wife, Michelle, and their two small children leave the house. She put them in her car and drove over to her mother-in-law's home on Weldin Road. Within minutes, Tom Capano was on the phone to Charles Oberly, his lawyer. Oberly showed up, but since he wasn't Gerry's own lawyer he had no special standing to help him get into Gerry Capano's house. Watching from a car parked in the street, Connolly also noticed Marguerite Capano's white

Mercedes drive by several times. He couldn't see inside the vehicle, but he was certain Tom Capano was behind the wheel.

Gerry, meanwhile, was on the floor of his garage with his hands cuffed behind his back. Allowed one phone call, he asked Donovan to dial Dan Lyons's number.

"Dan, this is Gerry," Capano said when Lyons picked up his phone.

"Gerry, how ya doin'?" Lyons asked.

"Fine," Gerry said sarcastically, "except I'm lying on the floor of my garage with my hands cuffed behind my back, a gun to my head and thirty FBI agents are rummaging through the house."

"Let me talk to one of the agents," said Lyons.

The raid that night generated another wave of publicity. Gerry was not arrested, but his guns and his pickup truck were seized. It was the first phase in a multipronged push to get him to come in and tell what he knew. A few days later, the Delaware Division of Family Services, citing reports of guns and drugs in the house, opened an investigation into whether Gerry and his wife were fit parents. That investigation, which Connolly said his office had nothing to do with, went nowhere and was quickly abandoned.

A few days later, however, there was a second, less publicized raid. Donovan and Alpert seized a rifle from Eddie Del Collo, a close friend of Gerry's. Del Collo was a convicted felon, and the rifle in his possession had been purchased by Gerry Capano—a classic straw buy, the kind the Sports Authority gun salesman had warned Debby MacIntyre about. It was illegal to buy a gun and give it to anyone else; buying it for a convicted felon who couldn't otherwise qualify for a gun permit was an even greater offense.

Connolly was boxing Gerry Capano in. Lyons knew it. Gerry Capano knew it. And Tom Capano knew it.

A few weeks after the raid on Gerry's house, Tom was with Louis at Pala's, a restaurant they frequented in Little Italy, to celebrate Louis's birthday. The Pala and Capano families had been friendly for years. The owners of the restaurant had been close to Tom's father and grandfather, and found it hard to believe what the papers were saying about Tom. There were, in fact, several old-line families from Little Italy who supported Capano almost until the end, refusing to believe that the oldest son of such a fine man as Louis Capano Sr. could be involved in such a heinous crime. There were even some who blamed Anne Marie Fahey, calling her a *"puttana"*—whore— and arguing that she had brought everything on herself by dating a married man.

During the party that night, Tom and Louis discussed the raid and the reports that drugs had been found in Gerry's house.

Tom Capano, who had put both his brothers in the middle of a murder investigation, told Louis, "I'm not going to accept responsibility for Gerry using drugs. He's on his own."

Louis tried to explain that Gerry was under tremendous pressure, that he was an emotional wreck, that the drugs were his way of trying to cope.

"Gerry's not gonna make it," Louis said.

Tom didn't want to hear it.

"Tell him to grow up and be a man," he said.

In the aftermath of the raid, Connolly sent out more than a dozen new subpoenas. Everyone who partied with Gerry, it seemed, was being called into the grand jury. All his close friends had gotten paper. So had his wife. The questions they were asked made it clear that the feds had been watching for quite a while. They knew about the parties and the drugs and the wild nights at the strip clubs in Philadelphia.

The undercovers, still in place, picked up more information as those called before the grand jury sipped beers in local bars and recounted the experience. Gerry was beside himself. He felt responsible for what was happening to his friends. He knew Del Collo could be seriously jammed up because of the gun. He knew several other friends could have problems because of the coke and marijuana. And he also knew—or at least suspected—that the feds were playing with his head. He knew, for example, that two women with whom he had had more than a passing acquaintance had been subpoenaed to appear on the same day as his wife. All three women waited together before they were called individually before the investigating panel. Michelle was unaware of who the women were. Gerry knew them well.

At the end of October, Gerry met with Lyons one last time. Lyons held nothing back. The former federal prosecutor knew how the game was played; he knew that his client had only one option. The pressure would continue to mount. Taken to its logical conclusion, Gerry would be indicted on gun and drug charges. His friends would either be charged or would be forced to testify against him.

"You're no longer bleeding," Lyons told Gerry Capano that afternoon. "You're hemorrhaging. What do you want to do?"

"Make a deal," Gerry said.

19

They arrested Tom Capano on Interstate 95 outside of Wilmington, as he was driving his brother Joe and Joe's wife to Philadelphia International Airport for a trip the couple had planned to Florida.

The FBI agents tailing Capano that morning were not aware of the vacation plans, and thought their target might be trying to flee. They put in a frantic call to Connolly, who had Louis and Gerry in front of a grand jury that morning. Connolly's beeper went off with a coded "911" signal on Wednesday, November 12, at a little after 10:00 A.M. Connolly returned the agents' call; when he heard their concerns, he ordered them to pick up Capano.

In less than a minute they pulled up alongside Capano's Jeep, ordered him to pull over, and placed him under arrest. Capano wasn't surprised. For months his lawyers had been saying it wasn't a question of if, but when. They said they were ready, even anxious, to confront the allegations, to blow away the ugly clouds of rumor, gossip, and innuendo based solely on unsubstantiated circumstantial evidence that had dogged their client for more than a year.

"Tom's been living in his own personal hell," PR consultant J. Brian Murphy had said just two days earlier.

In a way, Tom Capano welcomed the handcuffs that were snapped onto his wrists that morning. Still supremely confident in his ability to beat the case, he wanted things to move forward.

They drove him back to the U.S. Attorney's Office in downtown Wilmington and spirited him in through a back door. But a UPS deliveryman had spotted Capano being led out of the car in handcuffs and called a local reporter; word of Capano's arrest was on the streets before he had even been formally charged.

Capano's lawyers, Charles Oberly and Joe Hurley, had gotten calls and were already waiting for him when he was brought in. They sat at a table in one of the conference rooms. Connolly, Richard Andrews, Alpert, and Donovan sat across from them. Connolly outlined the case and the reason for the arrest. He played two tapes, one in which Gerry Capano told about the boat trip on the morning of June 28, 1996, and another in which Louis described how Tom had asked him to lie in his previous appearances before the grand jury—and how, at Tom's request, he had gotten rid of the bloody sofa that had been placed in the construction site Dumpster.

Tom Capano showed no emotion as he listened to the words of his brothers.

"You're gonna believe them?" Capano said disdainfully after the taped statements of Gerry and Louis had been played.

They were liars, his lawyers would say later, who had been pressured by the federal government, overwhelmed by the massive power of the U.S. Justice Department, the Internal Revenue Service, the Drug Enforcement Administration, and the Bureau of Alcohol, Tobacco and Firearms, all of whom had been called into the case.

Connolly eyed Capano from across the table, taking the measure of the man. It had taken seventeen months to get him into that seat, and Connolly wanted him to know that he wouldn't be able to just walk away. As the session was ending and authorities were preparing to transport Capano to the Gander Hill Prison for an initial arraignment, Connolly left the room. Moments later he came back, carrying a white Igloo marine cooler, identical to the one that had been used to transport Fahey's body.

The cooler had been purchased at the Sports Authority out

on Route 202 three days earlier. It was the last one in stock. Now Connolly was using it for dramatic effect, to make a point he was sure Capano, a former prosecutor, would understand. There was nothing Capano had done that Connolly, Donovan, and Alpert didn't know about. There was nothing he could hide. They had gone and would go wherever they had to go to make the case. Any shred of evidence that was out there, they would find. Any witness who could offer even the smallest detail, they would question.

Capano shrugged. It was a meaningless gesture, grandstanding. It didn't prove anything. As he was being led away to prison, Connolly caught his eye. The last time they had been in each other's presence was back in September 1996, when Capano, playing the role of an outraged and protective father, had chided Connolly for forcing his teenage daughter Christine to appear before a grand jury.

"How do you sleep at night?" Capano had asked disdainfully as he escorted his daughter to court that day. Connolly had ignored the question. But now, as Capano was being led away in handcuffs, Connolly looked directly at him. "By the way," the prosecutor said, "I sleep very well at night."

The arrest had been set in motion two weeks earlier, when Gerry Capano told Dan Lyons to work out a deal with the government. Lyons said he would place a call to Connolly's office, but he wanted Gerry to understand what was involved.

"If you make the decision to go in," he said, "you have to make a full disclosure. You can't hold anything back. If you do, it will come back and bite you in the ass."

Lyons knew from discussions he'd had with Louis Capano's lawyers that there were certain things Gerry had told Louis that he hadn't told him, things that were relevant and important to the investigation. "If you're holding anything back to protect your brother, you're making a big mistake," Lyons told Gerry. Gerry looked away.

Lyons repeated what he had said during several earlier meetings.

"I don't care about Tom Capano. My only loyalty is to you. Is there anything else that I need to know? Did your brother ever talk to you about killing someone and using your boat to get rid of the body?"

Gerry leaned forward in his chair and let out a big sigh. His head sagged and he stared at the floor.

"I think Tom mighta said something like that before [the morning of June 28]," Gerry said in a slow, halting voice. "Maybe he said it. Possibly he said it."

Lyons pressed Gerry on the issue, which he knew was crucial to the case. It went to the question of premeditation. If Tom Capano had planned in advance to kill Anne Marie Fahey, then what many believed might have been a crime of passion could in fact have been a cold-blooded execution. The events that occurred before the night of June 27, 1996, before the dinner date at the Ristorante Panorama and the trip back to Grant Avenue, would determine whether Tom Capano could be charged with first-degree murder and whether he could be sentenced to death.

Finally, Gerry blurted out that Tom had asked him if he could use the boat to dispose of a body if he had to kill one of those people who he said had been extorting him and threatening his children. Gerry didn't remember when, but he knew it was months before Tom showed up at his home on the morning of June 28, 1996.

Lyons arranged for Gerry to take a lie detector test, which he passed. A few days later, he called Connolly's office and opened negotiations on a cooperating agreement.

On Saturday, November 8, he and Gerry showed up at the U.S. Attorney's Office for what amounted to a six-hour debriefing session. Connolly thought he already knew most of what Gerry was going to tell him, but he was shocked to hear about the cooler. He asked Gerry to describe it. In passing, Gerry said it was the kind of ice chest you'd find at a Sports Authority.

During a break, Connolly was sitting around with Donovan, Alpert, and Ron Poplos, the IRS investigator who worked the financial end of the investigation and who had studied all of Capano's credit card purchases.

"You won't believe this," Connolly said as he started to tell the story about Fahey's burial at sea, about the ice chest and the shotgun slug and the chains and the anchor.

"Wait a minute," Poplos said. "I've got a receipt for a Sports Authority purchase from back in April."

The next day, Sunday, November 9, Poplos was at the Sports Authority confirming that the receipt matched the purchase of a white Igloo marine cooler. Poplos bought an identical ice chest that day, the last one the store had in stock, and brought it back to the U.S. Attorney's Office.

Connolly, Donovan, and Alpert stared at the chest for a long time. They tried to imagine how Capano had gotten Fahey's body inside. They had a female FBI agent, a woman who was smaller than Fahey, try to sit in the cooler. She couldn't.

"It was chilling," Connolly said. "He couldn't have gotten her body in there without crushing some of her bones."

Louis Capano had been away for the weekend. He had been with his wife, Lauri, who was playing in a golf tournament out West. When he returned to Wilmington and learned that Gerry was cooperating, he called his lawyer and arranged a similar deal for himself. Louis's biggest disappointment, said several people familiar with what was taking place at that time, was that he didn't get to go in first. Or, at the very least, that Gerry hadn't waited so that they both could have gone in together.

Gerry signed a cooperating agreement on November 8, agreeing to tell all and to plead guilty to a charge of failing to report a felony. If he lived up to his end of the agreement—if he testified fully and truthfully—the government agreed to recommend a sentence of three years' probation.

Louis's deal, signed on Monday, November 10, also required his full and truthful testimony. He would plead guilty to witness tampering, admitting that he tried to get his ex-girlfriend, Kristie Pepper, to lie to investigators. Under the terms of the plea bargain, he would face a sentence of one year of probation. Both Louis and Gerry taped statements for prosecutors at the time they signed their agreements.

As Tom drove to the airport on November 12, he was unaware that his brothers were at that very moment waiting to appear before a grand jury. Connolly, however, had asked the FBI to place Tom Capano on twenty-four-hour surveillance once Gerry Capano had signed on with the government. One reason was the risk of flight, but the other was Gerry's concern about his brother's state of mind. Gerry said he was worried that Tom might try to kill himself if he learned that Gerry and Louis had given him up.

Gerry left for Florida after he finished testifying before the grand jury on November 12. He didn't want to be around for the firestorm that was coming. Louis headed for Arizona. Both brothers were immediately ostracized by their family, and labeled "rats" and "stool pigeons" by those in the community who still believed in Tom Capano's innocence. But even some of those true believers were beginning to have their doubts.

"I hope this isn't over a piece of ass," said one longtime woman friend of the Capano family who, like many in the city, still could not believe that Capano had killed Fahey simply because she refused to continue an affair with him.

It was, of course, and always had been, more complicated than that. It was about control and manipulation and getting one's way. And it was, most of all, about Tom Capano's arrogance; about his belief that status, power, and wealth equaled privilege and that the privileged did whatever they wanted.

On Wednesday morning, November 12, Ferris Wharton had just sat down for what he expected would be a long, tedious, four-hour meeting on administrative and policy matters when his boss, Delaware Attorney General Jane Brady, stuck her head into the meeting room and signaled for him. He got up from the table and started to walk toward the door, leaving behind the files he had brought into the meeting that morning.

"You better take those with you," Brady said. "You won't be coming back."

Brady and Wharton had been summoned to the U.S. Attorney's Office. When they got there, they were told that Tom Capano had been arrested. Greg Sleet, Rich Andrews, and Connolly provided an outline of the case for the two state officials. Connolly told them that while he could not share information gathered by the federal grand jury, he would be able to let them hear the taped statements made by Gerry and Louis Capano, the statements that were the basis for Tom Capano's arrest.

Sleet, the U.S. Attorney for Delaware, told Brady that a decision would have to be made, and made fairly quickly. Either his office could proceed with federal charges—in this case a kidnapping that resulted in a murder—or the state could take over the prosecution and Capano could be charged with first-degree murder. The first-degree murder charge was the stronger of the two, and the one best supported by the evidence.

Brady asked for some time alone with Wharton. Both knew that this would be a highly publicized and politically charged prosecution, and Brady was still reeling from the effects of another high-profile murder case that was not going very well for her office. A University of Delaware student and her Gettysburg College boyfriend, Amy Grossberg and Brian Peterson, had been charged with killing their newborn son and dumping the infant's body in the trash receptacle of a motel where the birth had taken place. Brady had announced that she would seek a first-degree murder conviction in the case, which was attracting national attention. But that now appeared impossible.

Lawyers for both Grossberg and Peterson had begun to angle for deals. Each young lover was apparently willing to testify against the other. And the bottom line was that there probably would never be enough evidence to support a first-degree murder conviction. Brady, even with the pleas that were eventually entered in the case, looked more like a braying politician than a tough prosecutor. She didn't want that to happen again with the Capano-Fahey case.

Wharton argued that it made more sense for the state to bring charges against Capano. He trusted Connolly implicitly. He also knew that if Connolly was recommending that the state take over a case that he had shepherded for more than seventeen months, then it was the right thing to do and the best way to win a conviction.

That afternoon, Capano was charged with first-degree murder. He would be tried on state charges. By the end of the week Brady also announced that she was accepting Sleet's offer to allow Connolly to be cross-deputized so that he could co-prosecute the case in Delaware Superior Court with Wharton.

Wharton, the veteran prosecutor who had willingly stepped

away from the investigation back in July 1996 because he knew it was the best way to move the case forward, was now back in the picture. He and Connolly were a perfect blend of patience and energy, experience and enthusiasm.

Capano's arrest was trumpeted in front-page newspaper headlines, and was the lead story on all the local television and radio broadcasts. The reports included details about Louis and Gerry Capano's cooperation with authorities, and sketchy accounts of Fahey's horrific burial at sea. Mention was made of the cooler, but not the bullet hole or the missing lid.

Connolly, Alpert, and Donovan were sitting around Connolly's office the next morning when the call came in. The three men were still pumped from the previous day's events. Connolly had written a note in the block on his desk calendar for November 12.

"It's over," it said.

But in many ways it was just beginning.

The call was for Alpert. Someone wanted to speak with the FBI agent involved in the Fahey case. As Connolly and Donovan looked on, Alpert began to scribble furiously on a legal pad.

"A bullet hole?" they heard him ask.

"The lid's gone?" he said.

"And where is it now?"

The Faheys had always believed there was a special force looking out for them and their missing sister. Maybe it was Anne Marie's spirit. Or the spirit of their mother or their grandmother. Or maybe the spirits of all three women had come together in heaven, or wherever spirits exist, to make sure that those left behind would have some peace and some satisfaction after the long, sad, and emotionally brutal ordeal.

Connolly had long felt some of the same forces at work. There were times when he and Donovan and Alpert felt as though Fahey was speaking to them, that her e-mails and her diary notes had been left behind deliberately to paint a picture and help them solve the case.

But this call went even beyond that. This was a *there-is-a-God* moment.

The guy on the line to Alpert was a friend of Ken Chubb's. Chubb owned a summer cottage down near Indian River, said the caller, and two summers ago, around the time that Fahey's body was dumped in the ocean, Chubb had bragged about this ice chest he and his family had found floating out in the ocean. It didn't have a lid. It was missing one of its handles. And it had this bullet hole through its side and bottom.

Ken Chubb had fixed the cooler up, said the caller. And he had used it when he went out fishing. He kept it in a storage trailer out behind his cottage. It was there right now.

Within minutes, Alpert and Donovan were in a car heading toward Indian River. Two hours later they were breaking into the storage trailer. They would not be able to contact Chubb until the next day, but that night the Igloo ice chest that Tom Capano had thrown off the *Summer Wind* was in Colm Connolly's office. Even after seventeen months, after two summers of fishing, the chest still had a bar code stuck to its bottom. The code linked it to the Sports Authority. The bullet hole was where Gerry Capano had said it would be. The original lid and one of the handles had been replaced.

It was the same cooler.

For six days it had floated on the Atlantic, heading west instead of southeast as Gerry had suspected. Instead of washing up on a beach in Cuba, it had been floating off Indian River during the Fourth of July weekend in 1996 when Ken Chubb found it.

The cooler had bobbed on the ocean's surface for nearly a week.

On November 20, 1997, Tom Capano made his first formal appearance as an arrested murder suspect when he was transported from the Gander Hill Prison to the Daniel L. Herrmann Courthouse on Rodney Square in downtown Wilmington for a preliminary hearing.

The proceeding, in a small second-floor courtroom packed with spectators, lasted less than five minutes. Capano, through his lawyers, waived his right to a reading of the charges. His lawyers said they would move as quickly as possible to secure bail. In the meantime, Capano, looking haggard and somewhat dazed, would remain in solitary confinement in a special wing of the Gander Hill Prison. Because he was a former state prosecutor, prison officials felt he could not be placed in the general population with the majority of the prison's 1,800 inmates. Instead he was housed in a special security wing reserved for protected witnesses and disciplinary cases. Inmates on the "1F" pod were confined to their cells for twenty-three hours a day. They were denied television and radio privileges, had no access to the prison commissary or library, and were granted the use of no more than six books per month. Capano would spend the next fifteen months living in the 1F pod in Gander Hill.

After the brief hearing on November 20, the Fahey family stood in front of a bank of microphones and cameras in front of the courthouse and offered their first public comments on the case. They praised the prosecutors and investigators, particularly Connolly, Alpert, and Donovan, and said they were confident of the outcome of the prosecution.

When they were asked what they thought of Tom Capano in court that day, Kathleen Fahey-Hosey, as she often would, cut to the quick of the matter.

"For someone who once stood tall in this community," she said, "he looked very small to me today."

The cooler was a key piece of evidence because it corroborated Gerry Capano's story. His testimony would make or break the case; Connolly knew that from the beginning. A piece of hard, cold, dramatic evidence to support his account was a godsend.

Tom Capano was indicted on first-degree murder charges on December 22, 1997. But even before the indictment was handed up, Colm Connolly knew two things for certain: If the case went to trial, Gerry Capano would be the linchpin to the prosecution. And the cooler—the ice chest that Ferris Wharton would dramatically describe as "Anne Marie Fahey's coffin"—would be the last piece of prosecution evidence that would be shown to the jury.

With Gerry and the cooler in place, Connolly and Wharton set about building the rest of their case. The investigation would continue right up to the start of trial, which didn't begin until October 1998. Judge William Swain Lee, a highly regarded jurist from Sussex County, had been assigned the case because all the judges sitting in New Castle County knew or had had some connection to Tom Capano. Lee would hear the case in Wilmington, commuting in each week from his home near Rehoboth Beach. The son and grandson of longtime Delaware politicos, the silver-haired jurist would prove an intellectual match for all of the high-caliber lawyers in the case, and more than up to the task of keeping Capano from taking over the courtroom.

One other piece of information brought in by Louis Capano when he agreed to cooperate became the focus of the investigators as the new year began. Louis said Tom had told him that in addition to the bloody sofa and some of Anne Marie Fahey's belongings, he had also disposed of a gun in the Dumpster at the construction site.

The team had long suspected that Capano had shot Fahey, and now they had some corroboration. But where had the gun come from? Gerry insisted that the gun he had given Tom had been returned. There was no record of Tom Capano buying a gun.

It was Diane Iardella who suggested that investigators run a check on the other people in Capano's life, including his mistresses.

"Let's see if any of them made a gun purchase," she said.

Herman Cryer, who worked with Diane over at ATF, got the assignment. He was told to visit all the gun shops in the Wilmington area and run a list of names against the purchase orders. Cryer started at one of the shops closest to the city, Miller's Gun Center out on Route 13 near the New Castle County Airport.

20

Tom Capano's last seduction began a few days after he dumped Anne Marie Fahey's body in the Atlantic Ocean. The target was Debby MacIntyre. For the next seventeen months Capano showered his longtime secret mistress—his Wednesday-night girl—with love, affection, and attention. Public attention.

Capano brought their affair out into the open, squired her around town, talked about their future together, said they would get married. Debby MacIntyre had been waiting for more than fifteen years to hear those words.

But there was more. Capano told her how much he needed her. He praised her for her loyalty, for the way she stood by him while so many other "friends" suddenly didn't have time for him. During this period, they were together four or five times a week. They talked on the phone two or three times a day. Capano acted as if he could not live without her.

And acted was the operative word, for unbeknownst to MacIntyre Capano had also begun a sexual relationship with Susan Louth, an attractive young legal secretary who worked in his office at Saul, Ewing, Remick & Saul. Louth and Capano were involved for about a year, from the summer of 1996 until she left Wilmington for a job on St. Thomas in the Virgin Islands in July 1997.

Just as she had been during most of her time with Capano,

MacIntyre was in the dark about the other woman. She bought into whatever Capano said, believed whatever he told her. Capano promised her that when this horrible "nightmare" was finally over they would leave Wilmington and start a new life together. He said he might give up the law. He told her he liked her idea of opening a bookstore at the Jersey shore. He joked that they'd have to live on her trust fund. His legal fees and his divorce from Kay would wipe him out financially, but he said that he would be happy to be a kept man as long as he could be with her.

The tradeoff was understood: *Stand by me,* Capano was saying, *and you'll get the wedding ring you always wanted.* Left unsaid was the more sinister but obvious corollary: *If you want the ring, keep quiet about the gun.*

The irony was that anyone who knew Tom Capano knew he hated the shore. He barely spent any time on the beach during the summer. Tom Capano was not about to become a beachcomber, not for MacIntyre or anyone else. But he was willing to let Debby believe he would do anything to be with her. And she was more than willing to take him at his word. She accepted his story about Fahey without question. He told her he had no idea what had happened to her. Maybe she had committed suicide. Maybe she had been abducted. More likely, he said, she had taken some of the money he had given her—thousands of dollars in cash—and gone missing. She was probably in some Spanish-speaking country, Capano said. She was fluent in Spanish and loved the culture.

All of it sounded plausible to MacIntyre, who wanted desperately to believe.

Once Capano was arrested, her position became more precarious. Now she was on her own, out there alone to think and brood and ponder. And while she may not have realized how crucial she was to the case, Capano surely did.

His lawyers had filed papers seeking bail. In Delaware, bail can only be denied in a first-degree murder case in which the death sentence might be sought. Prosecutors would have to show at least part of their hand in order to keep Capano behind bars pending trial. Gerry and Louis would be the key witnesses at the bail hearing, which was set for the first week of February 1998.

MacIntyre was the wild card.

As the hearing approached, it was unclear where she fit into the picture. Capano wanted her as a defense witness. In letters and phone calls from prison, he had entreated her to appear on his behalf. At times, in fact, it sounded as if Capano were coaching MacIntyre, telling her what to say. She might take some flack when the length of their relationship became known, he wrote, but she would have to weather that storm for their love. Her testimony was important. Among other things, he wanted her to "remember" the cooler, about how he had bought it as a gift for Gerry because of all Gerry had done for his daughters the previous summer at the shore. He wanted MacIntyre to testify that she had seen the cooler at his home on Grant Avenue and that they had discussed his plans to give it to Gerry once the summer season began. It was a thank-you gift for all the times Gerry had taken Tom's daughters out on his boat, all the times he had let them use his Jet Skis. That was the explanation for the cooler. Nothing sinister. Just a way for one brother to thank another.

He also "reminded" MacIntyre about how much he disliked the rug that was in the great room and how annoyed he got when pulls and tugs appeared in the fabric. That was why he got rid of it.

The government, of course, would argue that the rug was replaced because it had been stained with Fahey's blood—and that the cooler, purchased in April, was a clear indication that Fahey's murder was premeditated, part of a plan that Capano had put in place weeks, if not months, before he killed her. The cooler, along with Gerry's testimony about how Tom had told him that he might need to borrow his boat to dump the body of the "extortionist," both went to the premeditation issue. The only way prosecutors could make a case for first-degree murder, and get his bail denied, would be to demonstrate premeditation.

Capano, locked in his cell twenty-three hours a day, was desperate to make bail.

And so the manipulation began. Even from behind prison

bars and in isolation, Tom Capano was operating with the same arrogance and pretentiousness that had defined his life. He still thought he could do whatever he wanted, to whomever he wanted, whenever he wanted.

And he still believed that those around him were there to do his bidding.

He wrote MacIntyre letters almost every day. Called as often as he was able. Bombarded her with his words, his thoughts, his emotions.

The letters said it all. They were a verbal self-portrait, one that prosecutors would later use to convict him. Sometimes melodramatic and full of self-pity, at other times snide and full of bravado, Capano tried to play on all of MacIntyre's feelings, to push all the buttons from their seventeen-year history in order to keep her in line—to keep her, if not physically, then mentally by his side.

There were several crude and salacious references to their sex life, to "toys" she liked to use to pleasure herself, to the manner in which they liked to make love, and to the way he liked to see her being made love to. If Capano had once enjoyed watching in person, from prison he became a mental voyeur.

In one January letter he wrote about how he imagined her "naked right now on all fours with your dinner date making you come like crazy doggy style." Just thinking about it, he said, drove him to a "relaxation" session. In response she wrote about the new sex toys she had recently acquired. One, she wrote, "is sort of disappointing and very similar to the one I have already [that] . . . is starting to wear out. But the other new one is longer and thicker and has little nubs near the base.

"You can imagine how well that works," MacIntyre wrote. "I tried it out immediately. . . . The little nubs are a whole new sensation. . . . It lasted awhile and was wonderful."

In a series of letters written in mid-January, Capano complained about his treatment in Gander Hill. In response, MacIntyre tried to be upbeat and positive. "Hi, handsome," she wrote at the top of a lengthy note encouraging Capano not to give up hope. She talked about watching *Homicide: Life on the*

Street, the Baltimore-based television show that was one of their favorites. "This is the first of our shows I have watched in weeks," she said.

With Anne Marie Fahey it was *NYPD Blue*. Even Capano's viewing habits were compartmentalized.

In other letters, MacIntyre wrote about the "mess your stupid and ruthless, selfish brothers have gotten you and themselves in"; in response to Capano's complaints about his wife's divorce proceedings, she warned that if Kay received a large divorce settlement she would "certainly go on a spending binge, compromising your kids' future."

Capano responded by criticizing the prosecution—Connolly was a "weasel," a "Nazi" and a "liar," he wrote at different times—as well as complaining about Kay and expressing his concern for his daughters, particularly Katie, who, he said, was not coping well with the situation.

Underlying all the messages and correspondence during this period were two central issues. MacIntyre had been subpoenaed to appear for an interview with the prosecutors on January 28 and to testify at the bail hearing on February 3. Capano wanted her at the hearing, but told her to duck the interview, to have her lawyer file a motion to block the prosecution's attempt to question her under oath.

Ultimately, MacIntyre sat for the interview, but did not testify at the bail hearing. Capano was not pleased.

By the end of January, Connolly, Alpert, and Donovan knew that MacIntyre had been lying to them and to a federal grand jury about her relationship with Capano. They also knew about the gun purchase, although they had not yet confronted her with it, and about the three-way sex with Keith Brady.

There were also phone records showing calls between MacIntyre and Capano late on the night of June 27 and shortly after midnight in the early hours of June 28. This was the period in which Capano was believed to have killed Fahey.

The question, of course, was what MacIntyre knew. The answer would determine how, and whether, the prosecution would try to use her to make its case.

"We wanted to get a statement from her under oath,"

Connolly said of the January 28 session he set up with MacIntyre, "but we weren't sure what we were going to do with it."

Accompanied by her lawyer, Adam Balick, MacIntyre showed up for the session that Wednesday without any idea that the gun was going to be brought up. When she was first asked about it, she hemmed and hawed, and then fell back on a version of a story that Capano had worked out with her a year earlier. She had bought the gun for self-protection, she told Connolly, because of the number of homicides and rapes she had been reading about in the paper. She bought it back in 1994 or 1995, she said, but had since thrown it away. She was worried, she said, that her son, Michael, or one of his teenage friends might find it. She didn't want an accident to happen. So she got rid of the weapon.

Connolly pounced, producing the gun purchase record from the Miller Gun Center indicating that the twenty-two-caliber Beretta had been purchased on May 13, 1996, just six weeks before Anne Marie Fahey disappeared and the day after MacIntyre returned from a weekend in Washington, D.C., with Capano. MacIntyre stammered some more. Her cheeks flushed. She admitted that she had been mistaken about the date, but insisted that her reason for buying the gun was self-protection.

"Where was it now?"

She said she had thrown it in the garbage can behind her house one day early in June.

Had she given it to Tom Capano?

No, she said, but she might have told him that she had thrown it away.

"Was this before or after the trash had been picked up?"

"Shortly before," she thought, but she wasn't certain.

So he could have retrieved the gun from her trash?

He could have, she said, but she didn't know.

With that, Connolly produced a twenty-two-caliber Beretta identical to the one she had purchased. He placed it on a table in front of MacIntyre.

"What would you say if we told you Tom Capano's prints were found on this gun?" the prosecutor asked.

Connolly's bluff unnerved MacIntyre. She didn't know

what to say. More important, she realized—perhaps consciously for the first time—that her purchase of the gun put her in the middle of a murder investigation. At the very least, she was facing possible perjury and gun law violation charges. But you didn't have to be a criminal lawyer to realize there was the potential for much more. If Tom had killed Fahey, she could be charged with being part of a murder conspiracy.

At that point, MacIntyre's lawyer terminated the interview and advised her not to answer any more questions. It didn't matter. Connolly had made his point.

When he learned of the questioning, Capano tried desperately to downplay its import, insisting—correctly, it would turn out—that Connolly was fishing and that he had nothing of substance. He was certain, he said, that the gun was a prop and wrote that the entire session "sounds like a bunch of crap to me."

He chided her for trusting her lawyer, who had been snookered by Connolly into letting her make a statement under oath that could now be used against her. And when he learned of the particulars—of the story MacIntyre had made up about throwing the gun in the trash and the possibility that he could have retrieved it—he told her she had been "dumb," "extremely dumb," and "world class stupid."

"I keep saying they [the prosecutors] cannot be trusted and, unfortunately, I'm always right. . . . And as for them having the actual gun—which we doubt—so what? They've got to connect it somehow and Charlie doesn't think—and I agree—they can, even if it does have my print on it somewhere."

Without Fahey's body—and without a ballistics test linking the bullet in her head to the gun MacIntyre purchased—Capano, the ex-prosecutor, knew no one could prove that the twenty-two-caliber pistol was the murder weapon.

The bail hearing that began on February 2 was a debut of sorts for the principal players in what would become the biggest show in Wilmington in 1998. It was the first time Connolly and Wharton would work in court together; the first time Gerry and Louis would squirm on the witness stand; the first time the prosecution would lay out its case against Tom Capano. And it marked the first time Judge William Swain Lee would have a chance to take the measure of the legal combatants who would do battle before him.

Lee was a graduate of Duke University, and a fanatic about Blue Devils basketball. The son of a doctor and the grandson of political figures, he had earned his law degree at the University of Pennsylvania and had been the Sussex County Republican Party chairman before being appointed to the bench.

Lee was also something of a bon vivant who, when he took off his robe, liked to kick back and relax over a drink and good conversation. But despite his wealth, family background, and position, he said the time he spent in the Marine Corps after law school had been what shaped his character. A young man of privilege, much like Capano, Lee said the Marines taught him life's most valuable lesson: What you do means more than who you are.

Lee saw himself as a referee rather than a participant; he ran the courtroom, but not the case. He enjoyed seeing good lawyers in action and tried not to get in their way. The bail hearing at which he presided that February was just a warmup for the trial: without a jury, the rules of evidence were loosened, requiring the prosecution to outline its case rather than prove it beyond a reasonable doubt. That would come later, with the jury in the room.

For the defense, the bail hearing was a chance to get a look at the state's case and its key witnesses. Gerry and Louis were the stars, of course. There would be other testimony, but much of it was read into the record from grand jury transcripts. Fahey's friends and coworkers and her therapists were spared a court appearance, although their words were presented to the judge through interview reports and grand jury records.

The hearing took place over five days in a high-ceilinged third-floor courtroom of the Daniel L. Hermann Courthouse on Rodney Square. The patterns that were established here would be carried over to the trial that began months later. The Faheys sat in the second row on the right side of the courtroom. The row in front of them was reserved for the courtroom sketch artists, whose drawings showed up on television news reports each night. Cameras were not permitted in Delaware state court.

The Capano family occupied the first two rows on the left side of the courtroom. The press had the row behind them, and several seats along a side wall. The remaining three rows were available to the public. The courtroom held about 150 people. On most days, it was full.

Capano would be driven over each morning in a sheriff's department van from the Gander Hill Prison about a mile from downtown Wilmington. He would be escorted in handcuffs and ankle shackles to a holding cell, where he was permitted to change out of his prison garb into a suit, shirt, and tie.

Led into the courtroom by sheriff's officers, he would arrive each day carrying a cardboard briefcase stuffed with legal papers. He would nod and smile to family members and friends, then take his seat at the defense table, where he blended in easily with his three lawyers, Joseph Hurley, Charles Oberly, and Eugene Maurer, another top local criminal lawyer who had been added to the Capano team.

State prosecutor Ferris Wharton set the tone for the hearing when he outlined the prosecution's theory of the case in an opening statement before Lee. Tom Capano, he maintained, was a controlling manipulator who could not and would not accept rejection, particularly from the women in his life. When Anne Marie Fahey tried to break off their relationship, he killed her.

"If he couldn't have her, no one would," Wharton said, succinctly summing up the essence of the case.

Gerry and Louis Capano did surprisingly well during their stints on the witness stand. For the first time they publicly described their roles in the controversial and highly publicized affair. Both held their own during verbal sparring matches with the defense lawyers, who argued that they were lying and that they had cut deals with the government because of their own legal problems.

Gerry, his thick hair cropped short, looked even younger than thirty-five and appeared terribly out of place in the courtroom. Clearly uncomfortable in the suit and tie that he wore that day, he fidgeted during breaks and stared at the walls, avoiding eye contact with anyone. Louis, his silver-gray hair thinning but cut stylishly, wore a suit that appeared tailor-made and was much more self-assured than his younger brother. He had, after all, been through something like this before. He knew how the legal system worked. Both of the brothers said they were upset about what they had to do, that they still loved their brother, and that for the longest time they had wanted to believe in his innocence. Neither brother appeared to make eye contact with Tom, who stared at them and then away in apparent disgust during their testimony.

Both Gerry and Louis had been ostracized by their family. From prison Tom had driven the wedge in deeper, insisting that his sister and mother "choose" between him and his brothers. He also talked of using his daughters to bring added pressure on Louis and Gerry—each was a godfather to one of his girls—by having the girls sit in the courtroom on the days they testified.

The media swarmed all over the event. The Capanos and the Faheys were confronted by newspaper photographers and television cameramen each time they entered and left the courthouse off Rodney Square. The Faheys, as always, took the high road, walking directly through the crowd with their lawyer. Occasionally they would comment; more often they would politely decline.

Once they settled into a routine the Capanos also learned how to cope with the annoyance, but during the first days of the hearing they were confrontational. Joe swung an umbrella at photographers who snapped away as he tried to get his mother out of her wheelchair and into a car after one session. And one of the Capano girls made an obscene hand gesture to another group of lensmen as she and her sisters made their way through a media gauntlet.

Tom Capano knew it would be chaos, but he was willing to put his family through it. He needed them there. He also needed MacIntyre—but she was a no-show.

The prosecution opted not to call her as a witness, using Alpert instead to outline her January 28 statement and detail the various stories she had told about her relationship with Capano and her lies about the gun. And, in an ominous note for the defense, Capano's team was told that MacIntyre would assert her Fifth Amendment right against self-incrimination and refuse to answer any questions if the defense put her on the stand.

On Friday, February 6, after four days of testimony, Judge Lee ruled that the prosecution had offered enough evidence to warrant a first-degree murder charge and ordered Tom Capano held without bail pending trial in October.

For a while, Capano wallowed in self-pity.

"I'm drained," he wrote during the bail hearing. "Someone told me this would be very debilitating and it is. . . . I've now got a cold and a cough . . . Maybe I will be lucky enough to die in my sleep tonight."

He also was offended by his brothers' behavior. Gerry, he said, had gone to Thee Doll House, the swanky topless bar in Philadelphia he and his friends frequented, the night after he testified. And the next night, after Louis had appeared on the witness stand, he and Gerry and some friends had dinner at the Columbus Inn, a Wilmington night spot where many of the city's elite could be found.

"Basically they were celebrating after sticking me with knives," Capano complained. "I thought it was abominable and really in bad taste."

But Tom Capano was most upset about MacIntyre's failure to appear on his behalf.

"I am beyond shock," he wrote. "The one thing I always thought, believed, loved, was that I could always rely on you and your unconditional love. . . . I would have bet my life on your unlimited devotion and loyalty. Perhaps that's exactly what I have done—at least my freedom—and now find that I have lost."

"Put me behind you and move on with your life," Capano wrote later in the same letter. "I expect to lose the hearing and remain here 'til trial, be convicted of something at trial and spend the rest of my relatively short life in prison. I would like to die before trial. . . . Please don't write any more. Let's just make a clean break. I do love you, but will try to forget. Please tell the kids I love them. I truly do. I'm so sorry. Forget me."

*   *   *

Tom Capano wasn't the only Capano brother finding it difficult to cope with the effects of the bail hearing. While Gerry had held up well in court, he lost his composure a week later in a blistering, alcohol-induced rant to his mother. She wasn't home at the time, so he railed away to her answering machine; his message was subsequently transcribed and turned over to the defense lawyers, who tried at trial to use it against him.

Mom, this is your son, your son Gerry. You'd better fuckin' call me. I'm tired of being the bad guy.

If you don't fuckin' call me you'll never see me or my wife or my kids again. What are you pissed because I told the truth? Because Joe fuckin' Hurley couldn't break me down?

As far as I'm concerned, you have three sons. One is a murderer in jail for fuckin' life. One you hate, and that's Louie. And Joey.

Like I said, you can go fuck yourself. Did you really think I'd go to jail for twelve fuckin' years? If you thought I was bad on the stand God fuckin' help you. If this goes to trial I'll think up even more shit to keep my ass out of fuckin' jail. And I'll make up fuckin' shit as I go along to keep Tommy in there for fuckin' life.

I hate him.

Gerry would later explain that he was drunk when he placed the phone call. He said he had left that expletive-laden message for his mother on Monday, February 9, three days after the bail hearing had ended and after he had spent a weekend brooding about his situation. He said he apologized to his mother for what he had said. It was never made clear if Marguerite Capano had accepted that apology.

What is clear is that the events of June 28, 1996, left a mark on Gerry. A short time after the angry phone calls, he visited a tattoo parlor and had an artist draw two anchors on the lower part of his leg. The drawing, said two people who knew him, was not an act of bravado, but rather one of shame.

"It was a way for him to always remember what he had done," said one associate of Gerry's.

It was his own personal stigmata.

*   *   *

Right after the bail hearing, Tom Capano began to regroup. While he urged MacIntyre to forget him, she remained uppermost on his mind. If she wouldn't testify *for* him, Capano knew, then all he could do was try to ensure that she didn't testify *against* him.

Gerry knew about the cooler and the body. Debby knew about the gun. Both had been told about the "extortion." Combined, their testimony went a long way toward proving the circumstantial case Connolly and Wharton had built. Tom Capano's chances of beating that case hinged on attacking Gerry's credibility and keeping Debby out of the prosecution camp. He knew he would have to get back in touch with her. The melodramatic "forget me and move on with your life" line was a temporary position, a stall for time.

Still reeling from the publicity that had put her in the middle of the sensational case, MacIntyre was now becoming known as the "other other woman" in Tom Capano's life—and she didn't like it. She bristled at a front-page profile that appeared in the *News Journal* two weeks after the bail hearing, even though the article was a balanced and, in many ways, sympathetic portrait of her.

More important, on the advice of her ex-husband, David Williams, she had changed lawyers. She was now represented by Thomas Bergstrom, a tall and imposing former federal prosecutor and ex-Marine who, like Dan Lyons, was not part of the old-boy Wilmington legal community. Bergstrom's office was in Malvern, Pennsylvania; he did most of his legal work there and in Philadelphia. Capano, in a description that was both humorous and pathetic, would later go to great lengths to demean and belittle Bergstrom, referring to him as "that loathesome lawyer". and the "Malvern malefactor."

Highly regarded and independent, Bergstrom took over MacIntyre's case in mid-February and did exactly what Capano feared most: He opened a line of communication with the prosecutors. Within two weeks, Debby MacIntyre had made a deal. On February 27, she and Bergstrom strode into the state office building just down the street from the courthouse and signed a cooperating agreement. She agreed to tell all that she knew and to testify for the prosecution. She also swore that she had nothing to do with the murder of Anne Marie Fahey. If she was telling the truth and testified honestly, prosecutors said, she would face no criminal charges for her grand jury perjury or her illegal gun purchase.

Debby MacIntyre had made her choice. She gave up the gun *and* the wedding ring.

MacIntyre spent nearly three hours that Friday being debriefed by Connolly and Wharton. At that point, with the trial still eight months away, the two prosecutors were confident they had what they needed to convict Capano.

But there be would more. Much more.

And most of it would come directly from the defendant.

Tom Capano knew what was coming. In a series of long letters written to MacIntyre after she had hired Bergstrom but before she had cut her deal, he implored, entreated, and begged her not to abandon him. He tried to tap into every fond memory from their years together. He wrote about the death of his father and her mother, about how he closed her mother's eyes on her deathbed, about how he loved her son and daughter as if they were his own.

"I loved you with every fiber of my being," Capano wrote on February 24. "We planned the rest of our lives together . . . I thought you were my best friend. I thought I was your best friend."

Capano told MacIntyre he could not believe she would give him up to an "immoral, unethical, self-important weasel" like Connolly, but said she was obviously listening to the "blandishments of your new found advisors."

And in breathless prose that rivaled some of Fahey's most saccharine diary comments, Capano told MacIntyre that he never believed his lawyers when they warned him after the bail hearing that she was going to give him up.

"I was so secure in the constancy of your love I smiled at my lawyers when they told me during the hearing that Adam said you were abandoning me. No, I said, it matters not what he says. The love of my life—my soul mate—will not abandon me when I most need her."

Sounding both maudlin and desperate, Capano wrote two days later with an ultimatum. He told MacIntyre she would have to choose between him and her lawyer. Then, in typical dramatic fashion, he offered to fire his legal defense team as well.

"Lawyers are a dime a dozen," said the one-time six-figure corporate attorney. "True love is rare."

Shifting gears again, he wrote, "Debby, I'm going to beat this somehow and have a life with you. Please don't give up on me. Please don't show me by your actions that you don't love me now and never really did. Please don't betray me a second time. Please trust me and love me and show me that we are one and always will be. I love you with all my heart and soul."

Capano wrote that letter from his prison cell on February 26, 1998. The next day MacIntyre signed her cooperating agreement with the government. In a letter she told Capano she still loved him, but that she couldn't and wouldn't lie for him.

"I'd like to think that I know you better than anyone, but maybe I don't," MacIntyre told Capano. "Yes, we are soul mates, for me there is no way that can be taken away regardless.

"Often I wonder why all this tragedy had to happen? What happened and why are you involved—will you ever be able to tell me? I think not and that will always keep us apart."

It was the closest MacIntyre ever came to confronting Capano about Fahey's disappearance and death. It was a question she didn't want to ask because, she finally admitted to herself, she was afraid of the answer.

That night, sitting alone in his cell after learning from his lawyers that Debby MacIntyre was cooperating, Capano composed what he thought would be his last letter to his longtime mistress. He opened with a line that proved prophetic.

"My world just ended," he wrote.

21

The phone call came in on Saturday night, February 28. Debby MacIntyre sighed. She had been expecting it, dreading it and wanting it at the same time. She paused before picking up the receiver to push the button on the recording device, the way Bob Donovan had showed her. Now she answered the phone and heard the familiar, prerecorded voice of the operator.

"Bell Atlantic has a collect call from an inmate at the Gander Hill State Correctional Facility," said the message she had become so familiar with over the past three months. ". . . To accept this call, dial one now."

She pushed the number one on her touchtone phone.

"Thank you," said the mechanical voice of the operator.

They had told her he would call, and they had urged her not to talk with him. She had said she wanted to hear his voice, wanted to explain what she had done. A part of her, she said sadly, still loved him. That hadn't changed. So they had convinced her to record the conversations in order to protect herself, in order to insure that later he wouldn't make up some outlandish claim about what she had said to him. Already there were rumblings that he would try to blame her for the murder. It was important, for her sake and for the case, that there was a record of the conversations.

Connolly, Wharton, Donovan, and Bergstrom had worked

out the arrangement. She had gone along. She was told not to question him about the case, not to solicit answers that might be relevant to the investigation. And she was told not to lie.

She failed on both counts.

But she recorded four conversations on four consecutive days. When the jury later heard the tapes, it was not so much what Capano said but how he said it that mattered. The anger, the arrogance, and the manipulation were all there. Tom Capano was talking to MacIntyre, but everyone who knew the story and heard the tapes couldn't help but think of Fahey and Marandola as well.

Tom Capano couldn't stop himself. He had been at it too long.

Partial transcript, February 28, 1998:

Capano: What did you . . .
MacIntyre: I told them the truth. I told them everything that I had told them before which is exactly the truth, except at the end, uh, they asked me about this gun and I . . .
Capano: What did you say?
MacIntyre: . . . I was truthful about it. I said . . .
Capano: Don't say that, just tell me what you said.
MacIntyre: I told them that, uh, I bought it and I gave it to you. You wanted it and I gave it to you.
Capano: Why did you say such a thing?
MacIntyre: Because you did.
Capano: Why did you, why did you go in there and . . . say that?
MacIntyre: . . . darling, I told the truth . . . I mean, I can't lie. If I'd gone to that bail hearing and said what I was, you know, thinking of saying, it would have been . . .
Capano: Do you know . . .
MacIntyre: . . . terrible.
Capano: . . . what you've done?
MacIntyre: I've told the truth.
Capano: No, no. Excuse me. Do you know what you've done to me?
MacIntyre: I've told the truth, Tom.

Capano: No, Debby, do you know what you've done to me?

MacIntyre: I don't know what you mean.

Capano: Did you read my letter?

MacIntyre [sigh]: But I told the truth.

Capano: No. Stop that . . . Do you know what you've done to me? Do you know what you've done to us?

MacIntyre: No. I don't believe that.

Capano: You don't believe what?

MacIntyre [sigh]: . . . Look, I told the truth . . .

Capano: Will you stop that?

MacIntyre: I told the truth and that . . .

Capano: . . . one more time, I'm gonna hang up. What did you, what, what did you, what do you mean you don't be, what, do you know what this has done to us?

MacIntyre: Well, I still love you.

Capano: How could you? . . . How could you love me and then betray me?

The conversation went around in that same circle endlessly. MacIntyre sounded tired and resigned, like someone who was used to taking a verbal beating. Capano was seething, his voice sharp and full of menace. She said she felt trapped and afraid. And again and again, to his growing consternation, she said she couldn't lie.

Then she did just that.

"Are you recording this conversation?" he asked.

"Am I what?" she said.

"Recording this conversation?"

"Yeah, right," she said, trying but not succeeding to sound sarcastic.

"Are you?"

"No, I am not."

Capano then went into the same riff he had used in his letter the night before. He told MacIntyre she was "destroying" him, that she had "abandoned" him, and that the prosecution was going to use her to bury him. He insisted, in his snide and arrogant way, that she had brought all of this on both of them, that "nobody had made her" do any of this, that she had listened to the wrong people, like her ex-husband

and her new lawyer, and that what was happening now was her own fault.

"This is all your doing," Capano said.

Somewhere along the way he had struck a nerve, and now MacIntyre lashed back.

"Wait a minute," she said. "Whoa, whoa, whoa, whoa, whoa, whoa, now wait a minute. Let's go back to this gun. Hah."

"No, no, no, no, no," said Capano, the fear and anger rising in his voice.

"Who made me get, give you . . .

Capano began to shout into the phone, trying to drown out what he knew was coming next, "No, no, no, no, no, no, no, no, no, no . . . "

Against that string of negatives on the tape is MacIntyre completing her thought.

"Who made me get, give you the gun?" she said.

Capano called her again that night, but MacIntyre said she panicked and turned the recording machine off by mistake. She did, however, record three other calls, one each on Sunday, Monday, and Tuesday, March 1, 2, and 3, 1998. The tapes were taken each day by Donovan; after they were transcribed he, Connolly, Alpert, and Wharton would run them back endlessly, listening and reading, looking for any other tidbit of information that would solidify the case.

On the March 1 call Capano tried to smooth over the problems of the night before and reestablish control, but it was a struggle. He chided MacIntyre for not being home when he first called that night.

"I have less than fifteen minutes because you're so fucking late getting home," he said, before catching himself and quasi-apologizing for losing his temper. Then, as if reading from a script, he asked MacIntyre a series of questions, starting with, "Do you love me?" and "Do you love me enough to fight for me?" and ending with a rant about Bergstrom and how she had to fire him. Capano gave her the name of a new lawyer whom he wanted her to hire. Capano said it was a small sacrifice for her to make, but it would mean everything to him. It would be a way for her to prove her love and would get their relationship back on track.

Capano badgered MacIntyre for nearly ten minutes before she agreed. But seconds later she said only that she would "think about" replacing Bergstrom. Capano's frustration was obvious.

"Are you willing to do this for me or not?" he asked. "It's me or him."

Capano told MacIntyre he had to get off the phone, that his time was running out. He needed her to promise that she would do this. MacIntyre stalled, wouldn't give him a straight answer.

"Debby, please, I'm begging you," he said. "How could this be more important to you than . . ."

There was a click and then the line went dead. Capano's phone time was up.

The last two phone conversations were, on the surface, mundane. Capano was conciliatory and took the position that despite the mistakes and the anger, they would be able to get past their problems and keep their relationship strong. MacIntyre said she wanted that, that she still loved him. He asked about her children, about her battle with the Tatnall School—the administration was trying to force her to resign, she said—and about her medical problems. She was being treated for a thyroid condition.

He talked about the horrible prison conditions, how he was singled out for mistreatment, how the food was atrocious. He again mentioned problems his daughter Katie was having at home, how she was an emotional wreck and nearly had to be hospitalized.

He also asked on several occasions about a trip MacIntyre was planning to Sanibel Island in Florida later in the month. She was leaving on March 18. Michael, her son, was going on a school trip to France that was to start on March 17. Her house would be empty for the ten days she was gone.

Capano joked about how the thought of her in a bathing suit on a beach in Florida excited him. He told her how much he loved and missed her. He asked her to start writing to him every night again and said he would do the same. He promised that they would be together in 1999 and then forever.

"I need desperately to hear you . . . tell me how much you love me and need me," he said toward the end of a rambling March 3 phone conversation. "I love you, I love you. . . . Good-bye my love. I will write you today. Write me."

The burglary plan was laid out in minute detail. There was a floor-by-floor diagram of the home and a description of what valuables would be found in each room. There were directions, and the numerical code for disarming the home alarm system, and for resetting it after the job had been completed. The haul would include jewelry, china, antiques, and electronic appliances. What wasn't taken had to be destroyed. Tom Capano wanted them to trash the house.

Debby MacIntyre's house.

Two days after professing his love for MacIntyre, Tom Capano sat in his cell in the 1F pod of Gander Hill Prison and, talking in a whisper through his door, discussed with Nick Perillo arrangements to break into MacIntyre's home on the 2400 block of Delaware Avenue in Wilmington.

Perillo was a forty-five-year-old career criminal. A former drug addict, con man, and burglar, he had spent the better part of the 1980s and 1990s behind bars. But he was a charmer, a smooth talker with an engaging smile, a thick shock of prematurely white hair, and a neatly trimmed white goatee. Perillo's banter was legendary in the circles in which he traveled. Several years earlier he had turned his charms on his court-appointed lawyer, who ended up marrying him. The marriage ended shortly after he got out of jail and returned to his life of crime; his wife the lawyer had him arrested for burglarizing her home after they separated.

On another occasion, his own mother had called the cops when she spotted him and two other men carrying a refrigerator out of a neighbor's house.

Perillo, in jail on another burglary charge, was facing a stiff sentence under the state's three-time-loser law when he crossed paths with Capano. He had wangled a cell in the isolation wing. It was better, he said, than being in the general population, where inmates were crowded on top of one another, four and five to a cell, some sleeping on the floor. He had made up a story about another inmate who was out to get him because of some past cooperation with authorities. He told the officials at Gander Hill he needed to be protected.

He did Capano a few favors, made some telephone calls for him when Capano's privileges had been restricted. Capano, in turn, had had his wife Kay send a $25 money order to the prison commissary in Perillo's name. Perillo was one of several inmates who had ingratiated themselves with Capano.

Now, around 10:00 A.M. on March 5, Perillo was on his recreational hour outside his cell when he stopped to talk with Capano, who was still locked down. Perillo had a piece of looseleaf paper and a pen, and began jotting down notes. Capano said the house would be "easy pickings." Perillo said he knew some people on the outside who could pull it off.

MacIntyre would be gone between March 18 and March 28, Capano told Perillo. That was when he wanted it to happen. No problem, said the con man.

Capano told Perillo that he wanted to "send a message" to MacIntyre because of her decision to cooperate with authorities. He called her a "stupid, dumb bitch." He said she was another "head case . . . just like Fahey." He was worried, he said, because MacIntyre "could blow this whole case for me."

Perillo listened with a sympathetic ear. He knew he would need more than his own hand-scribbled note to get the attention of Capano's prosecutors. Three or four days later, Tom Capano obliged. During his recreational hour he slid a six-page, meticulously detailed set of directions and diagrams under Perillo's cell door.

"March 18–March 28, Earlier is Better" was the heading on the first page, which then included thirteen itemized steps for burglarizing and trashing MacIntyre's home, starting with the code for the burglar alarm. Capano, ever the control freak, left nothing to chance.

"Total of 5 TVs, best one in the master bedroom," said item number nine. "Must shatter floor-to-ceiling mirror on wall in master bedroom, absolutely required," read item ten. "Locate and remove plastic bag with sex toys and videos in a closet in the master bedroom or under bed," read the next item. Then, "all art is original and valuable. Must remove all or slash and destroy. Jewelry in top drawers of furniture in dressing room of MBR but may be hidden in closets or built-ins."

Capano also wrote that the burglars could take their haul away in MacIntyre's Jeep Cherokee, which would be parked in the driveway. The keys, he noted, "should be on rack in kitchen or in pantry closet with opener."

The instructions were followed by five pages of diagrams, beginning with a street map that located the home on Delaware Avenue and including a floor-by-floor diagram of the house with notations on what valuables would be found in what rooms. The drawing of the second floor once again mentioned the floor-to-ceiling mirror and repeated the order, "MUST BE SHATTERED."

It was the mirror in which Capano and MacIntyre used to watch themselves make love.

Nick Perillo's lawyer arranged a meeting for him with the prosecutors on March 11. He arrived with the directions and diagrams. It was his ticket out of Gander Hill, and his guarantee for a reduction in the sentence he was facing in his pending case. It also insured him a momentary but important appearance in the spotlight during the Capano murder trial several months later.

Capano's lawyers could do nothing but concede the burglary plot. The hand-printed directions and diagrams, including the numerical code for disarming MacIntyre's home alarm system, were things Perillo could never have come up with on his on. So the defense's spin was that Tom Capano was in a battered emotional state, was not thinking correctly, and had momentarily lashed out angrily at his former mistress. But he had changed his mind and had told Perillo to forget it even before the con man started talking with the prosecution.

More easily challenged was a second, more serious allegation that also came from an inmate at Gander Hill. Wilfredo "Tito" Rosa, a drug dealer who had begun cooperating with authorities, was also housed on 1F pod. He told authorities that Capano had promised to arrange for someone to pay off the $90,000 mortgage on his home and look after his wife and child if Rosa would arrange to have two people killed.

The targets of the murder plot, Rosa said, were Gerry Capano and Debby MacIntyre.

Like Perillo, Rosa took the plans to the prosecution rather than the fictitious hit men he told Capano he knew. But unlike Perillo, Rosa had nothing in writing. In the end, it was his word against Capano's: a cocaine dealer against a suspected murderer.

Capano's lawyers said that Rosa had fabricated the entire story in an attempt to curry favor with authorities.

If Capano was distraught and not thinking clearly when he plotted with Perillo on March 5, he had recovered his senses enough two days later to begin planting the seeds for his defense.

"Debby did it" was his strategy.

He raised the prospect in a letter to Susan Louth on March 7. And came back to it in more detail in another letter written ten days later.

Louth and Capano had begun writing to one another in February. She was still in the Virgin Islands, working for a law firm there. Capano's letters to Louth included a lot of self-pity—he said he had considered suicide after being denied bail—and his usual sophomoric prattle about sex, especially oral sex. Capano, like a teenage boy whose hormones were in overdrive, appeared to be fixated on the topic.

In his March 7 letter to Louth, he ripped MacIntyre for abandoning him, but than casually noted, "Well, at least she loved blow jobs and swallowing—couldn't get enough of it." He then asked Louth to talk with her friends and spread the word about the "jealous, older mistress angle" that he said two television stations were already reporting. The stories reported that Capano's lawyers were going to contend that MacIntyre had killed Fahey and that Capano was covering it up for her.

In another letter, Capano again ripped MacIntyre through the words of an elderly female cousin who had written him.

"She told me she believes I'm guilty of only two things: extreme stupidity and taking my pants down too often," Capano wrote. "Think she's right? She also told me she saw Debby MacIntyre's picture(s) in the paper and thinks she looks

like a shrew and a backstabber. Pretty perceptive. You think I
should tell her that she swallows and loves it?"

Later in the same letter Capano asked Louth to spread the
word among family members and friends who lived in the
Wilmington area that the Debby-did-it/jealous mistress theory
"makes sense to you."

As the second anniversary of Anne Marie Fahey's disappearance approached, her family set about the gruesome but
necessary task of having her declared dead.

There were several practical reasons for the move that had
to do with the settling of Anne Marie's estate. There was also
the emotional issue of trying to finalize what they all knew in
their hearts was true. There could be no funeral Mass, no burial, no cemetery plot. But there could at least be the legal
acknowledgment that Anne Marie was dead.

Finally, there was the civil suit that everyone knew was
coming, the wrongful death suit that—as in the O. J. Simpson
case—would allow the family of the victim to seek legal retri-
bution.

"The only thing that matters to them," Kevin Fahey had
said months before Capano was arrested, "is their money. If
you want to get their attention, that's where you have to hit
them."

On June 18, Chancery Court Judge Myron T. Steele ruled
that there was sufficient evidence to indicate that Anne Marie
Fahey had been murdered. Without mentioning Capano by
name, Steele wrote that there was "clear and convincing evidence" that Fahey had been the victim of "murder at the hand
of another person." But Steele also pointed out that the legal
burden for him to reach that conclusion fell far short of the
criminal standard of "beyond a reasonable doubt," and that his
opinion would have no impact on the pending criminal case.

A week later, Weiss filed a wrongful death suit in which Tom
Capano and his three brothers, Louis Jr., Gerry, and Joseph,
along with several Capano construction and real estate companies, were named as defendants. Under Delaware state law there
is no requirement to fix a monetary figure to the litigation, but
word quickly spread throughout the city that the Faheys would

ask for millions. The case was put on hold because of the pending criminal trial; at this writing, it remains unresolved.

The filing of the civil suit, while not unexpected, was the least of Tom Capano's concerns in June 1998. In April, Joseph Hurley had unexpectedly asked to step down as one of Capano's defense lawyers. Hurley, a master at working the media and never shy about offering a quip or comment, was surprisingly circumspect about his reasons for bowing out of what would prove to be one of the biggest and most highly publicized murder trials in Delaware history.

He would say only that he and Tom Capano had differed over trial strategy.

Early in June, after interviewing several highly regarded lawyers from throughout the country, Capano hired Joseph Oteri, a top criminal defense attorney from Boston. Like Capano, Oteri was a Boston College Law School graduate. That and an Italian surname were perhaps the only things the two men had in common.

Oteri, in his sixties, urbane, sophisticated, and quick on his feet, emerged as the lead defense attorney in the case. A Florida lawyer, Jack O'Donnell, a friend of Kay Capano's and a former law school classmate of Tom's, was also added to what was now being described as Tom Capano's "million-dollar defense team."

The four lawyers, Oteri, O'Donnell, Oberly, and Maurer, spent most of the summer of 1998 preparing for trial. They met on a weekly basis with Capano in Gander Hill Prison, and held frequent strategy sessions to plot out Capano's defense.

Oteri, picking up where Hurley had left off, used every opportunity to challenge the credibility of Gerry and Louis Jr., arguing that both had made deals to save themselves.

When word leaked in June of Capano's prison plots to harass MacIntyre through Nick Perillo and, allegedly, to have his brother Gerry and MacIntyre killed, Oteri went on the offensive. He challenged the veracity of both prison snitches, although he conceded that Capano, in a weak moment, had given Perillo the directions and diagrams.

Rosa, however, was totally unreliable, Oteri said.

"He's a scumbag," the dapper defense attorney said. "He would give me and you up if he thought it would help him . . . This thing never happened."

On Monday, August 31, a state grand jury handed up an indictment charging Capano with three counts of criminal solicitation. The counts included the plots to have MacIntyre and Gerry Capano murdered and the plan to intimidate Mac-Intyre by having her home ransacked and burglarized.

Five weeks later, on October 6, 259 potential jurors showed up for the start of jury selection in the Anne Marie Fahey murder case, a process that would take more than three weeks.

Capano, who turned forty-nine on October 11, showed up in court each morning pale, gaunt, and seemingly disoriented. He whined and complained about his treatment in prison, claiming that he had become a "marked man" to prison authorities, who had singled him out for abusive treatment. "They can inflict death by a thousand cuts," he said dramatically during one go-round with Judge Lee. On another day he refused to shower or shave, and appeared in court in his orange prison jumpsuit. On two other occasions he threatened not to come to court at all.

Capano was receiving daily doses of two antidepressants, Wellbutrin and Paxil, along with the tranquilizer Xanax. His lawyers had expressed concern about whether he would be mentally alert enough to participate in his trial.

But as the jury selection continued, Capano seemed to warm to the task. He joined in discussions with his lawyers before they decided to accept or reject potential jurors. He argued with Oteri and Oberly, and he began to challenge Judge Lee openly, charging at one point that Lee was arbitrarily rejecting Catholics.

But it was a reference to Anne Marie Fahey that offered the best example of the arrogance and disdain that Capano would bring to the trial.

Throughout jury selection, Lee consistently referred to Anne Marie Fahey as "the victim." Capano finally rose to correct him.

She was, he said, "the alleged victim."

22

The trial opened on October 26, 1998, with a bombshell from the defense. Oteri, launching the first salvo in what would be Capano's ill-conceived all-or-nothing defense, shocked the packed courtroom that morning by conceding what Capano had been denying for more than two years.

Anne Marie Fahey was dead, Oteri told the jury. She had died in Capano's home at 2302 Grant Avenue on the night of June 27, 1996. What's more, Oteri admitted, Tom and his brother Gerry had dumped Fahey's body in the Atlantic Ocean the next morning, just as Gerry would testify in the trial. However, Oteri said—and now the entire courtroom was hanging on his every word—Fahey had died not at Tom Capano's hand, but as a result of a "horrible, tragic accident." There was, Oteri added, "one other person who was there that night . . . one other person who knows the whole truth."

Oteri did not identify that person during his forty-five-minute address to the jury, but he set the stage for the Debby-did-it defense that Capano hoped would result in his acquittal. Oteri also told the six men and six women who would decide his client's fate that for the past two years Capano had lied to everyone and anyone who asked about the incident.

"Tom Capano is not terribly proud of that night," Oteri said. "He faced an integrity test and he failed."

Oteri closed by asking the jurors not to prejudge his client, not to be swayed by testimony about a lifestyle and morals that might offend them. They would hear that Capano had been having an affair with Anne Marie Fahey, and that Capano had cheated repeatedly on his wife. They would also hear that there were times when Capano and Fahey had fought and argued.

Theirs was a "normal relationship," he said. There were good times and bad times. There were "rocky patches." Anne Marie Fahey was no kid. She had worked in Washington, D.C., that "cesspool." She had had other lovers. She was a thirty-year-old woman who had had many life experiences. She was someone who gave as good as she got when she and Capano argued. Anne Marie Fahey, Oteri said, knew just what she was doing when she decided to start the affair with his client.

"She was on to a good thing and she used it," Oteri said. "More power to her."

Oteri's surprise opening dominated the first day of the trial. The concession that Fahey was dead and that her body had been dumped at sea took some of the steam out of the prosecution's case. In effect, Capano was conceding a big part of what Connolly and Wharton wanted to prove. But the two prosecutors quickly decided that they would not alter the way they intended to present the case to the jury. They wanted to limit Capano's ability to maneuver and to twist the facts. They wanted to lock in as many elements of their case as possible. It was obvious that Capano had decided to build his defense around the prosecution's evidence. He would give up whatever was provable, and spin his story around the unknown and the unknowable.

Capano had only a small window of time to play with in crafting his new story—the period between 9:15 P.M. on June 27, when he and Fahey left Panorama, and 5:45 A.M. the next morning, when he showed up at Gerry's door. His life would depend on what he made of that time.

After opening arguments, the focus of the trial shifted from Capano to Fahey. For the first week, in fact, as Connolly and Wharton alternately questioned a string of witnesses, it was Fahey's life that was held up to public scrutiny. The secrets she had desperately sought to hide from family members and friends during her short life were laid out for twelve strangers sitting in a jury box, and for the public that was voraciously following the case each day in the newspapers and on television.

From the testimony of her psychiatrist and two psychologists and from her own diary notes, which were read sadly from the witness stand by her sister, Kathleen, a picture of Anne Marie began to emerge. The jurors and those who packed into the third-floor courtroom each morning learned of Fahey's traumatic and impoverished childhood. They heard clinical and anecdotal testimony about her depression, anxiety, and self-doubt. Anne Marie's emotional frailty and her inability to cope with life's ups and downs were themes that Connolly and Wharton returned to again and again.

Capano, sitting at the defense table with two lawyers on either side, showed little reaction, although he did eye Kathleen Fahey-Hosey when she stepped down from the witness stand and, Kathleen later said, mouthed the word "bitch" as she walked by.

Occasionally, during the early days of the trial, Capano would look at the jury, trying to make eye contact. The panel included three young women about Fahey's age, and it was apparent that Capano was trying to charm them. He would also nod for emphasis when a Fahey diary note that portrayed him in a particularly good light was read. But he was clearly annoyed and bristled at many of the characterizations that were made from the witness stand by Fahey's friends and therapists, who knew him only from Anne Marie's descriptions of him.

With each day the crowds grew larger and the lines of spectators trying to get seats in the ornate courtroom grew longer. Dozens of local residents who had been following the Capano case in the media for more than a year began showing up at 7:00 A.M., an hour or more before the doors to the Daniel L. Herrmann Courthouse opened and nearly three hours before testimony began each day. On some mornings the line of spectators hoping for a seat in the courtroom snaked down from the electronically monitored third-floor security entrance and along the circular stairway, down to the second-floor landing. Everyone wanted a seat in what quickly became the best show in town.

People magazine had a reporter staffing the trial. The *New York Times* and the *Washington Post* did occasional takeouts. There was daily local newspaper, radio, and television coverage and periodic national reports on the major networks and National Public Radio.

Outside the courthouse, directly opposite Rodney Square and stretching from one end of the block-long courthouse to the other, was an armada of television trucks. Each day, during the lunch break and again around 5:30 P.M., a half-dozen reporters, their hair coifed, their makeup in place, would do their standups. The public couldn't get enough.

Most trials establish their own rhythm. There is an ebb and flow to the proceedings. In most cases, there are few surprises. The prosecution, the defense, and the reporters covering the case usually know in advance what's going to be said, what witness will be used to establish what point. But with the Capano trial there was a constant buzz and at least one surprise a day.

Gerry Capano's testimony, for example, was a repeat of what he had said at the bail hearing. But on cross-examination, Oteri pulled out a transcript and badgered him at length about the "go fuck yourself" phone call he had made to his mother, the contents of which had never before been made public.

Keith Brady, everyone knew, was going to be questioned about the phone call he had received from Capano after Fahey disappeared, and the detailed note he had kept about that July 2 conversation. But then came the questions about his three-way encounter with MacIntyre and Capano, and an embarrassing discussion of his reluctant participation and his inability to become aroused sexually.

MacIntyre testified about the gun and about her long-term relationship with Capano, admitting she had lied repeatedly on both counts before agreeing to cooperate. But it was her disclosures about the three-way sex with Brady and her encounter with her old boyfriend from Boston as Capano watched from a window that created one of the biggest stirs. She said she did it because Capano asked her to, and because she was afraid of losing him. The defense argued that she did it because she liked it and because having sex with two men had always been a fantasy of hers. During a break in MacIntyre's testimony, Oteri—who could be crude outside the hearing of the jury—referred to her as a "twitchy twat." In front of the jury he referred to her "sexual escapades."

And so, for a time, the death of Anne Marie Fahey got lost.

The stories about sex, pornography, adultery, and voyeurism began to overwhelm the trial. They dominated the talk at places like O'Friel's, Kid Sheleens, The Logan House, or Deep Blue, popular bars and restaurants where people would gather for a drink after work or an evening out on the town. Everyone knew about the Capano case. Everyone had a story to tell. Everyone had an opinion about the testimony that continued to rock the city of Wilmington.

Brady, the father of two young children, took a leave of absence from his job as First Deputy Attorney General, the second-highest law enforcement position in the state, on the day he testified. MacIntyre had been forced out at the Tatnall School back in February. Both paid a professional price for their encounters with Tom Capano.

So did their families.

Kay Capano, whose divorce would be finalized in the midst of the trial, and Brady's wife both had to suffer the public disclosure of their husbands' infidelities and their seamy, X-rated actions. MacIntyre's teenage son, Michael, and Capano's three youngest daughters—all of whom were attending private schools in Wilmington—had to cope with the snide remarks, smirks, and giggles of classmates.

Your mother does it doggy-style.
Your father likes to watch.

The question in Wilmington's small and incestuous political and social circles was, Who would be next? What other mistress would surface? What other sexual escapade would come out? Who would be pilloried in tomorrow's headlines? Who would be the fodder for tonight's gossip?

That was what the case had come down to.

Anne Marie Fahey, whose body was rotting at the bottom of the Atlantic Ocean, was an afterthought.

MacIntyre, as expected, was confronted with the allegation

that she was there when Fahey was killed, that she had played some role in the as yet unexplained "accident." In questions and answers that sounded as if they were cribbed from an old Perry Mason episode, Eugene Maurer ended his lengthy and rambling cross-examination with a series of staccato queries that were, in fact, accusations.

"Didn't you go to 2302 Grant Avenue with a firearm on June 27, 1996?"

"Do you deny your firearm discharged that night inside that house striking [Fahey]?"

"Do you deny that you discharged that firearm?"

"No, sir," and "No, I did not," MacIntyre said repeatedly as Maurer danced around and hinted at what the defense maintained had happened on the night in question. "Mr. Maurer," MacIntyre said finally, "I did not know of Anne Marie Fahey until July 2, 1996."

The prosecution spent a little more than five weeks presenting its case. Connolly and Wharton called 81 witnesses and showed the jury 235 pieces of evidence. The testimony extended over nineteen days. Judge Lee routinely took Fridays off so that he could return to Sussex County and deal with other, unrelated court matters that were on his schedule. Two trial days were lost because of elections, and another day was lost when Connolly got sick. The young prosecutor caught the flu. There was also a three-day recess for the Thanksgiving holiday.

The witnesses ranged from Gerry and Louis Capano to Nick Perillo, who testified about the plot to harass MacIntyre. The jury also heard from a physics teacher who, using formulas involving volume and density, explained why the cooler didn't sink. Given the size of the plastic ice chest, it would have taken about 430 pounds to cause the cooler to drop to the bottom of the ocean; the chain, the anchors, and Fahey's body combined added up to less than half that. An official with the U.S. Coast Guard testified about ocean currents and drifts in the area around Mako Alley, and speculated on the direction the cooler floated. He also described the futile attempt by the Coast Guard, using sonar and a small submarine, to locate the chain, anchors, and Fahey's body, or whatever was left of it.

Anne Marie Fahey's friends and coworkers, the salesclerk who sold Tom Capano the pantsuit from Talbots, the waitress from the Panorama, the marina gas attendant who filled up the *Summer Wind* in Stone Harbor on the morning of June 28—everybody and anybody who could add anything to the case was called to the witness stand.

The last prosecution witness was Ken Chubb. He testified on Wednesday, December 2, 1998, and recounted how he had found a cooler floating in the Atlantic Ocean off Indian River over the Fourth of July weekend of 1996. With that, Connolly brought out the large white ice chest with the makeshift lid and the patched bullet holes in its side and bottom, and placed it on a table in front of the jury.

It was a cold and stark reminder of what the case was all about. It was impossible to look at the cooler without thinking of Fahey's body stuffed inside.

When court adjourned early that Wednesday afternoon, the Faheys were allowed to remain in the courtroom to privately view the cooler that they had heard so much about. They had never seen it before.

Ferris Wharton had described it as "Anne Marie Fahey's coffin." It was as close as her family was ever likely to get to her body. Alone with their thoughts and warmed by the presence of one another, they joined hands and said a prayer for Annie.

Outside the courthouse that afternoon the Faheys spoke out publicly for the first time since the start of the trial. It was sad and troubling to see the cooler, they said, and to contemplate their sister's final resting place. But it was important for the jury to understand just what Tom Capano had done.

"Today the focus came back to Anne Marie," Kathleen Fahey-Hosey said as she stood on the courthouse steps on a bright, sunlit, and surprisingly warm December afternoon. "Anne Marie was shot. Anne Marie was stuffed in a cooler. Anne Marie was dragged through a house. Anne Marie bled all over a room. That's what these five weeks have been about.

"I don't care who he slept with or how sick this man is," Kathleen continued, disdainfully refusing to even refer to Capano by name. "He murdered Anne Marie and that's what I think was important that got across today."

Speculation began immediately about how much of a defense Capano's lawyers would mount, and whether Capano would take the stand. There was a split in the defense camp: Capano was leaning toward testifying. Charlie Oberly argued that under the right circumstances that made sense, but he wanted Capano to prepare for what would certainly be a grueling cross-examination. Oteri adamantly opposed Capano testifying. He didn't like criminal defendants on the witness stand, particularly defendants who were lawyers. Maurer and O'Donnell also opposed Capano taking the stand, but not as strongly. Oteri wanted to present a limited defense and rely on a strong closing argument that would focus on reasonable doubt and the lack of any direct evidence about how Fahey had died. Oberly, on the other hand, thought the accident had to be explained, and argued that if Capano was properly prepared, then it was worth the risk.

Ultimately, they all knew, the decision rested with Tom Capano.

Judge Lee recessed the trial for two days after the prosecution rested. The defense, he said, would have that time and the weekend—a total of four consecutive days—to make final preparations for its case. He told Oteri and the rest of the defense team to be ready to begin on Monday, December 7.

Capano showed up in court that morning testy and agitated after battling with Oteri and his other lawyers for most of the weekend over trial strategy. Capano, ever the control freak, was resisting the counsel of his million-dollar defense team. He was giving orders. He was deciding how the case would be tried, who would be called as witnesses, how they would be questioned. His attorneys had had enough.

That Monday morning, before the jury was brought into the courtroom, Oteri stood up and asked that he and the other defense lawyers be permitted to withdraw from the case because of "deep differences" with their client over how the defense should be presented.

Lee asked Capano if this were true. Capano said it was. Choosing his words carefully, but not very diplomatically, he told Lee that Oteri wanted to use a "scalpel" to fashion the defense case.

"I want a chainsaw," Capano said.

"Anyone in the situation I'm in should use every legitimate weapon," he continued. "I'm on trial for my life. If I were a soldier in a foxhole and I had ten hand grenades, I'd use every one of them instead of five.

"I do not want to sit in jail three years from now for something I didn't do saying, 'I should have done this. I should have done that.'"

Spectators in the packed courtroom groaned, but Capano continued.

"I am on trial for my life," he said.

Lee questioned Capano and Oteri at length, asking if their differences were "irreconcilable." Oteri said it appeared they were. Capano wavered, offering some hybrid solution that would allow him to mount his own defense but keep his defense lawyers. It didn't make any sense, and no one saw how that could be accomplished legally. The debate went back and forth for several hours. The jury was sent home for the day. Lee was flabbergasted. "I'm trying to figure out just what the hell it is that you want," he said to Capano at one point. Finally and reluctantly, the judge said he would give Capano the night to consider his options. Court would resume the next morning, Tuesday, December 8. At that point, Lee said, he wanted Capano to be prepared to tell him how he wished to proceed.

The next morning, like a spoiled child who had gotten the attention that he wanted, Capano backed off. Never mind, he said. He would proceed with his defense team in place.

The flap was the first public airing of the differences that had existed in the defense camp for months. Periodically during the trial, members of Capano's team privately complained about Capano's behavior: He refused to listen, rejected advice, and spent all of his energy trying to control and manipulate his lawyers.

"He's an asshole," one said in disgust and frustration. Another member of the team was most troubled by the fact that Capano showed no remorse for what had happened.

One of the jokes that circulated around the courthouse during the trial was about how well the defense attorneys got along with one another. Despite their egos and the fact that each was accustomed to being at center stage, Oteri, Maurer, O'Donnell, and Oberly worked well together. And this, the courthouse wags would say with a smile, was due in no small part to the fact that each defense lawyer recognized they had a common enemy—their client.

Connolly, Wharton, and Bob Donovan, who sat with the prosecutors at their courtroom table each day, were not surprised. Capano, they knew, had to manipulate and control any situation. That was the reason they all were sitting before Judge Lee. It always came back to that. The key was making the jury see it.

In all, the defense would call thirty witnesses during the first seven days of its presentation. But in retrospect it all meant very little. It was just a prelude for the inevitable confrontation that was set in motion back in July 1996, when Colm Connolly joined the investigation.

Connolly against Capano was what this case was all about.

The straight-arrow prosecutor versus the corrupt, self-absorbed corporate attorney. Notre Dame versus Boston College. Character and integrity versus status and celebrity. Good versus evil.

It could end no other way.

The story was shaping up like a movie script. In fact, members of the media passed time at lunch casting the leading roles (leading contenders: James Woods as Capano and Andie McDowell as Fahey in the feature film; Armand Assante as Capano and Kim Delaney from *NYPD Blue* as Fahey in the television version). The case had seen lover pitted against lover, brother against brother. There had been sex, lies, both video and audiotape.

But the story could not end without a final, definitive confrontation.

At 11:50 A.M. on Wednesday, December 16, Joe Oteri stood up before Judge Lee and set that confrontation in motion.

"The defense," Oteri said, "calls Thomas Capano."

23

For two days Tom Capano danced around the issue, teased and enticed the jury, held out the promise, then pulled back. Finally, he got to it: his version of the truth.

Debby did it, but she didn't mean it.

That's what Tom Capano wanted the jury to believe.

For nearly two hours on the morning of December 21, his third day on the witness stand, Capano related the story of what he claimed had happened in his house on the night of June 27, 1996. He said that he and Fahey had returned to Wilmington after dinner at Panorama and decided to go over to his house to watch *ER* on television. He said he dropped Anne Marie off at her apartment at a little before 10:00 P.M. She was going to change, but her apartment was so hot that she decided not to. He waited outside in his Jeep for her. She was only inside for a few minutes. Then they headed over to his place.

Capano said his house was cool. The air conditioning had been running all day. Anne Marie took off her shoes and her pantyhose and settled in on the couch facing the television in the great room. Capano said he took off his sports jacket, tie, and shoes and sat in a recliner—"the Daddy chair," he called it—next to the couch. About halfway through the show, he said, he moved over and sat next to Anne Marie, who put her head on his shoulder and fell asleep. He heard the phone ring, but didn't answer it.

After *ER* had ended, and with Annie still snuggled on the couch, he got up and went to the powder room on the first floor. He then quietly used the phone to check his voice mail. Debby MacIntyre had called. He called her back.

The conversation was brief and not especially pleasant. She wanted to come over, as she often did at night. He told her it was not a good time, that he had "company right now."

"Maybe later," he said as he hung up.

He returned to the couch where Fahey was dozing and put his arm around her shoulder. The news was on television. And the next thing he knew, Tom Capano said, an angry Debby MacIntyre was standing in front of them in a fury.

"She must have come in the front door," he said. "She had the key. She was pretty ballistic. We didn't even realize she was there until she started yelling."

With that, Capano launched into his jealous-older-woman defense, the one he had referred to in his letters to Susan Louth a few months earlier.

"Who's this?" he said MacIntyre shouted. "What's this all about? Is this why you couldn't see me?"

Capano said he tried to calm MacIntyre down. Her face was flushed, he said, her neck beet red. He said he told her that he and Anne Marie were friends and that they had been out to dinner. He told her to take it easy, to relax.

But MacIntyre, he said, was enraged.

Anne Marie, meanwhile, was perplexed and more than a little annoyed.

"Capano, what the hell is this?" she said. "I don't need to put up with garbage like this. I wanna go home. I wanna go now."

With that, Capano said, Anne Marie reached down and began to put her pantyhose back on. (Several female reporters in the courtroom later noted that this was one of the least credible parts of his story. No woman, they said, would go through the less than flattering process of putting on pantyhose in front of another woman she did not know. None could imagine Fahey doing that in the circumstances Capano described.) MacIntyre, now distraught, had pulled something out of the small handbag she was carrying, Capano said. Both Capano and Fahey looked up and saw that it was a gun.

"Oh my God," Fahey said, more in disbelief and incredulity than in fear.

Capano said he stood up to face MacIntyre. Fahey, he said, was seated to his right.

"Debby was off the wall," Capano said. "She was not coherent. I tried to explain that Annie and I were friends, but she wasn't listening. She started to cry."

"All these years I've waited for you," Capano said MacIntyre blurted out through her tears. "I've got nothing left to live for. I might as well shoot myself."

With that, Capano said, MacIntyre—who was left-handed—began to raise the gun toward her head. Capano said he grabbed for the weapon to try to stop her. The gun discharged.

The bullet struck Anne Marie Fahey in the side of her head, just above and slightly behind her ear. She collapsed.

"Anne Marie was motionless on the sofa," Capano said.

Panic set in. He frantically tried to revive her, administering CPR, gently slapping her in the face, trying to wake her up.

"Annie," he said. "Annie, come to."

Fahey's eyes were open, but she did not react to his slaps or his voice. She had no pulse. Capano put a small pillow under her head and again tried to revive her. He gave her mouth-to-mouth and ordered MacIntyre to perform chest compressions. For several minutes, he said, they both worked over Fahey's body. But it was hopeless.

"I came to the realization that there wasn't a chance," Capano said.

Somewhere in the middle of his panic and anxiety and fear, Capano said, he decided that he had to cover up what had happened. That was why, he said, he did not call 911 and ask for help.

"It was the most cowardly, horrible thing I have ever done in my life," Capano said of his decision not to call for help. "My life flashed before my eyes. I always thought I was a guy with some guts and I wasn't. I knew Anne Marie was dead. I was being selfish. I decided not to call the paramedics and the police. I wanted to protect myself and also to protect Debby."

The explanation hung in the courtroom, begging the questions that would undermine Capano's entire defense. Whom did the coverup protect? And from what? At that point Capano was separated from his wife, free to date whomever he wanted without the risk of social scandal. He was a man of power and wealth, with plenty of connections within the Wilmington Police Department and the state Attorney General's Office. He had credibility with both those agencies. And if his story was to be believed, he had done nothing wrong that night. In fact, he had tried to stop one woman from committing suicide. If the gun had discharged by accident and this horrible tragedy had occurred, MacIntyre was culpable, but under the circumstances not nearly to the degree that would warrant the massive coverup that followed. With his money and influence, no one doubted that Capano could have easily arranged bail for MacIntyre, and that in a worst-case scenario she would have been charged with a lesser homicide offense, most likely involuntary manslaughter. In all probability, she would have faced an even less serious charge. Capano knew the way the system worked. More important, he knew how to work the system. He had maneuvered behind the scenes for both his brother Louis in the political payoff scandal and his brother Joe in the rape and kidnapping case that was pleaded down to much lesser offenses.

"It was absolutely, positively, I am certain, accidental," Capano said of the shooting that took Fahey's life.

Yet for more than two years, he claimed, he covered it up.

Capano spent another day and a half on direct examination, testifying in detail about how he had "compartmentalized" his actions in the hours following the tragedy in order to function and get through what he knew he had to do. He said he sent MacIntyre home and drove over to Fahey's apartment shortly before midnight and put the Talbots gift box and the groceries he had bought in her apartment. He also said he had dialed *69 on her phone to find out the last person who had called her. When a man answered—it was a friend of Scanlan's from whose home Scanlan had called Fahey that night—Capano said he hung up the phone.

MacIntyre, he said, came back to Grant Avenue early in the morning and helped him remove the bloody sofa and rug from the great room. By that point, Capano said, he had already placed Fahey's body in the cooler. He said he had covered her with a blanket and folded her up in a fetal position.

For his final question on the fourth day of his direct examination of Tom Capano, Oteri asked poignantly, "Tom, did you kill Anne Marie Fahey?"

"No," Capano said, his voice sad and somber. "A thousand times no. I loved Anne Marie Fahey."

Colm Connolly stood in front of Tom Capano and smiled. Capano was not happy.

"Is something funny that I'm missing here?" Capano asked as Connolly was wrapping up his second day of cross-examination. "You seem to be smiling a lot."

As he had repeatedly for two days, Connolly ignored Capano's comment and stayed focused on the task at hand. The young prosecutor asked another question.

That's how it played out for four tense and dramatic days in a packed third-floor courtroom. Spectators waited in line for hours each morning for a chance to see some of it. Capano and Connolly, face-to-face, a heavyweight battle that had been at least eight weeks—and more accurately, two and a half years—in the making.

From the start, Connolly had wanted to cross-examine Capano. And Wharton, to his credit, realized that was the best way to go. The state prosecutor, who technically was in charge of the case, allowed the cross-deputized federal attorney to have the plum. They had discussed the strategy in detail. They knew what points needed to be made. But more important, they knew that the case would hinge on how the jury perceived Tom Capano. For months, Wharton and Connolly had been portraying him as smug, arrogant, and self-absorbed. The consensus in the prosecution camp was that Connolly would be in a better position to bring that out.

"We knew how he [Capano] felt about Colm and we figured we could use it to our advantage," Wharton said. "We were right."

Connolly opened with a surprise, referring back to a murder case that Capano had prosecuted back in 1976 when he worked in the Attorney General's Office. It was another example of how detailed and thorough the prosecution had been in putting together its case.

As soon as Capano took the witness stand and told the story about the "horrible accident," Connolly and Wharton had started to brainstorm. They knew that it would be important to show the jury that Capano knew about forensic evidence and understood how it could be used to prove or disprove the manner in which a shooting occurred. Things like the angle and trajectory of a bullet, the blood splatter in a room, the presence or absence of powder burns—these all could be used to build or tear down a story.

Connolly wanted to show the jury that by dumping Fahey's body and the murder weapon, by removing the rug and the couch, and by cleaning up the room, Capano was doing everything he knew to distort what had happened. If he were telling the truth, those pieces of evidence would have supported his claim and helped prove that Fahey had died as a result of a horrible accident. Instead, Capano made sure that all anyone could do was wonder.

But in researching the one murder case that Capano had prosecuted, Connolly and Wharton stumbled onto even more. It was another one of those examples of good fortune, or some power beyond anyone's control, leading them in the right direction. Wharton read Capano's closing arguments in the 1976 murder trial, and was startled to find references to a missing gun and to the fact that the victim's body had been dumped in the water. Connolly went over the closing in detail, then, with Capano on the witness stand, questioned him at length about the case. He implied that Capano had borrowed the scenario from the 1976 shooting when he killed Fahey.

Capano was perplexed and annoyed. At first he insisted he had not made the closing argument in that trial. When Connolly began to read from the transcript, quoting him directly, Capano backtracked.

"I'm not going to talk about it," he said. "I remember next to nothing about that case."

In fact, the defendant was Robert "Squeaky" Saunders, one of the inmates Capano's defense lawyers had called to try to discredit Perillo earlier in the trial. Saunders was convicted of killing a coconspirator in a bank robbery, and evidence indicated that he had gotten rid of the gun and had dumped the victim's body in a creek that flowed out into the Atlantic Ocean. What he hadn't known, however, was that the creek was lined with a sluice gate. The body never made it out to sea. It was recovered by the authorities, who arrested Saunders.

In arguing before the jury in that case, Capano had said that Saunders knew that one of the "most important things was to get rid of the gun" and also knew that if you dump a body in a river that leads to the ocean, "the body is going to disappear."

Capano shook his head, insisting that once again, Connolly was distorting the record. That murder trial, he said, "has no connection to this case and the events of June twenty-seventh."

But by then Connolly was off and running.

The prosecutor picked away at Capano's account of the "accident" that led to Fahey's death, taking Capano through the same events in painstaking and minute detail. He returned again and again to the letters Capano had written and the phone calls he had made to MacIntyre from prison. He went over Fahey's diary notes and their e-mail messages. Whenever there was an inconsistency in Capano's answer, Connolly would pounce. But the exercise was largely form over substance. And that was what Capano missed as he sat on the witness stand at the end of the second day questioning Connolly about "what was funny."

"No, no, no, no, no, no," Capano had said during one classic confrontation after Connolly alluded to Capano's apparent cavalier and uncaring actions—the dumping of the body, the pizza and video with his daughters, the sex with MacIntyre—in the hours that immediately followed Fahey's death. "I'll play your game, Mr. Connolly, but not this one. I did deeply love Anne Marie Fahey. You never knew her."

The irony was that over the last two years, Connolly had gotten to know both Fahey and Capano only too well. His recall during cross-examination was staggering. It seemed as if he had memorized each of the more than 100 letters, phone calls, and e-mail messages that were now in evidence before the jury. While questioning Capano, Connolly bounced from one to another, chiding, challenging, and confronting the witness. Like a boxer pounding a speed bag, Connolly verbally tattooed Capano, pointing out each word, phrase, or description that was at odds with the facts and the evidence.

"People do make mistakes," a flustered Capano said after one exchange; then he paused and added sarcastically, "Excuse me. Most of us do." But by then Connolly was already framing his next question. Judge Lee admonished Capano several times for failing to respond to a question, or for answering a question with a question.

Connolly suggested that Capano had used everyone close to him to thwart and block the investigation, including his daughters. Capano turned cold and told Connolly, "Do not ask me questions about my children." When Connolly persisted, Capano said, "Don't go there."

Still, the prosecutor pushed on.

The jury saw and heard it all, including a comment from Judge Lee that underscored the point Connolly was trying to make. "Mr. Capano knows the rules," Lee said at one point. "And Mr. Capano must abide by the rules."

But Tom Capano, the prosecution had been saying over and over since his arrest, was someone who played by his own rules.

It was during his next-to-last day on the witness stand that Capano lost it. He had had nearly a week to regain his composure. Court had recessed from December 30 to January 4 for the New Year's holiday. But Capano still didn't get it. He still didn't understand that how he acted on the witness stand could be even more damaging than what he said.

Connolly understood it only too well. He knew which buttons to push. That afternoon, after taking Capano through several hours of testimony and rehash, the prosecutor again returned to Capano's daughters. Wasn't it true, Connolly asked, that Capano could have spared them from being questioned by authorities if he had simply conceded that he would not use them as alibi witnesses?

"Do you really want to get into this?" Capano asked, his voice taking on a cold, hard edge. "You tormented my daughters."

There was an objection by the defense and a brief sidebar discussion out of the hearing of the jury. Then the cross-examination resumed and Connolly again asked about Capano's children.

"You heartless, gutless, soulless disgrace for a human being," Capano shouted. Judge Lee had had enough. He called for order and told security guards to remove Capano from the courtroom. Trial ended abruptly that day, and the next morning, before the jury returned, an exasperated Lee delivered a verbal tongue-lashing to the defendant.

"There will be no apologies [in front of the jury]," Lee told Capano. "You are simply to answer the questions. . . . He [Connolly] will be permitted to ask questions subject only to your attorneys' right to object. . . . Those rulings are not subject to your approval."

Lee said that if Capano persisted in trying to "manipulate the state's questions to your purposes," he would impose "Draconian sanctions."

"I recognize you find yourself in a position which is a cause for anxiety and for anger and for all the other emotions which you've put on display in this courtroom. . . . I have attempted to give you every consideration. . . . Do we understand each other?"

"Does that mean you want a response from me?" a smug and pouting Capano asked the judge. Lee froze him with an icy stare, then looked past him to one of the courtroom attendants and said, "Please bring in the jury."

The reprimand from the judge and an attempt by Oteri to rehabilitate his client's testimony on redirect did little to change the message that Capano conveyed to the jury from the witness stand.

Before he stepped down and returned to the defense table, Capano offered a rambling and sometimes disjointed argument that included his take on Jesuit philosophy and his view of local, state, and national politics.

In an explanation that captured both his arrogance and his self-indulgence, he told Connolly that the involvement of the federal government had kept him from coming forward sooner with the "truth" about the case.

"Once you guys got in it was obvious what was going on," he said. "It was all politicized. . . . If the president of the United States gets involved, I'm diving as deep as I can."

Capano also suggested that Anne Marie's family, particularly her sister, Kathleen, and her brother Robert, shared the blame for turning the investigation into a political football. If Kathleen had not called her friends in state government and asked for their help after discovering Anne Marie missing, he complained, and if Robert had met with him back in July 1996 when he asked, things might have been different. If the FBI and the U.S. Attorney's Office had not "blasted" their way into the case, Capano said, he would eventually have told the Wilmington Police what had happened.

Anne Marie Fahey, of course, still would have been dead. And her body still would have been at the bottom of the shark-infested Atlantic Ocean. But Capano said the "nightmare" that the investigation had become would have been avoided.

Sure, he had lied repeatedly over the past two years, Capano said as Oteri tried to bring a positive close to testimony that he and everyone else in the courtroom knew had been extremely damaging. "But there was a thing called a virtuous lie."

Capano said he had learned about this from the Jesuits at Boston College. Then, in a condescending aside, he asked Oteri, "Should we assume the jury knows who the Jesuits are?" They were, he quickly explained, the intellectuals of the Catholic Church. "There is," he said smugly, "no such thing as a dumb Jesuit." And they had taught him, he said, "that it's okay to lie sometimes."

Take, for example, World War II. If a family hiding Jews from the Nazis lied to protect those they were shielding, that was permissible. More than that, it was noble and virtuous.

Capano said he had lied about what had happened to Fahey to "protect" MacIntyre. And while he was hard-pressed to explain why he wanted to have Perillo harass her and why he continued to keep silent after she started to cooperate, Capano stuck to his "virtuous lie" defense.

"It's a good thing to be loyal to those you love," he said shortly before stepping down from the witness stand. "It's also good to be loyal to the truth. Sometimes those things collide . . . It's not easy to decide how to choose one over the other."

Tom Capano chose.

Now it was up to the jury.

"A lie is only evil," he said, "when it's based on evil intent."

24

Eight days after Tom Capano stepped down from the witness stand, the jury got the case. Deliberations began on Thursday, January 14, 1999, after a day of closing arguments from the prosecution and defense.

The jurors, six men and six women, were sequestered in the Christiana Hilton just outside of Wilmington. They had access to a hotel conference room, where they conducted their deliberations. In the room were the more than 400 pieces of evidence that had been introduced by the prosecution and defense during the twelve-week trial. The evidence included the transcripts and the tapes of the phone messages between Capano and MacIntyre, Capano's letters, the e-mail messages sent by Capano and Fahey, Fahey's diary, and the cooler.

The jurors spent three days sifting through it all. At one point a female member of the panel tried to sit in the cooler; like the FBI agent in Connolly's office, the woman—who was much smaller than Fahey—had a hard time squeezing her body into the space. It was hard to believe, as Capano had testified, that he had not broken any of Fahey's bones when he stuffed her body into the rectangular plastic container.

For three days, while the jury deliberated, time stopped in place for those directly involved in the case. All anyone could do was wait and wonder. The lawyers hunkered down in their offices trying to keep busy. Family members, whose lives had revolved around the daily routine of the trial for nearly three months, tried to find some way to fill the sudden void in their day.

It was over, but it wasn't finished.

On Thursday night, after the first full day of deliberations had ended without a decision, Mark Fahey sat at the bar in Kelly's Logan House. There had been an ice storm that day, but the slippery driving conditions hadn't kept people at home. The Logan House was jammed. A popular nightspot whose ambiance was a cross between an Irish pub and a fraternity house, Kelly's was located just across the street from Trolley Square and up the block from Toscana's, a popular restaurant mentioned frequently during the trial as a place from which Capano and Anne Marie often ordered takeout.

Sitting at the other end of the bar sharing drinks with a half-dozen reporters were Joe Oteri and Jack O'Donnell, the two out-of-town defense attorneys who had become well known in the bars and restaurants that constituted Wilmington's night life. A jukebox blared in the background as the regular crowd, a mostly twentysomething group dressed in jeans, sweaters, and flannel shirts, sipped beers and circulated.

"How can they do what they do?" Mark Fahey asked as he eyed the two lawyers who were defending the man he was certain had killed his sister. "Don't they know who he is?"

They were just doing their jobs, he was told. It was nothing personal. Mark Fahey's eyes filled with tears. He shook his head. Not personal?

Within an hour O'Donnell had worked his way down the bar, until he was seated next to Fahey. They fell deep into conversation, these two Irishmen who at another time and in another situation probably would have been friends. As they spoke, sharing private thoughts about the public spectacle that had brought them to this same place, someone—by chance or design—punched another number into the jukebox. And against the din of conversation, the clanging of glasses, and the occasional shouts and bursts of laughter that are so typical of a night at the Logan House, there came the unmistakable voice of Frank Sinatra and the strains of that song of lost love, "The Summer Wind."

*   *   *

The jurors deliberated for a total of roughly twenty hours between Thursday and Saturday, debating the different points that were made and the conflicting testimony that had been aired during the thirty-seven days they had sat listening in the courtroom. By late Saturday afternoon they were ready to vote, but they opted to have dinner before returning to cast their ballots. Their decision was unanimous. After it was over they gathered around the cooler, which someone had placed on top of a coffee table. Anne Marie Fahey's office planner, her wallet, and some pictures were placed inside the chest. The jurors gathered in a circle around it. They each placed a hand on the cooler, and together they said a prayer.

At around 7:00 P.M., Judge Lee got the call informing him that the jury had completed its deliberations. He was two hours away at his home in Rehoboth Beach; one of the defense attorneys had gone to Atlantic City; several others were out to dinner. Lee decided that the verdict would not be announced until the next morning, and ordered everyone back into court at 9:30 A.M.

Todd Spangler, the reporter covering the case for the Associated Press, moved the first bulletin over the wire around 7:30 P.M. Television and radio stations broke into their broadcasts to announce that a verdict had been reached, but that the jury would not be back in court to announce it until the next morning.

The city started to buzz.

Conventional wisdom had held that the longer deliberations took, the better it would be for Capano. The jury had been out for three days. Was that long or short? All anyone could do was speculate.

"I don't think it looks good," said one tuxedo-clad politico later that night as he stood sipping a glass of white wine in the ornate ballroom of the Hotel duPont just across Rodney Square from the courthouse.

"What do you think?" his wife, clad in a sequined gown, asked a reporter.

It was perfect.

The verdict had come in on the night of the Grand Gala. And now, after listening to a performance by the Broadway star Betty Buckley, the city's toniest inner circle and its constella-

tion of aspirants had all gathered for the postperformance fes-
tivities, the adult promenade that all but defines the city Tom
Capano once boasted of owning.

While Capano sat alone in his cell at the Gander Hill prison
less than a mile away, his former colleagues, coworkers, political cronies, and perhaps even two or three of his unnamed mistresses danced, drank, smiled, and laughed their way through
the social event of the year. Occasionally, one would pause and
look up from his or her drink to speculate on Capano's fate.

"I just hope it's not a hung jury," said one partygoer. "No
one wants to go through all of this again."

The hearing took less than ten minutes. In fact, it took
longer—nearly an hour—for everyone to file into the courtroom than it did for the jury to announce its verdict.

Outside, a crowd had begun to gather around 7:00 A.M.
Some people came right from church. Others skipped breakfast
to be there. Some who had been out late the night before never
went to bed. It was sunny and mild, the January air crisp but
comfortable.

Marguerite Capano set the tone for her family when she
arrived in her wheelchair and was pushed through a crowd of
reporters. "My son's innocent, she's a drunk," the white-haired
matriarch said without further elaboration. The assumption
was that she was referring to MacIntyre.

The Faheys were tight-lipped as they entered. Several
people, not knowing what to say, awkwardly wished them well.

Capano was stone-faced as he walked into the courtroom,
flanked by a squad of sheriff's officers. He nodded toward his
family, who had jammed into the first two rows behind the
defense table. He said a few words to his lawyers, then sat
down. Oteri later said that Capano had "fully believed he was
going to be acquitted." If he did, he was one of the few in the
room who felt that way.

The jurors, led by a forty-five-year-old pipe fitter who had
been chosen foreman, arrived a little before 10:00 A.M. None of
its members looked at Capano as they filed into the seats in the
jury box they had been occupying since October 26. Minutes
earlier Judge Lee had cautioned the spectators packed into the

hushed courtroom not to engage in any type of outburst when the verdict was delivered.

"One way or the other, some people are going to be very upset," Lee said.

With the jurors in place, Lee turned immediately to the matter at hand.

"Have you reached a verdict?" he asked the foreman.

"Yes sir, we have," he said. "Guilty as charged."

And with that, it was over.

There were quiet sighs in the courtroom, but no outbursts. Outside in the hallway, however, after a courtroom attendant announced the verdict to an overflow crowd that had not been able to gain access, a cheer went up.

Lee thanked the jurors for their work and gave them two days off. They were to be back in court on Wednesday for the start of the penalty phase of the trial.

Capano, his face drawn, showed little emotion. As he was being led out of the courtroom, his mother, his sister, and his three oldest daughters stood sobbing and hugging one another, three generations of Capano women crying over the golden boy. His ex-wife, there for her girls, stared silently.

Outside on Rodney Square the atmosphere was festive, as if it were all some kind of pep rally or tailgate party. There were now nearly 300 people standing around waiting for something, although none was able to say exactly what it was. Cars drove by, honking their horns. When the Fahey family emerged from the courthouse, they were cheered. When Wharton, Connolly, Donovan, and Alpert walked out, the crowd burst into applause.

Television reporters, broadcasting live, scrambled for interviews with anyone and everyone connected with the case. In the middle of it all Debby MacIntyre showed up; she granted a half-dozen different interviews, appearing on every local and most national broadcast feeds.

On each, she told the same story: She was glad it was over. The Tom Capano she had loved no longer existed. She had been lied to and deceived. And now she was looking forward to getting on with her life.

"It would be off the mark to say she was there to gloat over the verdict," wrote Tom Ferrick, a columnist for the *Philadelphia Inquirer*, in a piece that ran the next day. "But not by much."

The Faheys, at a news conference in the cafeteria of the building where David Weiss's law firm had its offices, praised the prosecutors and investigators, but said the conviction was a hollow victory. It had been 934 days, they said, since Anne Marie disappeared.

Weiss said the case demonstrated that "no matter where you are from or how privileged your background may be, justice applies to everyone."

The family, he said, was concerned that the trial and the sensational media coverage had presented a distorted picture of their sister. He said the Faheys understood how and why it happened, but they wanted to set the record straight.

"Anne Marie was a lot more than Tom Capano's mistress," Weiss said. "If one's value is measured by those who love you, Anne Marie was truly a wealthy individual."

"Tom Capano put a lot of people through a lot of distress, suffering, and pain," Connolly said as he stood in front of a bank of microphones and cameras on the courthouse steps. Flanked by Wharton, Donovan, and Alpert, he thanked everyone who had worked the case, made a point of mentioning Doug and Diane Iardella without going into detail about their roles in the investigation, and said the case was a testament to faith and perseverance.

"It was kind of a rollercoaster," the boyish prosecutor said when asked to describe the long and at times frustrating investigation he had spearheaded. There had been times, he admitted, when the public perception was that "we were grasping for straws." But that, he said, was a misconception.

"We developed a long-term plan," Connolly said. "If you want to get to the truth, it often takes time."

But what was the truth?

What really happened on the night Anne Marie Fahey was killed?

The assumption is that Tom Capano told as much of the

actual story as he possibly could. Most lies are built on a foundation of reality.

A plausible scenario, based on Capano's testimony and what little else is known about that night:

They were miserable at dinner, perhaps because Fahey was telling him it was over. Maybe he mentioned the Jackson Browne concert in August, and she told him to forget it. Maybe the thought that he was trying to insure himself a place in her life that far in advance pushed a final button, and she decided, as Michele Sullivan had been suggesting, to make a clean and complete break. Maybe she had just had enough.

They drove back to Wilmington, just as he said. He convinced her to come over to his house. Maybe he held out the prospect of the Talbots gift. Maybe he told her he had some groceries. Maybe he mentioned both those things, even made a promise to accept the new relationship—to just be friends.

She went into her apartment to change, leaving her floral dress over the chair where it was later found. Nervous, she expected to come right back. She put on a T-shirt, shorts, and running shoes. Authorities and family members would later believe those items were missing, but could not be certain. No one, not even Anne Marie Fahey, keeps a complete wardrobe inventory.

They drove over to the home on Grant Avenue. Capano told her to sit down and relax. He turned on *ER*, one of "their" shows, but she wasn't interested. *Those times are over*, perhaps she said, and perhaps she finally meant it.

Desperate now, and at the end of his rope, Capano began to whine. He told Fahey he couldn't live without her, that he might as well be dead. Then he pulled out the handgun, just as he said MacIntyre had, and he threatened to kill himself.

"Oh my God," Fahey would have said, more in disbelief than concern. "Capano, what the hell is this?"

Fed up with his antics, and finally mustering enough courage to confront him, she refused to fall for his ploy. Instead of evoking sympathy, he had made her angry. Perhaps her comments bordered on ridicule.

"I don't need to put up with garbage like this," she said. "I wanna go home. I wanna go now."

And so it must have hit him. He was Anne Marie Fahey's Thursday-night dinner date. He would never be anything more than that. He could spend money on her, take her to fine restaurants, but there would be nothing more than that. The great manipulator had been manipulated. Fahey wanted to play him the way he had played Debby MacIntyre. She wanted him there when she needed him, but only on her terms.

Capano flipped out. He ranted and raved, paced back and forth. His voice rose. Looking for an escape, Anne Marie may have bent over, perhaps to tie a shoelace, or to put on the sneakers she had taken off when they first arrived and he encouraged her to sit down and watch some television. Maybe to pick up a small handbag or wallet that she had brought with her. Capano, now behind her, pointed the gun and fired. The bullet entered her head just above and behind her left ear. She collapsed back onto the couch. Dead. She never knew what hit her.

Did it happen that way?

Only Tom Capano knows.

His version of what took place after Fahey was shot— except for his account of MacIntyre's involvement—is probably accurate. No doubt he panicked. No doubt he tried, however briefly and halfheartedly, to revive her. And no doubt he never considered calling 911. He couldn't. There was no way to explain what had happened.

The penalty phase of the Tom Capano murder case began on Wednesday, January 20, and lasted a week.

The prosecution opened with Linda Marandola, who told the jury the story of her experiences with Capano. The jury had not been permitted to hear about them during the trial; Judge Lee had ruled that the most damaging events—the harassment and threats from 1980—had occurred too far in the past to be relevant to the Fahey murder. But during the penalty phase, when the character and background of the defendant are at issue, they were permissible.

The penalty phase hearing was a chance for the prosecution to argue the aggravating circumstances in the case that warranted a death sentence—in this case, premeditation and planning. Prosecutors were also allowed to show how the defendant's background was relevant, in which context the Marandola incident showed a pattern of abuse. And they were permitted to call family members of the victim to the witness stand to describe the impact the crime had had on them.

Under Delaware state law, the jury in a first-degree murder case can only "recommend" a sentence, and its two options are life without parole or death by lethal injection. That was what Capano was facing. Unlike the verdict, the recommendation did not have to be unanimous. The actual sentence would be imposed by Judge Lee, who, according to the law, was obliged to give "great weight" to the jury's recommendation, but was not bound by it.

Kathleen, Robert, and Brian Fahey were called as witnesses by the prosecution on the second day of the penalty phase hearing.

Their testimony brought the trial back to where it had begun. It put the focus back on Anne Marie.

But this time the picture was different.

This time the jury was spared the sad tale of a young woman struggling to find herself in a complicated world where celebrity had somehow become more important than character, where status had more value than integrity.

This time the jury heard about family and love and the sadness of loss.

This time the jury saw the faces of those who mourned the death of Anne Marie Fahey, heard them cry out not for revenge—although there are those who would say revenge was certainly justified—but for some sort of explanation, for a way to understand the hows and the whys of a tragic, sad, and incomprehensible murder.

And this time, the jury cried.

At least four of the twelve jurors sitting in the courtroom that day were reduced to tears by the poignant and gut-wrenching testimony of the three Faheys. None mentioned Capano, who sat jotting notes on a legal pad at the defense table as they spoke. Robert and Brian Fahey hardly even looked his way. Kathleen, on the other hand, froze him with a chilling stare as she stepped down from the witness stand. This was after she had brought tears to the eyes of jurors and spectators—including several of those sitting in the press aisle—with an impassioned explanation of how the death of her sister had left her two young sons, Kevin, five, and Brendan, three, anxious and afraid. They constantly asked her, she said, if the "bad man who killed Aunt Annie" and dumped her body in the ocean "was coming to get them."

"My kids' innocence is gone," she said. "My kids are surrounded by this evil presence. I can't understand it myself. I can't explain it to them."

And, she said sadly, "I can't fix it for them."

"These kids are five and three," she said, her voice cracking. "These kids should not be worried about a bad man coming to get them. They should be worried about Power Rangers."

"They ask, 'Mommy, why did the bad man put Aunt Annie in the cooler?'" She said she had no answer for them.

"I can't comprehend how the bad man could do that to my sister," she told the jury. "I can't understand it myself. How the hell am I supposed to explain it to them?"

None of the Faheys mentioned the life-or-death sentence that was central to the hearing. Instead they spoke of Anne Marie, making the point that Weiss had made after the verdict: their sister was more than just the scheduling secretary for Tom Carper and the secret mistress of Tom Capano. They wanted the jury to know that. They worried that Anne Marie herself might have gotten lost during the trial, amid the hours of sensational and salacious testimony about power, politics, greed, sex, lust, and betrayal.

Their sister was dead. Capano had killed her. And they didn't want all the talk about extramarital affairs, voyeurism, three-way sex, and pornography—all the things that had turned the trial into a series of tabloid headlines and risqué jokes—to diminish either Anne Marie's life or her passing.

In that sense, the Faheys' testimony was cathartic. Anyone who had sat through the trial could sense it. It was a chance to wash away the grit that had built up since opening arguments back on October 26. The Faheys had been there for it all. They had been stoic and resolute. They brought a quiet grace and dignity to a case that badly needed a dose of civility.

There was sorrow and anger, but there was also a sense of propriety about what they said and how they said it. This was a family that had largely raised itself, a group of siblings who made it on their own after their mother died when they were children and their father disappeared into the despair of alcoholism.

It was the Capano family that had wealth and status, that grew up with a sense of belonging and, ultimately, of entitlement. The Faheys, on the other hand, were an up-by-their-bootstraps group who had made a place for themselves through fortitude and perseverance.

Each morning they brought that same quiet determination into the courtroom. Now they had a chance to show the jury who they—and Anne Marie—were.

Robert, his face flushed with determination, spoke of his family's love of the New Jersey shore and of how he could no longer take walks along the beach because he knew "my sister's out there, probably in a million pieces." He talked about the "black hole" of despair and uncertainty that had engulfed his family. And about their struggle to emerge.

Brian, the youngest and the closest to Anne Marie, offered the jury a bright and shining picture of his sister. He wanted her remembered not as a victim of Tom Capano, not as his mistress or as one of his many lovers, but as the warm and loving and funny and caring individual that she was.

A week earlier, after the verdict had been announced, he had mused about what had been lost. One of the things he regretted most, he said, was that Anne Marie would never get the chance to be somebody's mother. "I was thinking how much fun it would be to have Anne Marie as your mother," he said. "She really loved life."

On the witness stand, he told the jury about her "vitality" and her "spirit."

To date, he said, he'd been able to "keep at arm's length" how much he missed her. He said he knew, however, that "that's still out there, still waiting for me." But for the moment, he told the jurors, it was important for them to know that his sister "was outstanding" and that "the world's going to miss her."

Outside the courthouse later in the day, Brian Fahey was still talking about Anne Marie. It didn't really matter, he said, what sentence Capano received. He and his brothers and sister were content to let the jury decide. What mattered, he said— and what may be the saddest part of a very sad and agonizing story—was that his younger sister was deprived of a chance to live her life, to experience success and failure, to strive for love and happiness.

Anne Marie Fahey was thirty years old, and she had just started to figure it all out. Life was a journey, not a destination. You were defined not by what you had, but by what you did. You were the choices that you made. Anne Marie Fahey chose not to be with Tom Capano. And he had killed her because of it.

"She had plans and dreams and hopes," Brian Fahey said. "We all do. She deserved a future."

Capano's lawyers tried to mount an equally emotional presentation, but in the end their client undermined it all, just as he had undermined the trial.

Capano's daughters, his sister, and his brothers—including Gerry and Louis—begged for his life. They all asked the jury to sentence him not to death, but to life in prison.

Each of Capano's four daughters got on the stand and pleaded with the jury to spare his life. They talked about what a great father he had been and how they still needed the opportunity to talk with him, to see him, to hear his voice. He loved them, they said, and they loved him. It was an argument that would seem almost impossible to ignore or rebut. But in the Capano case the prosecution had a way.

Before the penalty phase had ended, Connolly and Wharton called Harry Fusco to the stand. Fusco, his skin sallow, his eyes sunk deep in his angular, thin face, was an inmate at Gander Hill whom Capano had befriended. He had helped Capano by calling home when Tom's phone privileges had been revoked. Fusco was later transferred to another wing in the prison, but continued to communicate with Capano's daughters with Capano's blessing. They sent him a picture, which he displayed in his cell. He wrote about how he loved them as if they were his own.

None of the girls knew about Fusco's background, but their father did. Harry Fusco was a convicted child molester. He was in jail for fondling at least five young boys and girls.

Even the former Kay Capano, who began using her maiden name—Kay Ryan—the day her divorce was finalized, pleaded for her ex-husband's life. "I'm as repulsed by his vile actions as you are," she told the jury. But she asked that he be allowed to live so that he could remain a part of their daughters' lives. Marguerite Capano also cried and begged the jury, still insisting her son was innocent.

Then Tom Capano took the stand and talked away any chance he might have had of avoiding a death sentence.

In a long and disjointed allocution in which he quoted the Roman philosopher Seneca, former U.S. Senator Hubert Humphrey, the Beatles, Saint Anthony, and an Arab proverb about friends and enemies, Capano sounded as if he were still trying to convince the jury of his innocence. Despite an admonition from Judge Lee not to discuss the trial or the verdict—that phase of the case was over—Capano did just that. And when he went off on another rant about how his daughters had been "harassed and lied to," Lee had had enough.

"That's it, we're done," the judge said abruptly.

Capano quickly apologized and said he would comply with the judge's order. Allowed to continue, he rambled on, self-indulgent and self-absorbed to the end.

"I never claimed to be blameless," he said. "I must and I do take moral and ethical responsibility for my actions." But he insisted he had not killed Anne Marie Fahey, and even his attempt to ask for leniency dripped with arrogance.

"I'm not going to sit here and beg for my life," Capano said. "I don't beg for myself. . . . My life is essentially shot." He asked that he be allowed to live so that "my daughters and my mother should not be punished for my sins."

But those sins, Capano implied, were a lack of courage on the night Fahey was killed—a night, he said, when "I lost my moral compass"—and a misplaced sense of loyalty.

"I chose the living over the dead," he said, still insisting that everything he did was intended to protect Debby MacIntyre.

"This is a tragedy for a great many people," he said at

another point. "If I could do anything to undo it, I would. If I could trade places with Anne Marie, I would."

While the jurors could not recommend such an exchange, they did suggest, by a vote of ten to two, that he join her. Their recommendation that Tom Capano be sentenced to death by lethal injection came after less than three hours of deliberation.

Epilogue

Judge William Swain Lee had the final word.

And he delivered it with style, distinction, and the moral outrage that the case demanded.

On March 16, 1999, he sentenced Capano to death by lethal injection, detailing in a twenty-one-page memorandum his reasons for accepting the jury's recommendation. At that point, Thomas J. Capano joined seventeen other inmates already on Death Row in Delaware's prison system.

But Lee, sitting on the bench in front of yet another packed courtroom, said he wanted to supplement his formal order with some personal comments.

"I believe that it is important for any reviewing court to understand what occurred in the courtroom that cannot be reflected in a transcript," Lee said. "The gradual revelation of the personality and character of the defendant clearly was a factor in both the verdict of the jury and its recommendation. . . . It is a significant factor in my sentencing today."

Tom Capano, Lee said, "embarked on a course of conduct" during the trial that rebutted his own presumption of innocence. "Intelligent, educated, affluent, accomplished, and charming by reputation, he proceeded to negate all of the advantages his life had provided during the harsh confrontation with reality which is a criminal trial."

Lee described Capano as "an angry, sinister, controlling

and malignant force which dominated the courtroom for months." He said Capano "degraded all of those who participated in the proceedings," undermined the efforts of his own lawyers, and ultimately and to his own detriment presented "a story of Anne Marie Fahey's death which the jury found incredible."

Lee talked about the "malevolence" of Capano's nature, and said that his "chainsaw" defense resulted in him "attacking, maiming, and destroying the character and lives of lovers, friends, and family who had, in his eyes, been disloyal to him in his times of need.

"The defendant fully expected to get away with murder and, were it not for his own arrogance and controlling nature, may well have succeeded," Lee said.

"He chose to use his family as a shield; make his brothers and his mistress accomplices; use his friends and attorneys for disinformation; attack the character of his prosecutor, make his mother and daughters part of a spectacle in an effort to gain sympathy. . . . He even bullied, berated and undermined the efforts of his own attorneys."

Lee said Capano "has no one to blame for the circumstances he finds himself in today except himself.

"The selfishness, arrogance and manipulativeness of Thomas Capano destroyed his own family as well as the Fahey family. . . . Tom Capano does not face judgment today because friends and family failed him. He faces judgment because he is a ruthless murderer who feels compassion for no one and remorse only for the circumstances in which he finds himself. He is a malignant force from whom no one he deems disloyal or adversarial can be secure, even if he is incarcerated for the rest of his life.

"No one, except the defendant, will ever know exactly how or why Anne Marie Fahey died. What is certain is that it was not a crime of passion, but rather, a crime of control. . . . He chose to destroy a possession, rather than lose it."

There was stunned silence in the courtroom as Lee unloaded. Only Capano seemed unaffected. He sat at the defense table jotting notes. The golden boy would leave the courtroom doing his best to appear unruffled.

THE SUMMER WIND   287

As they left the courthouse for the last time, the Faheys declined to be interviewed. But as she walked past a group of reporters, Kathleen Fahey-Hosey—as she had done so often during the long and tortuous case—cut to the heart of the matter.

"He said in fifteen minutes what we've been feeling for two years," she said of Lee's comments.

Judge Lee knew that his order for Capano's execution would automatically be appealed, and that any sentencing date he set would be moot. Nevertheless, the judge did not miss the chance to add a final poignant touch to the proceeding.

He set Capano's execution date for June 28, 1999, the third anniversary of the day Tom Capano and his brother Gerry took a ride on the *Summer Wind*, the third anniversary of the day Tom Capano wrapped Anne Marie Fahey's lifeless body in a chain and anchors and dumped it in the Atlantic Ocean, the third anniversary of the day he threw the cooler overboard and never looked back.

Without a lid, missing a handle, with a bullet hole through its side and bottom, the large white plastic ice chest had floated for more than six days.

The thought had never entered Tom Capano's mind.

The cooler wouldn't sink.